This new work by Travis West i[s a]
winsome invitation to a practice [whether we know]
it or not! The rhythm of workin[g six days and resting the]
seventh is one of God's greatest [gifts]
in the human community. By entering into this rhythm, we
participate in God's nature and God's best for our world. The
Sabbath was made for us, Jesus tells us; this book will help us
receive it as the gift it is.

RUTH HALEY BARTON
Author of *Embracing Rhythms of Work and Rest: From Sabbath to Sabbatical and Back Again*

I hardly have words for this stunning invitation to reimagine,
to reorient, to redeem the time we view with such scarcity, and
to be restored and refreshed to our depths. I'll never again view
Sabbath as something to do but see it now as an invitation to a
new way of being in the world, a new way of inhabiting God's
vision for wholeness in all creation and people.

CHUCK DEGROAT, PhD, LPC
Professor of pastoral care and Christian spirituality; executive director of
the clinical mental health counseling program at Western Theological
Seminary; author of *Healing What's Within*

Reading this book feels like having a dear friend gently lead
us into God's presence. Without downplaying our busyness or
our pain, it welcomes us into God's rest, into the goodness of
his life and love. This is so different from what we normally see
and experience in the world and the church. We all need this
book—*I* certainly did!

KELLY M. KAPIC
Author of *You're Only Human*

I need *The Sabbath Way*; you need *The Sabbath Way*. With cultural and economic forces that seem outside our control, we need to hear Travis West's encouragement and wisdom to slow down, pause, breathe, and re-member our bodies, minds, and souls. This is not a call to enhance performance. It is a call to enhance our humanity. *The Sabbath Way* is a deeply spiritual and deeply humanizing project, and a timely gift to a culture desperately in pursuit of its next accomplishment.

> **EMERSON B. POWERY, PhD**
> Dean of the School of Arts, Culture, and Society; professor of biblical studies at Messiah University

Travis West's years of study and practical thought on the subject of shalom come together in *The Sabbath Way* to create a readable, practical, and beautiful message that we all need now. Phrases in the book such as "*Shalom* is the wholeness found on the *other side* of justice" resonated with me, and I will repeat them often in the coming years. In short, your life will be better if you take *The Sabbath Way* to heart!

> **RANDY WOODLEY, PhD**
> Speaker, activist, and author of *Shalom and the Community of Creation*, *Becoming Rooted*, and *Journey to Eloheh*

I didn't know how much I needed to read *The Sabbath Way*, but page after page, I realized it was written for me. If you are living in the Western world in the 2000s, I bet it was written for you, too. With warmth, intimacy, and compassion, Travis West reframes Sabbath into a vital, joy-blooming, life-changing practice in service to delight and whole-being-ness. Nothing puritanical here—*The Sabbath Way* is wholly current, filled with references to contemporary music, poetry, sociology, psychology, and theology, plus dozens of reflection questions to help you personalize your own Sabbath practice. I am challenged and inspired by this book. It's a radical, compelling invitation.

> **ROSEMERRY WAHTOLA TROMMER**
> Author of *The Unfolding* and host of *The Poetic Path* on the Ritual app

For those of us who dwell in the land of the Protestant work ethic, now hopped up on the steroids of capitalism and consumerism, production, and competition, Travis West calls our distracted hearts to holy attention and redirects our frenzied souls to the balm we urgently need, revealing how the Sabbath way is the way of Jesus: abundant, satisfying, delightful. Deeply biblical, thoroughly human, and altogether compelling, *The Sabbath Way* excavates the fourth commandment from its legalistic ruins and reintroduces us to this exquisite gift from God that has the power to restore us to Eden and usher us into the Kingdom of Heaven.

PASTOR ERIC E. PETERSON
Colbert Presbyterian Church

Travis West recommends Sabbath as a practice of individual and communal flourishing. Drawn from a deep well of both personal experiences and wise companions across many centuries and traditions, this book is wise yet strikingly accessible. It insightfully mines the voices of Scripture, poets, philosophers, pop culture, psychology, personal anecdotes, and common sense and then weaves it into a stirring call to a Sabbath practice that feeds both soul and society.

LEANNE VAN DYK
President Emerita, Columbia Theological Seminary, Decatur, Georgia

Of the many books that have appeared about the Sabbath in recent years, *The Sabbath Way* distinguishes itself as being personal and invitational. Travis West shows that Sabbath's disruption will be transformative and lead to a deeper experience of the loving and life-giving presence of God in the world. Throughout the book, he shows that the way of the Sabbath is the way of Jesus, is the way of love.

REV. DR. THOMAS BOOGAART
Dennis and Betty Lou Voskuil Professor Emeritus of Old Testament at Western Theological Seminary

Imagine stepping off the treadmill of busyness, even for a day, and finding space to breathe, connect, and simply be. In *The Sabbath Way*, Travis West invites you into this sacred rhythm of rest and delight—something our hurried lives desperately need. Woven with personal stories and deeply human reflections, this book shows how the Sabbath can anchor your week and nourish your soul.

    JOHN SWINTON
    Professor of practical theology and pastoral care at the University of Aberdeen, Scotland

In a world consumed by hurry, stress, and endless demands, we desperately need a sacred rhythm that brings radical rest and renewal. *The Sabbath Way* comes at the perfect time, inviting us to rediscover the peace and joy found within this divine gift. With Travis's thoughtful wisdom and practical insights, this book serves as both a guide and a companion, helping us reconnect with the deep rest our souls were designed for.

    BRAD GRAY
    Founder of Walking The Text and author of *Make Your Mark*

THE SABBATH WAY

Making Room in Your Life for Rest, Connection, and Delight

TRAVIS WEST

FOREWORD BY WINN COLLIER

TYNDALE REFRESH®

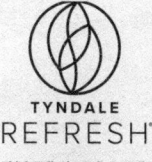

Think Well. Live Well. Be Well.

Visit Tyndale online at tyndale.com.

Visit Tyndale Momentum online at tyndalemomentum.com.

Tyndale and Tyndale's quill logo are registered trademarks of Tyndale House Ministries. *Tyndale Refresh* and the Tyndale Refresh logo are trademarks of Tyndale House Ministries. Tyndale Refresh is a nonfiction imprint of Tyndale House Publishers, Carol Stream, Illinois.

The Sabbath Way: Making Room in Your Life for Rest, Connection, and Delight

Copyright © 2025 by Travis West. All rights reserved.

Cover illustration of watercolor leaves copyright © Liliya Rodnikova/Stocksy.com. All rights reserved.

Interior illustration of labyrinth copyright © by Thurmanukyalur/Wikimedia Commons. All rights reserved.

Author photograph copyright © 2024 by Megan Rice. All rights reserved.

Cover designed by Lindsey Bergsma

Edited by Christine M. Anderson

All Old Testament Scripture quotations are the author's own translation.

Unless otherwise indicated, all New Testament Scripture quotations are taken from the New Revised Standard Version, Updated Edition Bible, copyright © 1989, 2021 by the Division of Christian Education of the National Council of Churches of Christ in the USA, and are used by permission. All rights reserved.

Scripture quotations marked KJV are taken from the *Holy Bible*, King James Version.

Scripture quotations marked NIV are taken from the Holy Bible, *New International Version*,® *NIV.*® Copyright © 1973, 1978, 1984, 2011 by Biblica, Inc.® (Some quotations may be from the earlier NIV edition, copyright © 1984.) Used by permission. All rights reserved worldwide.

Scripture quotation marked NLT is taken from the *Holy Bible*, New Living Translation, copyright © 1996, 2004, 2015 by Tyndale House Foundation. Used by permission of Tyndale House Publishers, Carol Stream, Illinois 60188. All rights reserved.

The URLs in this book were verified prior to publication. The publisher is not responsible for content in the links, links that have expired, or websites that have changed ownership after that time.

For information about special discounts for bulk purchases, please contact Tyndale House Publishers at csresponse@tyndale.com, or call 1-855-277-9400.

Library of Congress Cataloging-in-Publication Data

A catalog record for this book is available from the Library of Congress.

ISBN 978-1-4964-7651-7

Printed in the United States of America

31	30	29	28	27	26	25
7	6	5	4	3	2	1

*For Mariah, my ever and always Sabbath companion—
in life and love, in sickness and health,
in work and play, in rest and delight*

Stand at the crossroads and look,
ask for the ancient paths—
where the good way lies—
and walk in it to find rest for your souls.

JEREMIAH 6:16

Contents

Foreword *xi*
An Invitation to Rest, Connection, and Delight 1
1. Walking the Sabbath Way 13

Part 1: Sabbath and Work 29
2. Orienting: What Is Work? 31
3. Disorienting Striving 47
4. Reorienting: Work, Rest, and Delight 63

Part 2: Sabbath and Time 79
5. Orienting: What Is Time? 81
6. Disorienting Clock Time 97
7. Reorienting: Time Is Love 111

Part 3: Sabbath and Community 127
8. Orienting: What Prevents Community? 129
9. Disorienting Dualism and Disconnection 145
10. Reorienting: Becoming the Beloved Community 161

Part 4: Sabbath and Creation 175
11. Orienting: What Has the Land to Do with Sabbath? 177
12. Disorienting Greed and Scarcity 191
13. Reorienting: Prerequisites for a Life of Gratitude 205

The Sabbath Is Calling 221
Acknowledgments 225
Notes 229
About the Author 243

Foreword

Some people talk about important ideas, but then some people *live* them. Travis West lives Sabbath. I once heard him mention in passing how every Friday he and his wife, Mariah, enter their weekly rhythm by covering all the clocks in their house. I perked up and leaned in. "We need help remembering we're entering a different kind of time," Travis said. "For twenty-four hours, we get to leave behind any dehumanizing, oppressive way of counting hours." His description sounded like relief, like beauty, like delight and possibility and hope.

In the Wests' home, they also engage their Sabbath vigil with other familiar markers (prayer, candles, walks, poetry, sleep, pleasures), but those details, helpful as they are, are not the primary illumination you'll encounter in these pages. These sentences carry fire because they emerge from a writer *living* Sabbath. "Sabbath isn't designed to 'fit' into our lives," Travis writes. "It is designed to take over our lives."

And let me bear witness: Travis has been taken over, in liberating and beautiful ways, by Sabbath. Amid an obsessively frantic culture, Travis moves with a restful cadence. In a fear-ravaged culture, he offers a courageous heart. In an age of rejection and estrangement, he creates and extends, again and again, a generous welcome. In a world fueled by shame, he's a persistent grace-monger. He's a friend you can trust. He sees the world with wide and curious eyes, with the glint of the lover, with the quiet wisdom of the sage. The Spirit has formed Sabbath deep in his soul.

Sabbath—this gritty, mercy-drenched, routine tempo—can, over years, shape and transform us into something more than we are now. "More than the Jews have kept the Sabbath," writes Hebrew journalist Ahad Ha'am, "the Sabbath has kept the Jews."[1] And it keeps us, remakes us, too. We are not consigned to a small, suffocating, selfish existence. We can become more awake, more human, more enlivened, more present to the world and its many wonders. The God of Sabbath will do this within us.

God is the central word here. Sabbath's fundamental gift is how this steady way reorients us to God, makes us more alert to God, fills us with the love of God. Sabbath, as the first Scriptures insist, is "unto the LORD [our] God."[2] Week by week, as we learn to let "all the voodoos of ambition sleep" (as Mary Oliver says),[3] Sabbath opens vast space within us, room to grapple with our sorrows and renew our laughter, a new capacity to bear disappointment and kindle hope. And Sabbath's grace reveals God right there, never far, amid every bit.

Sabbath is no ham-fisted religious edict imposed on flailing creatures from a remote, disinterested deity, but rather is part of God's own life, woven into God's own way of being. God rested first, and now we follow God's lead. And this resting life is good news for everybody. "Sabbath-keeping is elemental kindness," writes Eugene Peterson.[4] Sabbath extends us kindness, but even more, Sabbath pours kindness into God's whole, wide world: toward our neighbors and into our community, over the economy, and into the land itself. In Sabbath, we stop our machinations. For a few marvelous moments, we stop pounding the hammer. We stop counting the dollar. We stop pressing our opinions. We stop and we listen. We love. We trust God. We're alive.

Thankfully, this book offers no technocratic treatise on how to meticulously follow the manual and get Sabbath just right. Instead, there's lyric and dance and mystery here. And laughter. Never trust a writer—or a pastor or a teacher or a politician—who never laughs. Travis laughs deep, the merry roar coming from way down in his belly, like thunderous joy. That same thunder and gladness strikes here.

Winn Collier

Author of Love Big, Be Well *and* A Burning in My Bones: The Authorized Biography of Eugene H. Peterson *and director of the Eugene Peterson Center for Christian Imagination at Western Theological Seminary (Holland, MI)*

An Invitation to Rest, Connection, and Delight

*The Sabbath is a day for the sake of life. . . .
It is not an interlude but the climax of living.*
ABRAHAM JOSHUA HESCHEL, THE SABBATH

I was a happy-go-lucky kid, the kind who naturally balanced being the class clown with being respectful of my elders and classmates. The youngest of three siblings, I found my mission in life when I discovered I could use laughter and levity to lift the mood and ease the ever-present tensions in my family of origin. These same skills enabled me to be a salve to hurting friends. Give me a lonely freshman and I'd soon have them screaming their brains out with joy at a school basketball game. Joy and delight were my life's currencies. I loved to make people laugh and smile. I wanted everyone to feel alive and free.

It's no wonder, then, that in college I fell hard for a woman who made me laugh as much as I made her laugh. With her, my joy and delight multiplied. Married shortly after college, we looked out on a future bright with possibility. She was going to be an elementary school teacher inspiring kids to marvel at the natural world (science) and express their wonder in beauty (art). I was headed to seminary to do . . . something? I didn't know what. I just knew I wanted to study Scripture and help people.

On July 11, 2003, we dumped all our life's eggs into one glorious basket and vowed to love each other "in sickness and in health." At the time, we had no idea how prescient the word order of that vow would be. We couldn't foresee then how the coming years would exile our joy and delight.

In Sickness (and in Health)

By the fifth day of our honeymoon, we knew something wasn't right. We were sleeping more than two healthy twentysomethings should, even in the aftermath of planning a wedding. We decided to cut our honeymoon short and return home to find answers. It turned out we both had mononucleosis. Not surprising, given the monthslong sprint leading up to the wedding. But the timing was terrible.

We had to quit our summer landscaping jobs since all we could do was sleep. Being recent college grads who'd paid for much of our own wedding, we had no savings, and our student loans were coming due. It was a wake-up call from the world of adulting, and we still felt like toddlers. But we weren't alone. Our church paid for a month's rent. My parents covered another. We signed up for government assistance to help cover groceries. It was a humbling and vulnerable season.

I recovered after a few months, but Mariah was not so lucky. By our one-year anniversary she still had active mono. They called it "chronic mono." Eventually they just called it chronic fatigue.

In the years that followed, our lives were consumed by appointments, tests, diagnoses, and medical bills—to say nothing of me starting seminary, then a doctorate; taking exams; writing papers, sermons, and lesson plans; and memorizing Greek and Hebrew flash cards. Beyond Mariah's baseline of systemic exhaustion, doctors discovered multiple digestive conditions, an autoimmune condition, a genetic toxin-processing disorder, multiple chemical sensitivities, severe anemia, and more. To date, her complex and mysterious condition has persisted for over twenty years. Of the many health-care professionals she's seen, one doctor's parting words at our final visit summed up Mariah's entire health journey: "It's not fun being a puzzle, is it?"

During the early years, we lived in a dual state of denial and hope. We were just holding our breath until she would recover and we could leave all this behind. But as the years wore on and nothing changed, reality sank in—and it nearly crushed us. Daily survival became our North Star. We longed for the levity of laughter, for the ease to chat with a stranger about the weather, to be able to do something—anything—spontaneously.

Searching for a Center

Looking back on those early years, I can now see that Mariah's chronic illness was the center of a much larger web of losses that left us feeling anchorless. Our wedding was bookended by the dissolution of our parents' marriages—Mariah's parents the year prior and mine the year after. Then, a couple years into Mariah's illness, several doctors made it clear that while her illness remained, she could not take the risk of getting pregnant for fear of losing her own life as well as the baby's.

During the critical years in which dreams are born, we lost not only our past, but also our future and our identity. Who was Mariah if she couldn't work, couldn't mother a child, or couldn't leave the house? Who was I if I couldn't provide for my family or even meet my wife's most basic needs? What could it possibly mean to experience joy and delight in the wake of such losses? When life felt so burdensome and serious all the time, would we ever laugh again?

We didn't know where to take our questions. What we did know was that we were exhausted, overwhelmed, and afraid—afraid the month would run out before my next check arrived, afraid Mariah would never recover, afraid this would be our life forever. We needed rest, but we knew our situation wouldn't be resolved by more sleep or better sleep, a three-day weekend, or a weeklong vacation (although any of those would have been nice). We needed a more radical form of rest—the kind of rest that could be an anchor for life, or a lighthouse to orient by as we navigated life's dark and stormy waters. Where would we find such a thing?

In the mysterious providence of God's timing, when we felt lost and the path seemed dark and foreboding, a light broke through the clouds to shine the way. During the summers after my second and third years of seminary, Mariah and I received *two* once-in-a-lifetime opportunities to travel together to Jerusalem. At the time, I thought I was there to take classes and explore a future vocation as a professor of Hebrew and Old Testament. In the end, our most formative experience happened outside of class and on the weekends, when we found ourselves so caught up in the present moment, we forgot to be anxious about the future.

Encountering Sabbath

Within our first week on the campus of a small community near Jerusalem where my class was held, we encountered the sacred and ancient rhythm of Sabbath. It was unlike anything we'd experienced before. From sundown Friday to sundown Saturday, the whole community shut down. The city of Jerusalem shut down. The whole country seemed to shut down. Buses didn't run. Jewish shops weren't open. The streets were empty. People spent time with their families and friends. The very air felt different because the atmosphere itself changed. We felt it. And it was amazing.

We fell into that weekly rhythm of rest with ease while we were there, but it didn't survive the trip home; we hadn't yet made it ours. We were like hungry people who'd been served fish for dinner. We were grateful, but we had no idea how to fish for ourselves. No one did Sabbath where we came from, and we didn't know how to live it when the world no longer stopped around us. As soon as we returned to Michigan, I reverted to my well-honed habits of busyness and overscheduling. The blissful summer of rhythmic rest evaporated like steam from the mugs of Earl Grey tea I started drinking to stay awake on less and less sleep.

It wasn't until we returned to Jerusalem the following summer—my *second* once-in-a-lifetime opportunity—that the rhythm of Sabbath rest clicked. We felt ourselves being re-membered. We committed then and there to reorient our lives around this practice. But truth be told, we didn't fully grasp what we were committing to. We knew our souls were hungry, but we still didn't know how to fish.

Our two summers in Jerusalem were like the infancy phase of our Sabbath practice. All we had to do was be there and Sabbath happened. But when we came home and stopping was up to us, we felt helpless. We didn't know how to answer the most basic Sabbath questions. How do we *start* Sabbath? Light a candle? Sing a song? Make a meal? Go to sleep? What do we *do* on Sabbath? Can we use our phones? Watch a movie? Take a nap? Scroll Facebook? Take a walk? Go to the mall? Take another nap? How do we *conclude* Sabbath? Say a prayer? Sing a different song? Take *another* nap?

Sabbath Enters Adolescence

When we got home that second summer, it felt like our infant Sabbath hit an overnight growth spurt, skipped right over childhood, and dove headlong into a tumultuous adolescence. Mostly this meant that our experience of it was as up and down as raging teenage hormones. Sometimes, on Sabbath, we were like parents reminiscing over their child's baby photos. We felt connected, laughed together, and were deeply grateful for the beautiful mystery of life. Other times, we ended up at each other's throats in a fight that left us exhausted and confused. This adolescent phase lasted over ten years as we struggled to raise our Sabbath child in a cultural climate that was hostile to its flourishing.

Perhaps I am straining the child metaphor to its breaking point (or beyond), but the metaphor feels apt for our experience. One unexpected gift the Sabbath gave us was something beautiful to nurture together in the aftermath of learning we couldn't bear children of our own, due to Mariah's chronic illness. We have committed ourselves to the Sabbath as parents to a child; we have sought to nurture it in our lives as best we can. And, as many parents will say, we have received much more than we've given.

The Sabbath wasn't our only child, though. In many ways, surviving Mariah's illness together has felt like raising a "difficult" child—it has taken everything and more, and yet it has taught us so much that when we look back on it, we can't imagine who we'd be without those scars. Throughout that long season of our Sabbath's adolescence, we experienced severe illness, extreme stress, financial insecurity, intense busyness, and sustained physical and emotional exhaustion. There was no other way for us to live through that season than one day at a time. And the Sabbath held us through it all. In our own way, we lived the truth of journalist Ahad Ha'am's statement "More than the Jews have kept the Sabbath, the Sabbath has kept the Jews."[1] During that period of life, more than we kept the Sabbath, the Sabbath kept us.

Sabbath Enters Adulthood

Our Sabbath entered adulthood when it moved from being an add-on, a weekly pit stop in our otherwise hectic and inattentive lives, to being the central organizing principle of our lives. It has become the pinnacle of our week, a day of intentional delight instead of a day to collapse into. As Rabbi Abraham Joshua Heschel proclaimed, "The Sabbath is a day for the sake of life. . . . It is not an interlude but the climax of living."[2] It organizes our priorities, clarifies our values, and helps us make decisions about how we want to use the time we have. It's what we wanted all along but didn't know how to find. To revert to an earlier metaphor, it was like we *finally* learned how to fish. And got a fishing boat. Then moved to a lake house!

That's not to say that our Sabbath practice is perfect. In fact, we've failed at Sabbath more than we've succeeded. At the same time, we've also learned that the Sabbath does not even compute the categories of "failure" and "success"! Instead, the Sabbath invites us to approach life playfully and not take ourselves so seriously. It invites us to come, eager and grateful, week after week, to receive its gifts of abundance, joy, presence, and delight. It invites us to embrace a more radical form of rest.

A Rest That Is Radical

Sabbath rest is radical because it means much more than sleeping in, taking naps, or chilling poolside for an afternoon. *Sabbath rest is radical because it means putting rest—and delight, and flourishing—first rather than last.* Sabbath rest is radical because it will not settle for being an occasional add-on to an otherwise busy and distracted life. It wants to be the metronome that establishes and maintains our life's rhythm. It wants to apprentice us to abundance our whole life long.

Sabbath rest is also radical because it's countercultural. To "remember the Sabbath" (Exodus 20:8) is to resist some of the dehumanizing cultural currents flowing in our world today. For example, the Sabbath elevates:

- being over doing,
- people over profit,
- presence over productivity,
- attention over distraction,
- abundance over scarcity,
- gratitude over greed,
- contentment over consumption,
- delight over division,
- connection over competition, and
- both/and over either/or.

While it's true that these countercultural values find expression in the Sabbath practice of resting for a day each week, radical rest is more than a weekly *practice*—it's also a *posture*. It is a day of the week *and* a way of living every day. A Sabbath practice and a Sabbath posture come together to form a Sabbath life. To live that kind of life is to walk the Sabbath way—a lifestyle anchored in rhythms that make ample room for rest, connection, and delight.

Reading *The Sabbath Way*

The Sabbath Way is divided into four parts, each exploring an area of life in which we need the Sabbath to teach us how to approach life differently by making room for the things we value most.

> **Part 1: Sabbath and Work.** A culture obsessed with productivity and achievement distorts our identity, but the Sabbath restores and preserves it.
>
> **Part 2: Sabbath and Time.** In a world of speed and distraction controlled by the clock and social media, the Sabbath teaches us that time is love and shows us the power of living with patience, presence, and play.
>
> **Part 3: Sabbath and Community.** Loneliness and exclusion wreak havoc on our hearts, leaving a trail of grief and pain. The Sabbath exposes the values behind these experiences and gently guides us toward meaningful connection and belonging.
>
> **Part 4: Sabbath and Creation.** Complex economic structures that incentivize greed and survive by scarcity are harming the land on which our lives depend. Sabbath reorients us from greed to gratitude and from scarcity to wonder as prerequisites to caring for the creation that cares for us.

To help you integrate the teaching into everyday life, each chapter includes a Sabbath practice. Use the practices as a launching pad to get started, and feel free to adapt them to your own needs and circumstances. Every chapter also includes reflection questions to help you process what you read. Use the questions for personal reflection, perhaps with a journal, or for group discussion. Since one of the Sabbath's gifts is connection with others, and since it's hard to sustain a Sabbath practice in isolation, I hope you find others with whom to read and discuss the book. Maybe even on your Sabbath! And with some delicious food!

Learning what the Sabbath wants to teach us also requires unlearning some of what we've been taught. This process of learning and unlearning is inherent to the threefold journey of discipleship modeled in Jesus' *life*, *death*, and *resurrection*. The language I use for this process is orientation, disorientation, reorientation. Each of the four parts includes a chapter on orientation, disorientation, and reorientation, respectively.

The *orientation* chapters explore how we have been formed by cultural values that are hostile to God's dream of creation's flourishing. The Sabbath invitation is to *see* our lives and the forces influencing our living more clearly. The *disorientation* chapters consider how the Sabbath's countercultural values disrupt our cultural *mal*formation and offer alternative values that are antidotes to our culture's values. The Sabbath invitation here is to *cease* patterns and behaviors that diminish us or others. Each *reorientation* chapter points toward the trailhead of the Sabbath way, inviting us to begin our life's pilgrimage toward *delight*, and what the prophet Jeremiah called "rest for your souls" (Jeremiah 6:16).

This threefold process might appear to be linear, but it's not. Although I've presented the process that way for the sake of clarity, we are always being oriented, disoriented, and reoriented throughout our lives. The ongoing nature of this process is reflected in the chapter titles, which use the active forms of the verb: *orienting*, *disorienting*, and *reorienting*. We can't just go through the process once and "get it." Just as we'll never perfectly live like Jesus, we'll never perfectly live the Sabbath either. That's why it's called a practice!

The Invitation

This book will not offer you "seven steps to a successful Sabbath." There is no cut-and-paste approach to Sabbath because every person, family, and situation is unique, and any attempt to standardize it is bound to feel oppressive or stifling to some. Instead, Sabbath is an invitation to let go of rigid rules and embrace delight, to let go of striving and embrace ease, to let go of distraction and embrace the present moment.

Sabbath is about learning to trust that God is God, and the world will not fall to pieces if we stop for a day to breathe and play. It's about believing that we are worthy of experiencing delight and that such a pursuit is worth our time and intention. It's about reconnecting with what brings us delight and draws out the child trapped inside the adult stressing over this and that. It's about recovering a sense of wonder and awe at the sheer miracle of life. It's about finding ways to feel God's abiding presence in the world and in our lives. It's about falling more deeply in love with God and with the world that mediates God's presence and love.

If all of this sounds like a pipe dream to you, like maybe this could work for other people with fewer responsibilities, less stress, fewer demands, more time, more money, and more flexibility than you, I want you to know I hear you. Or, if you've spent years deferring or denying your desires to the point that you don't even know what you long for anymore, I want you to know I see you too. I've been there. And a critical part of what got me from there to here was my commitment to showing up each week to the Sabbath with as much of myself as was available to me, and then bringing as much of that as I could with me into the week. And every week, the Sabbath met me there and helped guide me here—and it continues to guide me onward.

But what's even more important is that God sees you—right where you are. The Spirit of God longs for you to be fully alive, and the world needs your unique vitality. Wherever and whoever you are—whether you're a parent of young children who is sleeping little and stressing a lot just to survive, a college student searching for your purpose and your people, a pastor continually guiding your flock toward wholeness yet neglecting your own life, or a retiree seeking a legacy in the sunset years of life—the Sabbath can meet you where you are and guide you toward what thriving and wholeness might look like for you in this season.

AN INVITATION TO REST, CONNECTION, AND DELIGHT

I believe in the power of the Sabbath to transform lives. I don't really understand it, but I trust it, and I've seen it happen over and over—to my students, to my friends, and to myself. It won't happen overnight, and it won't be accompanied by fireworks or a laser light show. But it will happen—slowly, often imperceptibly, over the course of time. As you lean into trust, into gratitude, into delight, and into presence, your heart will expand, your delight muscles will get strong and toned, you will grow in self-compassion, your commitment to justice will deepen, and your increased capacity to love your neighbor as yourself may surprise you—and your neighbors!

My hope for you is that after reading this book you will be inspired and convinced that living the Sabbath way is possible for you. More than possible, that it's your birthright. My hope is that you will take to heart the words of the prophet Jeremiah, who saw that his fellow Israelites stood at a threshold between the status quo and abundance, and he begged them to enter in.

> Stand at the crossroads and look,
>   ask for the ancient paths—
> where the good way lies—
>   and walk in it to find rest for your souls.
> JEREMIAH 6:16

My hope is that you will find ways of experiencing the rest your soul craves. The Sabbath can't make your children fall asleep at night or stop them from crying; it can't resolve tensions between coworkers, secure a raise, or complete your never-ending to-do list; it can't snap its fingers and make your stress go away, resolve the tensions in your marriage, or heal the body of someone you love. What it can do is give you space to process these dynamics and the complex emotions they create. It can reconnect you to gratitude by teaching you to live in the present moment. It can remind you of your priorities and expose the ways your life is out of sync with them. It can empower you to live as an act of protest against forces that equate your value with what you do. It can make room for you to laugh and cry and sing and dance and sleep and play—in short, it can reorient you toward what brings you joy and delight, what makes you *you*.

I am with you at the crossroads. The Sabbath is calling. Will you come?

1

WALKING THE SABBATH WAY

*The Sabbath . . . cannot survive in exile,
a lonely stranger among days of profanity.*
ABRAHAM JOSHUA HESCHEL, THE SABBATH

My sister is a busy woman. She and her husband have four kids, ages ten to seventeen. They live outside of town in a house with some property, along with a dog and several chickens. My brother-in-law works full-time outside the home, and she works part-time from home—in addition to her full-time gig of managing all the logistics of their home life with kids in different schools, meals, cleaning, chores, and so on. It's a lot.

We were talking recently about the Sabbath, and she expressed what so many people today feel when considering the Sabbath. She desperately wants it, and even needs it, but with life full to the brim and overflowing—with homework; sports, music, and theater practices; church classes twice a week; and all-day tournaments on Saturdays—if Sunday afternoon isn't given to laundry and cleaning, the house will quickly fall to pieces. There just isn't a nook or cranny big enough for all the overflow that would be created by giving an entire day to Sabbath each week. And if she attempted it, the other days would become so full that she would either collapse exhausted into Sabbath each week, or never truly be able to rest knowing what insanity awaited her as soon as Sabbath ended.

I hear similar laments from my students when I require them to practice two twenty-four-hour Sabbaths during our unit on Genesis 1. Everybody has busy and full lives managing schoolwork with internships and family obligations, in addition to side hustles and the desire to also have a life while being a grad student. Life is just too full to fit the Sabbath into it.

Perhaps you can relate to my students and my sister. Whether you're a parent, a grandparent, or single; whether you're a college student, a grad student, or a pastor; whether you're an accountant, an architect, or an acupuncturist, I imagine you often feel like life is so full there simply isn't room to block off twenty-four hours on your calendar without creating a cascade of chaos on the remaining days that will erase whatever rest you found on the Sabbath.

Herein lies both the reality and the problem. My sister and my students are right. They *don't* have time for Sabbath. Just like you don't. I see the pace of their lives and all they attempt to do in a week. I see their exhaustion and hear their longing for something different. I know that reality intimately myself.

However, the uncomfortable truth is that the only way any of us can fully experience the gifts of Sabbath is to *stop trying to fit it into our lives*. Sabbath isn't designed to "fit" into our lives; it is designed to take over our lives—in the best way imaginable. But our lives are not designed with the Sabbath in mind. Quite the opposite, in fact. The cultural, political, philosophical, and economic forces that shape our lives and our choices are forming us in ways opposed to the Sabbath, which makes it very hard to rest. The irony of contemporary Sabbath practice is that rest is really hard work.

Anyone who wants to experience all that the Sabbath offers will have to reorient their lives around it. They will have to fit their lives into its pattern and values, not the other way around. And that will be costly, even radical. A rest that is radical isn't easy or convenient. The Sabbath way is a narrow way; it demands something of us. If we walk it, we need to be willing to go where it leads. We need to let go of things that might feel important or even necessary. We need to *make* room for Sabbath in our lives.

The Compassionate Interrogator

What I said to my sister, in response to her lament that life is too full to fit Sabbath into it, is that if she allowed it to, the Sabbath would probably ask her some important but uncomfortable questions. It will do so because it is what I call a compassionate interrogator. Before it got to the uncomfortable stuff, though, Sabbath would remind her to breathe, relax her body, and really feel into this moment. It would remind her that its ultimate desire is for her to live a joyful, vibrant, and meaningful life—characterized by its foundational values of presence, attention, gratitude, delight, rest, connection, and wonder. It would remind her that its work is to shepherd her toward those values along her life's path. It would ask her to describe, in practical terms, what a joyful, vibrant, and meaningful life would look like for her and her family *during* this demanding stage of life.

Then it would look at her with great compassion and ask (with genuine curiosity, not condescension) if all the activities and classes and tournaments and rehearsals are necessary or helpful toward living into that vision. In other words, it would interrogate the fullness-to-overflowing that characterizes her family's life. It would invite her to consider what the sources and motivations for all the busyness and striving are, to help her get clarity on what is inherent to this stage of life and what is not. At the end of the conversation, it would invite her to explore what she and her family are willing to give up to move toward her Sabbath-inspired life vision.

I have had many such difficult conversations with the compassionate interrogator over the years. They generally begin with the self-awareness naturally created by slowing down and stepping away from the responsibilities of work and the distractions I seek during the week. By moving slower and being on a different schedule, I am naturally inclined to pay more attention to my body and my soul. And in that space, I notice things such as fatigue, aches and pains, or habituated ways of thinking or acting that are harmful to me or others. That noticing is the first thread of the conversation.

When I'm feeling courageous, I pick up the thread with my wife, Mariah, or my spiritual director, or my Sabbath journal. More often than not, those conversations lead to the same realization author Anne Lamott's son had while watching her rush to yet another appointment, leaving behind her a wake of dropped papers and spilled coffee: "You are going too fast, and carrying too much."[1]

Each time, that realization presents me with a choice: *Will I persist along the path of the status quo, of going too fast and carrying too much? Or will I change my life to enable a deeper resonance between my living and Sabbath values?* That is a very hard choice to make. Many, many times I have opted for the first option and just kept pushing through. But on the occasions that I have chosen to embrace the Sabbath way by slowing down and prioritizing Sabbath values, I have inevitably become a better spouse, a better friend, a better professor, a better neighbor—because I have become a better version of myself.

What I have been describing here is the reciprocity between the two aspects of the Sabbath way—a Sabbath practice and a Sabbath posture. The *practice* is the day itself, set aside from the workweek with its unique obligations and temptations, which gives us the time and opportunity to practice cultivating the Sabbath values and to experience delight. The *posture* is how we integrate those values into our workweek—whether we are paid for our work or not. Living the Sabbath way requires taking seriously both the practice and the posture, the day itself and its implications for every other day.

Sabbath Is a Practice

The Hebrew verb *shavat*, from which the noun *shabbat* is formed, means "to cease, stop." Stopping in a culture obsessed with speed, advancement, ambition, productivity, and unrestrained growth is a deeply countercultural choice. Stopping is hard work. This is why it requires practice.

The Commitments of a Sabbath Practice

To call Sabbath a practice is to do more than acknowledge its countercultural character. When we engage the Sabbath, we are engaging our purpose as human beings, created in God's image, and kin of all creation. To take Sabbath seriously is to explore the whole of your life under its illumination. Sabbath is the most ancient of all spiritual practices, woven into the fabric of creation. We tend to reduce spiritual practices to "doing devotions," essentially a ten-minute add-on to life that we squeeze in wherever we can make it fit. But Sabbath is not an add-on to life; it is life's core organizing principle. It is the center to which the rest of life is tethered, the center around which it revolves to find balance.

To walk the Sabbath way is to fall headlong into transformation. It is to invite disruption. It begins by losing our way, since the way by which we have come is what Psalm 1 calls a perishing path. It is to embrace the truth that only what is lost can be found, so we must lose our way before we can find the Sabbath way. This process of disorientation and reorientation will not happen overnight or on accident. Rather, it requires *time*, *intentionality*, and *consistency*.

Time. Traditionally, a Sabbath lasts for twenty-four hours, although there is also a Jewish practice I love that extends Sabbath an extra hour, making it a twenty-five-hour day. This playful practice affirms the Sabbath as an anticipation of eternity and the life to come. Either way, Sabbath requires time. A full day is important because it often takes several hours to slow down enough internally to become present. But if that seems impossible, start by giving Sabbath what time you have and go from there.

My wife and I begin our Sabbath on Friday evening, usually around 7:00 p.m., and conclude it around the same time on Saturday. Sometimes, when we can, we extend it until we go to bed on Saturday. A playful strategy we employ to change our relationship to time during our Sabbath practice is to cover our clocks. This creates something of a "timeless day" that helps us pay attention to our bodies and their rhythms. We eat when we're hungry, not when the clock tells us to. It also helps me realize how often I look to see what time it is! I wrote this haiku to explore what I was learning:

What time is it now?
Clocks are covered, time stands still
It's presence o'clock

The gifts of a Sabbath practice unfold over a lifetime. The Sabbath is not like Thanos, the great purple villain of the Marvel Cinematic Universe. It can't snap its fingers and make your life serene. And you aren't Thanos either. You can't snap your fingers and make your Sabbath perfect or use it to make all your problems go away. Real, lasting change happens slowly, over time. It requires intention, humility, and a sense of play—being willing to fail and try again next week. Sabbath apprentices us in the ways of delight, wonder, and gratitude over the course of our lives. Our primary responsibility each week is to make the space and show up to it.

Intentionality. Sabbath practice requires intentionality because the space will not make itself. In the Bible, Sabbath time is holy time, time that is set apart from the linear, production-oriented time of our workaday lives. It takes intentionality to set this time apart.

This can be done simply by establishing a threshold ritual that marks the transition from "regular time" to "Sabbath time." Traditionally, this is done by lighting candles, saying a prayer or blessing, or singing a song. My wife and I keep Sabbath decorations in storage during the week, and part of our threshold ritual is setting out our Sabbath plate, candles, and handmade pottery on a handmade towel. The act of setting it up indicates that Sabbath is here. Seeing the beautiful items on display throughout the day reminds us what time it is.

It also takes intentionality to show up differently to Sabbath time than to the habituated ways we're accustomed to living. I recently heard Pastor Rich Villodas quote Ronald Rolheiser's description of our current lifestyle as "pathological busyness, distraction, and restlessness."[2] Sabbath time is slow time. It's about being present here and now. It's unproductive and inefficient time. It takes effort to show up in these ways. It takes effort to keep the noise of the rest of life from creeping in and taking over—whether it's the buzzing phone or the mental buzz of next week's to-do lists.

Consistency. As a spiritual practice, Sabbath is not intended to be a one-off thing we enjoy here and there on a whim or when we have time. It is not an appendage to life but the beating heart of life, providing energy, support, and nourishment to the whole "body" of our life. Built on the pattern of God's practice in Creation, Sabbath establishes the rhythm by which our days are lived. In Genesis 1, it is the climax of God's creative work, the height of the crescendo, the moment toward which all of creation was headed. As an ancient Sabbath song put it, Sabbath is "last in creation, first in intention."[3] A week without Sabbath is like a concerto or a movie—or anything—without a climax: incomplete and unsatisfying.

The Fruit of a Sabbath Practice

When we set aside *time* with *intention* and *consistency*, we make room in our lives for the fruit of Sabbath to grow. This fruit is the substance of a life well-lived. It involves the purposeful cultivation of *connection, attention, a yes to life,* and *delight*.

Sabbath cultivates connection. When we set aside Sabbath time with intention, we direct it toward connection. I like to imagine that connection happening in four directions: upward, inward, outward, and downward. We direct our attention *upward* by connecting with the Spirit of God, discerning God's presence in our life and the world, and by slowing down and listening to what the Spirit is saying.

We connect upward and *inward* by engaging in activities that make our souls come alive, which is when we are most connected to the divine image in us. We pause each week to pay attention to our heart, body, and life. Instead of waiting for an illness or emergency to stop us in our tracks, we practice stopping every week to connect to our body and its needs. We honor our humanity by making room for our delights and our sadness.

We connect *outward* by engaging other people—our families and friends, our neighbors, or even strangers. We slow down internally to practice really seeing the people around us, in all their complexity and beauty and uniqueness.

Finally, we connect *downward* with the earth, which John Calvin referred to as the "theater" of God's glory[4] and the stage of God's own Sabbath delight in Genesis. We fall in love with creation week after week so that we come to recognize the manifold ways creation cares for us, even as we seek to care for it.

Sabbath cultivates attention. Sabbath practice is about learning to pay attention—to the world, to each other, and to our own lives. We tend to live in the past or the future instead of the present. When we feel regret, guilt, or resentment we are stuck in the past. When we feel anxiety, fear, or worry we are caught in a future we are making in our minds. The only moment that truly exists is the present moment, and when we are not present to it, we are not fully alive. What's more, when we aren't living in the present, we cut ourselves off from love, joy, delight—even from God—for they are accessible only in the present. This is true whether the moment is full of sadness, joy, pain, awe, or ease. Sabbath cultivates the inner capacity to be present to our lives, whatever they hold, while pointing us toward delight and joy.

Sabbath cultivates a yes to life. A Sabbath practice is ultimately about living well, with purpose and meaning. For previous generations the emphasis in Sabbath was given singularly to stopping, not to the cultivation of certain values. Sabbath was about saying no. Period. But the Sabbath I have come to embrace is a Sabbath that says no *in order to* say a much more important "Yes!" The *no* is penultimate; it serves the *yes*. The *no* is an act of protest against the values and structures and habits that diminish us, keeping us exhausted, distracted, and unsatisfied. The *no*—to devices, the economy, work, hurry, or a scarcity mindset—enables a *yes* to abundance, playfulness, gratitude, presence, and connection. The Sabbath *no* is about making room in our lives; the Sabbath *yes* is about filling that room with what makes us feel alive.

Sabbath cultivates delight. Ultimately, a Sabbath practice prioritizes delight in our lives. Sabbath delight is not a happy-clappy denial of difficulty, an escape from stress, a luxury reserved for the wealthy or naturally carefree, or a way to numb our pain. It is the experience, unique to each of us, of being fully awake to life, whatever it holds. It's being fully present, fully ourselves in any given moment. Sabbath delight is a fulsome delight. It includes adjacent emotions such as gratitude, wonder, connection; and joy. Poet Ross Gay has called it "the pleasurable evidence of life . . . love . . . connection."[5] It can involve play, but it can also involve silence, or even sadness. This kind of delight is the horizon toward which a Sabbath practice orients us. What a gift to have a weekly reminder that experiencing delight deserves to be a priority since it is fundamental to what it means to be a human being alive in the world!

In our world today, prioritizing delight, pleasure, gratitude, playfulness, and contentment is an act of protest against the grind, the rat race, the slog of unrelenting productivity, busyness, obligations, and expectations. It's an act of defiance against how we've been convinced we are supposed to live. Embracing delight sometimes requires an act of the will, an act of discipline and intention. But as we practice delight week after week, our delight instincts grow, our priorities begin to shift, and we may find that we want to bring our delight with us everywhere! Which brings us to Sabbath as a *posture*.

Sabbath Is a Posture

When I say that Sabbath is a posture as well as a practice, I'm suggesting that Sabbath is not content to exist as an isolated event, an add-on to a life marked by the "pathological busyness, distraction, and restlessness" Ronald Rolheiser observed. Rather, a Sabbath posture links the values cultivated on a Sabbath day to how we show up to the rest of our lives— to work, to our kids' school, to the grocery store. The goal is a sense of congruity between our Sabbath day and every other day.

Finding a Sabbath Posture

I discovered the idea of a Sabbath posture several years ago while reading Abraham Joshua Heschel's magisterial book *The Sabbath*. I had felt for some time that Mariah's and my Sabbath practice was incomplete but wasn't sure how or why. Then I read the following quote from Heschel, and it clicked. He said the Sabbath "cannot survive in exile, a lonely stranger among days of profanity. It needs the companionship of all other days. *All days of the week must be spiritually consistent with the Day of Days.*"[6] Those words were like the sun breaking through the clouds, clearing the fog, and revealing the path that is the Sabbath way. I knew in that moment that our Sabbath day and the rest of our life were *in*consistent, operating out of incompatible values, making our Sabbath practice feel like whiplash and the start of the week like jumping on to an already-running treadmill. No wonder my wife and I tended to fight so often on Sabbath!

Let me be clear, though. Adopting a Sabbath posture does *not* mean quitting your job, abandoning your responsibilities, and enjoying Sabbath all week long. A Sabbath posture is about showing up to your life in a Sabbath-y kind of way—unhurried, compassionate, kind, generous, playful; and yet serious, earnest, understanding the value of hard work *while not letting it define you*. It's about working in such a way that "a Sabbath mood / Rests on our day, and finds it good," as poet Wendell Berry so beautifully put it.[7]

It may sound like I'm suggesting Sabbath necessarily begins with a practice and extends to a posture, which is how it worked for us. But it can go the other way as well. Someone who cannot yet envision how to incorporate a Sabbath practice into their lives can nevertheless begin to adopt a Sabbath posture throughout the week, which could grow into a Sabbath practice. They can be explored simultaneously.

A Sabbath posture involves interrogating the pace of your life, the decisions you make—and the why behind those decisions. It's about setting an intention to arrive to work or the coffee shop or your in-laws' place as the best version of yourself available to you. Maybe it's finding a Sabbath moment on a Thursday to pause, breathe, and witness an entire sunset at the end of an especially busy day—and *really being there*. Maybe it's engaging the more radical process of reorganizing your life to give more space and time to the things that mean the most to you or make you feel most alive and connected—even if they aren't lucrative or won't increase your chances for promotion. Inhabiting a Sabbath posture is about enacting in your daily life the Sabbath values—gratitude, a sense of abundance, a spirit of play, and a commitment to meeting each moment as fully as you can—while honoring your own limitations and those of the people around you.

A Sabbath posture is like having a mini-Sabbath sitting on your shoulder throughout the week reminding you of Sabbath truths: that you are not what you do; that your life is bigger than the challenge you are facing; that you are the beloved of God; that this moment, whatever it holds, does not define you—for better or for worse. It's the voice inviting you to move slower between meetings and feedings, to look—really look—at the people around you, to see them in their full humanity and complexity, and to love them for who they are, not who they could be.

Improving Our Posture Takes Time

A few years ago, my wife and I each spent several months trying to improve our physical posture. Whether we were sitting or standing, we would try to be as upright as we could comfortably be. It was a lot harder than I thought it would be. For months, we corrected our posture dozens of times every day. If we were together and one of us remembered, we would ask the other, "How's your posture?" The answer would come in the form of standing or sitting up a few inches taller.

The habit of bad posture is incredibly hard to break. In fact, as I typed the sentence about sitting up "a few inches taller" I realized I was slouching! I find that my posture worsens—and my unconscious instinct to slouch increases—with the level of stress I'm under.

It is the same with life. We all have our ways of slouching through our lives. And most of us are so accustomed to it that we don't even notice anymore. A Sabbath practice is a weekly reminder of what it feels like to stand our life up straight. The more we can carry that posture into the week, the healthier and more whole our lives will be. And just as it is with physical posture, we need to remind ourselves repeatedly what values we want to live into from moment to moment.

The internal voice I often hear reminding me to stand up straight is an invitation to slow down, to be present to my life *as it's happening* instead of rushing through day after day. I feel that tug toward slowness and presence when I'm walking through the hallways of Western Theological Seminary so quickly that people shift to the side to let me pass—or to make sure I don't run into them! I feel Sabbath inviting me to leave on time when I'm tempted to cram in a few more emails before my next meeting, and I inevitably show up late and frazzled. I remember my Sabbath posture on my commute home as I watch people senselessly weave through traffic while I set my cruise control to the speed limit and breathe into the transition. I inhabit a Sabbath posture when I set my phone to airplane mode in the evening and truly pay attention to my wife, my neighbor, or my nieces.

Adopting a Sabbath posture is about finding ways of allowing our Sabbath day to nourish our workweek, and our workweek to nourish our Sabbath day. Doing this is *not easy*! And it's important to remember that this work is never done—and the point is not perfection! The point is to pay attention to our life's posture and to be curious about how we are living and why we've made the choices we've made. Then we can find meaningful ways of cultivating joy, gratitude, wonder, contentment, and delight in the very midst of our everyday lives. We can remember that each day is a new opportunity to do this, so if we fail one day, we can give ourselves grace and try again tomorrow. Because Sabbath is for anyone who longs to bring their life back down to size, to experience connection, and to live with greater contentment and delight.

Sabbath Is for Everyone

My conviction is that the Sabbath is universal—it's for *everyone*—but there is no uniform way to practice it. I do not advocate a one-size-fits-all approach. The Sabbath way will look different for parents with toddlers than with teens, for college students than retirees, for single parents than two parents in the same home, for single people than for couples without kids. It will look different for painters than for pastors, for bankers than baristas, and for electricians than educators. My sister can't cut and paste into her family the Sabbath my wife and I practice. Since we don't have children, our practice wouldn't translate well into her home, and vice versa.

I suspect that even if we did have kids, my sister still couldn't cut and paste our practice because how we define work and what we find delightful are also different! I find taking walks, watching birds, and reading poetry to be endlessly delightful. I consider most yard work and all home renovations to be "work," even though they aren't my "job." Others may feel the exact opposite and want to fill their Sabbath with yard work and renovations while avoiding poetry and birding like the plague.

At the same time, I can appreciate how previous generations sought to make Sabbath practice consistent by imposing strict rules—whether written or unwritten—that governed what people could and could not do on Sabbath. Within the Christian tradition in the United States, this is part of the legacy of the Puritan Sabbath, which was an essential thread in our cultural fabric for many generations. While it was well-intentioned, the focus often shifted toward controlling how people lived, which reduced the practice to prohibitions and abandoned delight. The tentacles of the Puritan Sabbath still cling to much of the contemporary Christian Sabbath imagination, prompting some to resist it out of fear of doing it "wrong" while others resist it because it feels restrictive in all the worst ways.

The Sabbath way, as we will explore it in this book, is a life marked by both a Sabbath practice and a Sabbath posture, which avoids the trap of Sabbath-as-control by offering a vision of Sabbath-as-ceasing *in the service of delight*. Now more than ever, we need to make space in our personal and collective lives to experience the enduring power of kindness, the sustaining grace of friendship, the awe-inspiring gift of wonder, the perspective-shifting nature of gratitude, the identity-awakening capacity of belonging, and the transformational potential of presence.

Above all, the Sabbath helps us to see and believe in a world that is alive with God's presence. Not only just to see, but also to train our hands to feel, our ears to hear, and our hearts to sense where God is and what God is doing, so that we might find life-affirming ways of joining in God's project of repairing the world. But to do this, the Sabbath must be more than a once-a-week practice disconnected from the rest of life. A Sabbath faithful to the biblical tradition is both a weekly practice and a posture toward all of life.

REFLECTION QUESTIONS

- Imagine sitting down for tea with Sabbath, the compassionate interrogator. How would you respond to the following gentle questions?
  - What would a joyful, vibrant, and meaningful life look like for you during this season?
  - Which of your activities and commitments are necessary or helpful for living into that vision of life? Which are not?
  - What motivates your busyness and striving?
  - How might you slow down your life, even if it means making hard decisions or possibly disappointing people?
- A Sabbath practice requires *time, intentionality,* and *consistency* to bear fruit. Which of these three would come most naturally to you in planning your own Sabbath? Which might you struggle with most? Why?
- Shifting our weekday posture toward a Sabbath-y way of being is how we begin to "stand our life up straight" throughout the week. Listed below are examples of practical ways to make that shift. In what ways might each of the examples challenge you?
- Driving the speed limit

- Being *truly present* in the presence of beauty
- Drinking coffee or eating a meal without doing other things
- Saying "no" when you want to say "no"

Sabbath Practice: Plan a Simple Sabbath

Make a plan for your first (or next) Sabbath. Be intentional about it, but don't overthink it! Start simply knowing your practice can change and evolve over time. Use the following prompts to make your plan.

- At what time on what day will your Sabbath begin?
- At what time on what day will your Sabbath end?
- What will you do as a threshold ritual to mark the transition from regular time to Sabbath time, and back again?
- What activities do you want to refrain from on Sabbath?
- What is one activity you (and your family/friends) can do to experience Sabbath delight?

PART 1

SABBATH AND WORK

2

ORIENTING: WHAT IS WORK?

Productivity is the unspoken virtue of our culture.
FELICIA WU SONG, *RESTLESS DEVICES*

Work, work, work, work, work, work!
RIHANNA, "Work"

Every life is shaped by patterns and habits that emerge from the contexts in which our lives are lived—our families of origin, our experiences in school and the workplace, our ambitions and disappointments, our opportunities and barriers to opportunity. Some habits we choose, such as when we go to bed or wake up, our exercise routines, family meals, or social commitments. Others may be imposed on us, such as when we arrive to and depart from a job, get the kids ready for the bus or pick them up from school, change diapers, or pay the rent.

Beyond these visible and largely external habits are also deeper, invisible patterns—ways of thinking or stories we tell about ourselves—that shape our lives in ways about which we are mostly unconscious. Mariah and I recently discovered that we had been locked into one of these invisible patterns for much of the past twenty years. Our pattern was created by a perfect storm of challenges. Her chronic illness prevented her from working while simultaneously creating significant medical and grocery bills. I was a full-time seminary student working several part-time jobs and always feeling behind—on assignments and our budget. We sent our roots down deep into the soil of scarcity.

The story we told ourselves about ourselves was that she never had enough energy or health to contribute meaningfully to life; I never had enough time or money to fulfill my obligations and provide for our needs. This story of lack was reinforced and redoubled from every corner of our lives. In a culture obsessed with productivity, her inability to produce told her that she was deficient and that something was wrong with her that needed fixing, deepening her shame around not making money and tempting her to push every limit to regain her health. In a culture obsessed with achievement and efficiency, I felt like I had to choose between professional advancement and being present as my wife's primary caregiver. Saying yes to her felt like saying no to opportunities to build my CV and make extra money, which my scarcity mindset told me we needed desperately. This sense of lack saturated our lives and created a pattern that marked our relationship for years.

The superpower of patterns like this is their invisibility. They evolve as our circumstances change. Because they influence our core sense of identity, they shape how we view the world and ourselves in it. Just like the Sabbath, the cultural values in which our lives are steeped also seek to shape our posture toward life. For example, even though Mariah and I have stabilized our finances, and my income now covers all our needs, we still struggle with a scarcity mindset because it has become a lens through which we view our lives.

But one very essential thing *has* changed: we are now aware of the pattern! We can *see* how the tentacles of scarcity squeeze our joy, diminish our delight, cultivate anxiety, and tempt us to seek distraction. And *seeing* the pattern is the first step toward breaking out of it.

It was our Sabbath practice that exposed the vise grip of scarcity in which we'd been caught. And it is our Sabbath posture that is helping us begin to live beyond it. Each week as we experiment with embracing our enough-ness, reconnecting to our bodies, decoupling our value from our productivity, and receiving the gifts of rest and delight, we are partnering with the Spirit in discovering the abundant life Jesus came to offer us. But I'll be honest, it is not easy! Our Sabbath is a weekly act of protest against the currents of diminishment that swirl about us every day. But we cannot cease from what we cannot see. Awareness fuels intention.

In light of this, our exploration of work begins with an invitation to *see* how our relationship to work is being formed by invisible cultural currents that are inherently anti-Sabbath. And by "work," I mean *things done daily*, the actions and behaviors that occupy our time and from which we seek to derive our identity and value—whether for a salary or a degree, as a volunteer, or as a parent raising children. Work is what we think of when someone asks, "So, what do you do?" Everybody works. Some get paid for it and some don't.

There are at least four invisible cultural currents we need to see more clearly to understand how work is forming—or *mal*forming—us, and how the Sabbath can help us break out of our unhealthy and unsustainable patterns. These four anti-Sabbath currents are: the lie that our work defines our identity, the fact that our work is disconnected from body and space, the temptation to believe we must earn everything, and the trap that confines us in a cycle of productivity shame.

Current 1: Our Work Defines Our Identity

How many conversations have you had with someone you just met that began with, "Hi, nice to meet you! So, what do you do?" In the social mores of North American society, "What do you do?" is a high-priority question. Outside of the rhetorical "What's up?" or "How ya doing?," it is very often the first question anyone asks someone they are meeting for the first time. This is at least partly because we associate identity with productivity. The expected response is a job title, which elevates paid labor as a social value over other ways of being in time.

Friends of mine from other parts of the world are less interested in what I *do* than in who I know. My family and friends are points of reference for them in learning who I am at my core. In parts of the world less affected by individualism and consumerism, identity begins with relationships, starting with your family and extending to your community, tribe, or ethnic group.

My point is not that one cultural value is good and the other bad. My point is that identity is a complex, dynamic, mysterious, and culturally specific reality, unfolding and evolving over time. It includes our relationships and experiences, our gifts and passions, our bodies and voices. It includes how we offer our inner lives to the world, whether through a paying job, in random acts of kindness, through volunteering, or in social media posts. It also includes all the private, hidden ways we interact with the world, which no one will ever see or know. When identity is reduced to a single, static reality, like what you do for a living, the vast and complex reality that is you is condensed into a single word: professor, painter, plumber, photographer, parent. Or, if you don't have an answer for "What do you do?," your identity can be erased entirely, and your value ignored or denied.

The late Catholic priest Henri Nouwen spoke passionately about the dangers endemic to a cultural milieu in which our *doing* in the world—as well as the economic, social, and consumeristic implications of our doing—shapes our identity and determines our value. Nouwen taught that we all spend our lives answering one fundamental question: *Who am I?* Drawing on the biblical account of Jesus' temptation by the devil in the wilderness (Matthew 4:1-11), Nouwen identified three lies American culture tells us in response to this question.

- *I am what I do.* Do something special: "Turn this stone into bread."
- *I am what others say or think about me.* "Throw yourself down from here"—so that others might see and be amazed.
- *I am what I have.* "Bow down and worship me, and all this will be yours."[1]

I imagine you feel instinctively the power these lies wield. Far from supporting and reinforcing our identities, they work in concert to colonize[2] us, extracting all the resources they can—our time, our attention, our energy, our finances—while providing us enough tastes of satisfaction to keep us searching and longing. Perhaps this is why substance abuse therapist Mary Bell described achievement as the "alcohol of our time."[3] While achievement gives us a feel-good high, the feeling is ephemeral; its absence leaves us longing for more.

When we believe that who we are is dependent on what we do, what we have, and what others say or think about us, we buy into a self-perpetuating cycle of scarcity. We will never be enough, because there is always more to do, more to buy, and more people to impress. And there will always be people who do more, have more, and are more impressive than we are.

The lies serve only themselves and the system that created them. Scarcity is the currency of consumerist economies. The greater the sense of lack, the more willing people are to do whatever they can to satiate that sense of deficiency, even for a moment. The power of the lies is inversely correlated to our ignorance of them: the less we see the lies, the more powerful they become.

This came home to me a few years ago when a dear friend and mentor shared the story about the day he learned what it *really* meant to work. Tom started working at Hendricks Supply Company, a sheet metal shop where his dad did the books, when he was around eleven (child labor laws were less enforced back then!). One of the tasks at Hendricks was feeding large pieces of sheet metal into a machine that bent and crimped them into the shape that would fit into a furnace. Tom loved working with Denny, an eighteen-year-old whom Tom idolized, to feed metal into the machine. Denny knew how to work and took his job very seriously.

At one point, Denny cut his arm badly on a piece of metal as they put it into the machine. After a brief pause, he motioned the others to keep the metal coming (a piece came out every ten seconds). Despite the blood dripping down his arm, Denny kept feeding the machine. Nothing was more important than the job.

Eventually, Tom's dad came by to check on them and immediately sent Denny to the ER to treat the wound. Later that night, on the drive home, Tom's dad reflected on the day. He marveled at the young man's work ethic. Taking advantage of the teachable moment, he put his hand on Tom's leg and said with great earnestness, "Did you see that Denny? He works like the *devil!*" In that moment, Tom knew what was expected of him. If he wanted his dad's attention, *he* would need to work like the devil too. He would need to work in a way that denied self, pain, exhaustion, and limits—to work until he dropped, then get up and work more. That kind of work would win approval and praise. Remember, Tom was only eleven years old!

This story is a microcosm of our crisis with work. Too many of us have been bleeding for our jobs and ignoring the pain for too long. The Sabbath invitation is to feel and embrace our inherent "enough-ness" *apart* from our work. A weekly Sabbath practice is an act of protest against defining who we are through the matrix of the three lies: *I am what I do. I am what others say or think about me. I am what I have.*

Current 2: Our Work Is Disconnected from Body and Space

In 1991, theologian Miroslav Volf explored the theological dynamics of what he called the "crisis of work" in the West.[4] Over three decades later, much of his analysis of the crisis remains relevant—even more so as the world has continued to evolve toward increasingly virtual spaces within an increasingly globalized context.

Volf traces the history of work through three eras of human history: agricultural, industrial, and informational.[5] To oversimplify the history somewhat, in the agricultural era almost everyone engaged in physical activity that was embodied and local. The fruits of each person's labors fed, clothed, and sheltered themselves and their neighbors. In the industrial era work became mechanized and skills were reduced to a narrow band of repetitive actions in service of efficiency, mass productivity (think the assembly line), and profit through market share expansion. The informational age abstracted work from its native contexts even further. It took the blueprint of the industrial age and expanded it exponentially through technology that refined production processes, increased the scale of production, and broadened the market to include the whole world.

ORIENTING: WHAT IS WORK?

I understand the trajectory Volf describes as an ongoing and accelerating process of *abstractification* of work. By "abstractification" I mean the process by which the contexts and the products of our work have progressively fewer concrete and recognizable connections to our basic human needs of survival, such as nourishment, shelter, and connection. Work has similarly been on a long trajectory away from the body and toward the mind. Mediated by screens and isolated in cubicles, so much of the work we do today is *mental* activity.

When so much of our lives is focused on mental activity we lose touch with our bodies, which are doorways into the present moment. The abstractification of work reinforces the power of the three lies, which are deeply entrenched neural pathways, or habituated ways of thinking. An effective way to jump out of these neural pathways is to reconnect with our bodies, whether through breathing, physical activity, movement, laughter, or play.

For most of human history (the agricultural era), intrinsic connections between work, the world, and human survival lent a sense of self-evident meaning to the work being done inside and outside the home and embedded that meaning in a community that shared the burdens of the work while benefiting from one another's labors. The work wasn't always easy—or enjoyable—but it was intrinsically meaningful by virtue of its explicit connection to the flourishing of the land and the neighborhood.

This is no longer the case. Work is increasingly *dis*embodied, *dis*connected, digitized, virtualized, and mechanized. For those who spend their days designing the next mobile app, entering data into spreadsheets for a multinational corporation, or answering phones at a tech giant's customer care center, the work may provide flashes of meaning, but it takes a bit of imagination to connect one's work with the flourishing of one's neighbor or neighborhood. If we are what we do, and what we do has no obvious or inherent life-affirming purpose beyond securing us a paycheck, we hemorrhage a significant source of meaning in our lives, draining work of its power to connect us to each other and to something larger than ourselves.

This disconnect between the work so many of us do, the bodies and places in which our lives are lived, and the meaning we all long to participate in is "symptomatic of a life that is fragmented and without a unifying context," as theologian Norman Wirzba put it.[6] The challenges so many of us face to find meaning and significance in our work are mirrors of the larger challenges we face to find meaning and significance in our lives.

Current 3: Our Work Teaches Us We Must Earn Everything

On a recent Sabbath morning, I left the house early for the walk that has become my Sabbath custom. I cut through the parking lot behind my house, then through the ball fields and into the forest flanking Rush Creek, which flows between Elmwood and Apio Lakes. As soon as I was out of earshot of the neighbors, I inhaled sharply and let out what Mariah and I call a "Sabbath sigh."

The Sabbath sigh is our embodied way of releasing the tensions of the week and acknowledging the goodness of the Sabbath, enabling us to be right here, fully present in this moment, as all intentional breathing techniques teach us to do. As I inhaled, I felt the tensions of the week. It had been a very full week. But as my lungs filled with air, I also felt a deep sense of gratitude for how I had showed up to the fullness. I had been faithful, done what I needed to do, and had performed my duties well. I was proud of myself and the week that was. I was also glad it was over! As I exhaled that Sabbath sigh, I heard myself say aloud, "Ahh, I *earned* my Sabbath this week!"

As soon as I said it, I stopped in my tracks. *What?!* I *earned* my Sabbath?! I had been practicing Sabbath for years, had taught seminary courses on it and preached about it in churches—and yet somehow the most basic aspect of the Sabbath had failed to sink into my soul. Sabbath rest is a gift of grace; it *cannot* be earned or bought. I was flabbergasted.

That flabbergassery prompted an insight into my instincts. It would have been one thing if I had simply felt deeply my gratitude for a week of hard work and a job well done. But I didn't do that. Or I did *more* than that, rather. I concluded that my hard work had *earned* me the right to rest. I had paid for it with my toil, and now it was my reward. The shift was subtle but fundamental. I had regressed from receiving rest as a gift to deserving it, and ultimately possessing it (I called it "*my* Sabbath"), all in the space of a breath. A gift, however, can only be received. To attempt to do otherwise is to violate its spirit and dishonor the giver.

While it was a simple slip of the tongue, it exposed a value, baked into the bread of our culture, that all the good things in life must be earned. We earn a paycheck in exchange for hours worked or projects completed; we earn grades in exchange for assignments finished on time; we earn praise for having a good work ethic, arriving early and leaving late, and being a team player. We earn the right to rest and play by completing our work. These are common, everyday exchanges. None of them are problematic in and of themselves.

The problem arises when earning is universalized beyond the specific instances for which it is beneficial. When it becomes an essential element of what makes a person or a life valuable or good, it begins to shape our instincts in progressively problematic ways. We begin to believe that anything can be ours if we just work hard enough—and if we work hard but do not get what we want, we grow resentful. We begin to view all of life as a transaction in which other people and creation are reduced to their utility as the reward for our ambition. We begin to believe that anything can be possessed, and the world is ours for the taking.

This progression is deeply American; it is expressed in some of our nation's darkest moments in history, from our relationship with the indigenous populations of the Americas to our pillaging of Africa's people and natural resources. It may seem like a hard pivot to go from feeling like I earned my Sabbath to the transatlantic slave trade. In some ways, of course, it is. But the two are not unconnected. A similar principle informs them both. When everything is filtered through a lens of earning and reward, it cultivates a sense of entitlement that animates greed and justifies ownership and possession. When that perspective is reinforced by power—whether social, political, spiritual, cultural, economic, or military power—its effects can be devastating. History is strewn with the casualties this perspective has justified.

Most of us live on a much smaller scale, however. We are more likely to get caught in the trap of trying to earn a gift than spearheading the next devastating historical event. When we expect everything to be earned, we distort or deny encounters with things that can *only* be given and received. The most important parts of our lives—what makes them meaningful and worth living—are, by definition, gifts. Grace, forgiveness, generosity, and love cannot be earned, taken, or owned. To possess them is to lose them. They exist only when they are freely given and received. The attempt to earn them erodes them, draining them of their transformative power. What was meant to be hallowed becomes hollowed out, like a tree in which termites have made their home: any gust of wind or passing storm is likely to bring it all crashing down.

Current 4: Our Work Traps Us in a Cycle of Productivity Shame

Another cultural current that shapes our lives in anti-Sabbath ways is a hyperfocus on productivity. Cultural sociologist Felicia Wu Song describes productivity as "the unspoken virtue of our culture."[7] Her use of the language of virtue is significant here as virtues name what we aspire to. When productivity is our aspiration, we enable it to define our identity and value—in our own eyes, and in the eyes of others. According to Song, productivity is "one of the most powerful lenses through which we evaluate the worth and success of someone's life."[8]

We all want to live lives worthy of the breath we are given. We want to be respected and affirmed by the people we know and love. We want to succeed in the work that has been set before us, whether we are a second-shift janitor, an ER triage nurse, a small business owner, or a stay-at-home parent. People want to do their best, but it seems like just about everyone is exhausted, stressed, anxious, and overwhelmed. When an exhausted and overwhelmed society attempts to fulfill the demands of a culture hyperfocused on productivity, the gap between expectation and reality widens. In a society like this, the consequences of underproducing are significant.

On her podcast *Hurry Slowly*, Jocelyn K. Glei explored a powerful cycle of self-sabotage many of us get trapped in when we find ourselves in the crosshairs of productivity culture and the limits of human energy and capacity. She calls this cycle "productivity shame," and offers several examples on the way to developing a definition.

Productivity shame is committing "to a schedule or workload that you intuitively know at the outset is unrealistic . . . and then later on you beat yourself up when you're unable to meet that schedule." Or it is setting "an incredibly challenging goal for yourself without creating any structure for emotional support or accountability, and then you blame your failure to meet those goals on a lack of personal willpower." Or how about "not defining what enough looks like in advance, whether it's for knocking stuff off your to-do list, or even making money with your business, and then berating yourself later for not having done enough." Glei then offers this definition: "Productivity shame is the act of setting utterly unrealistic goals or schedules for yourself and then beating yourself up when you fail to meet them."[9] I feel the sting of these self-sabotaging habits in my own life almost every day. I suspect you do too.

The connection between feeling like we haven't produced enough and feeling like we are not enough is why the word *shame* in "productivity shame" is so important. Sociologist Brené Brown, a leading shame researcher, clarifies a fundamental distinction between shame and its would-be doppelgänger, guilt. Guilt has to do with behavior. Its message is, "I did something wrong." Shame, on the other hand, has to do with identity. Its message is, "I *am* wrong."[10] When we are what we do and we're convinced we aren't doing enough, shame makes its home in our hearts. That shame feeds the cycle of ceaseless doing and fuels our futile efforts to earn our worth and find that elusive "enough." This cycle is unsustainable. It is *not* working.

What's at Stake in Seeing Our Work

Many of the cultural forces shaping us, including those I've described here, have a vested interest in our diminishment, distractibility, and dissatisfaction. Their objective, among other things, is to lull us into believing that surviving the slog until the next vacation is all we can hope for. Even more insidious is believing that the cycle of "work-work-work-work-work-vacation" *is* the good life.

Ultimately, what's at stake is having no answer for T. S. Eliot's existential question: "Where is the Life we have lost in living?"[11] Do you know where your life is going? Do you know where it went? Have you misplaced your life while living it? If so, you are not alone.

Jesus said he came that we may have life, and life abundant (see John 10:10)! The Sabbath is one of the Bible's most powerful strategies for receiving this gift. I think this is why so much of Jesus' ministry took place on Sabbath days. Jesus wanted to draw our attention to its transformational power. He healed on the Sabbath to demonstrate that healing and wholeness are at the heart of a Sabbath life, and that rest, just like healing, is a gift we cannot earn. Jesus wanted to reorient Sabbath observance from a mechanism of control, perfection, and spiritual status to an experience of delight, abundance, and belonging.

Delight, abundance, and belonging—along with gratitude, connection, and joy—are at the heart of the life Sabbath offers us. But so many of us have lost the trailhead to the Sabbath way in the course of living and working in the world.

A Sabbath practice is an act of protest against defining ourselves and our worth through the matrix of the three identity lies, which will always tell us we are not enough, and that the way to wholeness and happiness is *doing more*. The Sabbath says we are first and foremost human *beings*, not human *doings*, and that we are complete and whole as we are, right now. The Sabbath reminds us that making partner or becoming a president or a phlebotomist will not make us whole. It invites us to believe with poet Brad Aaron Modlin that "*I am / is a complete sentence.*"[12]

Every week, we have an opportunity to practice showing up to life differently. Every week, we have an opportunity to reflect on how we showed up to our work the previous week, and to learn from it and explore other ways of working in the future. Even though so much is at stake, the Sabbath invitation is to play with life, to experiment and try things out, to not take ourselves too seriously. We will inevitably fall back into old habits of anxiety and busyness and distraction. But each week we have an opportunity to reorient back toward the Sabbath way—a way marked by slowness, gratitude, abundance, and delight. Staying on that path will require some hard choices. Sabbath delight exists only on the other side of Sabbath ceasing.

REFLECTION QUESTIONS

- Henri Nouwen named three identity lies: *I am what I do. I am what others say or think about me. I am what I have.*
  - » Which lie is most challenging for you to resist? Why?
  - » Recall a time when you were seduced into believing one or more of these lies. What impact did the lies have on your thoughts and behaviors, your relationships, your sense of self-worth?
- The way we see our work is shaped by the four cultural forces listed below, each of which is largely invisible to us.
  - » *Our work defines our identity.* What aspect of your work gives you the most meaning or sense of value and identity? How would it impact your sense of identity if you were to lose that aspect of your work?
  - » *Our work is disconnected from body and space.* How connected is your work to your body, to the flourishing of yourself and others, to a purpose larger than yourself?
  - » *Our work teaches us we must earn everything.* In what ways are you most tempted to earn what can only be received as a gift (such as grace, forgiveness, generosity, or love)?
  - » *Our work traps us in a cycle of productivity shame.* When, recently, have you experienced productivity shame—feeling like you aren't enough because you haven't produced enough?

- In what ways is your view of work an *adversary*, something that makes it harder for you to experience such gifts as delight, abundance, belonging, gratitude, contentment, and joy? In what ways is your view of work an *ally*, something that makes it easier for you to experience these gifts?

Sabbath Practice: Make a Plan to Protest and Play

To work in accordance with the Sabbath way is to protest by resisting the identity lies and cultural forces that fuel our anxiety, busyness, and distraction. The Sabbath way also invites us to play with life, to experiment and try things out so we can embrace slowness, gratitude, and delight. As you anticipate the week ahead, use the prompts below to identify how you can protest and play.

- **Protest.** Listed below are the three identity lies and examples of simple actions you can take to protest those lies. Each includes at least one physical activity to break you out of the lie's well-worn neural pathway and back into your body, where its power has less effect over you.

    » *I am what I do.* During a busy part of the day sit quietly for five minutes of intentional breathing. As you breathe, remind yourself, *"I am" is a complete sentence.*

    » *I am what others say or think about me.* Write "I am loved" or "I am enough" on a card and post it where you'll see it during the day. Every time you see it, stand on one leg for two minutes. The silliness and physicality will break the lie's power.

    » *I am what I have.* Give something away—an object, or a compliment—and notice how it feels. Shake or wiggle your body for thirty seconds; feel the rush of life in you and affirm your inherent enough-ness.

- **Play.** Listed below are three Sabbath values and examples of simple actions you can take to experience these values in the context of daily work.

» *Slowness.* Do only one thing at a time, and smile while you do it; notice how smiling changes your attitude. Out of the blue, ask a coworker a silly question, such as, "What color are you today?" Walk slowly to your next meeting—or perhaps skip to your meeting and see how it changes how you show up.

» *Gratitude.* Tell your boss or coworker something about them for which you're sincerely grateful. Ask a coworker (or a stranger you encounter through your work!) what they're grateful for today.

» *Delight.* Bring in treats to share or a vase of flowers for the office, just because. Write a coworker a silly, encouraging note and put it at their workstation while they're away. Wear a color, an accessory, or a playful item of clothing you wouldn't normally wear to work. Invite a coworker to join you for a coffee break or to do something outside of work.

Choose one or more of the examples or create your own way to play and experiment with Sabbath values in the context of your work this week.

If you find it helpful, write down your daily observations about your acts of protest and play in a journal. At the end of the week, review your written observations and reflect on how your acts of protest and play impacted the way you showed up to work.

3

DISORIENTING STRIVING

Six days you shall work.
GOD, EXODUS 20:9

It is a sacred act to pause. And it has become a radical act to stop, or even to slow down.
KRISTI NELSON, WAKE UP GRATEFUL

A few years ago, I decided to teach a new course titled "The Art of the Sabbath." I had sensed for years that our seminary students were exhausted, overwhelmed, and feeling burned out even *before* they accepted their first call to full-time ministry. I felt a responsibility to help my students imagine what a healthy approach to ministry might look like, one that honored their human limits while preserving their passion and capacity to pour into the people they would minister to for the long haul—people who were *also* exhausted, overwhelmed, and on the verge of burnout. At the same time, I felt like my own Sabbath practice was stagnant and uninspired. I hoped that teaching this class would stimulate new creativity and intentionality in my practice as well. What I did not anticipate was the extent to which shining a Sabbath light on my students' lives would end up exposing my own life's unhealthy patterns.

The whole semester was an extended immersion in irony. I realized how driven I was by perfectionism as I worked relentlessly to create the *perfect* content to convince my students to embrace their imperfections. I felt ashamed when boasting to myself that I worked a fifteen-hour day that included writing a lecture about the perils of productivity shame. I raced through my days while advising my students to s l o w d o w n and reject the premise that a go-go-go lifestyle is the path to success. I felt the sting of conviction when teaching my students to resist the self-sabotage of overcommitting and saying yes to everything as compensation for a persistent fear of deficiency, when that was precisely what I had done for years.

The nagging sense that my life was out of sync with the subject matter of the class haunted me all semester, but I was too busy to stop and listen. Well, to be truly honest, I was too afraid to stop and listen. I was certain the Sabbath would wag its finger at me and say, "Aha! I caught you, you hypocrite!" As ridiculous as it sounds, that fear drove me. So I kept my head down and pushed through, striving to make this the best, most transformative, most restful class ever.

Eventually, I ran out of gas. Around week twelve of the fourteen-week semester I crashed and threw my hands in the air, shouting to the proverbial skies that I couldn't do it anymore. I couldn't sustain the pace or maintain equilibrium under the pressure I had put on myself to be perfect and always have it together. When I finally stopped and listened to what the Sabbath was saying to me, what I heard sounded a lot different than what I'd expected.

The Sabbath didn't want to expose me as a fraud and a failure. It wanted me to slow down, take a breath, and listen to my anxiety and my fear. It wanted me to see my struggles with Sabbath-keeping not as a moral failure but an opportunity to empathize with my students, to normalize *their* struggles by sharing mine—and then for us to pause together and listen to what our struggles could teach us about how we've been formed and where we needed to grow.

Ultimately, I learned that a primary purpose of the Sabbath is to disrupt the habituated ways we show up to our lives. Our work-related habits are some of the most deeply formed and unconscious of all our habits. And the stakes are high when these habits are tied to our livelihoods and the nurturing of our children and family life. But for so many, the status quo—the pervasive cultural forces shaping how and why we work—is, well, not working. The Sabbath's goal is to provoke us to protest these forces and the anti-Sabbath ways they compel us to live so we can begin living beyond them. Changing our habits and resisting the pull to produce, to rush, to stress, to control is challenging, slow work. It can feel like we are cracking open. And yet, as songwriter Leonard Cohen reminded us, the cracks are "how the light gets in."[1] They're also, as poet Brian Andreas reminds us, how our "love spill[s] out into the world."[2]

For us to understand how the Sabbath does this, we need to go back to the biblical understanding of work, and particularly to the context in which Israel's Sabbath originated. That's where we learn how God used the Sabbath to disrupt the formative power that the culture of work in Egypt had over the people of Israel. Then we will be able to see how the Sabbath also disrupts the formative power the culture of work exerts on us today.

Work and Rest in Exodus

Within the biblical imagination, work and Sabbath are two halves of an inseparable pair. Neither can be fully understood apart from the other because each one provides the essential context in which the other's purpose is clarified and fulfilled. In both versions of the fourth commandment, which offer some of the Bible's most explicit teaching on Sabbath rest, work and Sabbath are uttered in the same breath: "Six days you shall labor and do all your work, but the seventh day is a Sabbath to the LORD your God" (Exodus 20:9-10; Deuteronomy 5:13-14).

It is interesting that rest is not the Sabbath commandment's only requirement. Work is also commanded. Work and rest need each other. Rest without work is just extended leisure, a sort of permanent vacation devoid of a larger purpose outside oneself. But without rest, work loses its limits and can become an addiction or an idol, even a form of slavery. The book of Exodus offers the Bible's most substantive reflection on the nature of work in relation to Sabbath. We must begin there to understand the Bible's vision for how Sabbath rest disrupts forms of work that diminish, deny, and deform God's good creation.

Throughout the book of Exodus, two words are used to compare the "work" the Israelites did in Egypt under Pharaoh's iron thumb with the "work" they performed in the wilderness constructing the Tabernacle for the Lord. In both cases the Israelites constructed building projects at the behest of a higher power, but the two types of work couldn't have been more different.

The Hebrew word *avodah* (ah-voh-DAH) is related to the word for "servant" and "slave" (*eved*) and describes Israel's forced labor under Pharaoh's yoke of oppression. *Avodah* is work that disregards the limitations of human capacity and the earth's resources. It is work without Sabbath: unceasing, exploitative, all-consuming, soul-crushing. It is work fueled by anxiety. Israel built storehouses to hold Pharaoh's surplus because Pharaoh was terrified of scarcity. *Avodah*'s only metrics are productivity and profit. Pharaoh cared about little more than how many bricks were built by the end of each day—and how much wealth he amassed by the end of each year.

Does this sound familiar? A work culture fueled by anxiety and scarcity, measured by productivity and profit, which is inherently exploitative and denies the dignity of both worker and land? According to Bible scholar Ellen Davis, Egypt is the biblical analogue of industrial work systems like ours in the US.[3] And the book of Exodus offers a resounding critique of such systems, which deny God as Creator by diminishing or dehumanizing that which God created good.

The critique Exodus is making comes in the contrasting form of work introduced after God liberates Israel from Egypt and gives them instructions for building the Tabernacle in the wilderness. Constructing God's house involved not *avodah* but *melakhah* (meh-lah-KHAH). In addition to "work," *melakhah* refers to "craftsmanship and handiwork." *Melakhah* is a word conveying immense dignity.[4] Its emphasis falls on skilled labor and its benefits—to the workers, to the community, to the earth that offers its resources, and ultimately to God from whose creativity all *melakhah* flows.

Melakhah is work defined by the limits of Sabbath—this work must give way to rest every *shabbat*. But the spirit of Sabbath also permeates *melakhah* with the sense that it is contributing to something larger. *Melakhah* is fueled not by anxiety but by God's abundant sufficiency. God works, then stops to rest and delight. We can too.

Not incidentally, *melakhah* is the term the poet in Genesis used to describe God's work in creation, from which God ceased on the Sabbath (see Genesis 2:2-3). When we *melakhah*, we *melakhah* with God, just as when we *shabbat*, we *shabbat* with God. *Avodah* denies this pattern of participation. Sabbath can help restore it. And when we bring Sabbath into conversation with the four ways the culture of work (mal)forms us today, the trailhead of the Sabbath way emerges.

Sabbath Disorients Our Cultural Formation

The Sabbath's work is to usher us into a life marked by delight, wonder, connection, gratitude, justice, and joy. But before it can do that it has to re-create our priorities in its image. So many of our priorities are created in the image of work systems infused with the ethos of Egypt. The only way we can break free from their metaphorical grip is to literally break free from work each week, and then pay attention to what it feels like when we do. This is Sabbath's first and essential gift.

When we cease from our work, we begin to create pathways around and through the barriers we discussed in the previous chapter. The Sabbath helps restore our true identity (*nephesh*, in Hebrew). It reminds us we have bodies with limits, confirms that radical rest is a gift we cannot earn, and teaches us to celebrate unproductive time.

Sabbath Re-Nepheshes Us

One of the most striking Sabbath passages in the Bible comes at the end of Exodus 31, in which God concludes a long section of directives related to the Tabernacle (Israel's "work" in the wilderness) with instructions on Sabbath. The passage includes many striking elements, from identifying the Sabbath as an everlasting sign of the covenant between

God and God's people to the repeated warning of the death penalty for breaking the Sabbath. Clearly, Sabbath is extremely important to God. But this is the verse that takes my breath away: "[Sabbath] is an everlasting sign between me and Israel that in six days the LORD made heaven and earth, and on the seventh day God rested and *was refreshed*" (Exodus 31:17, emphasis added). That final word is profound—God was "refreshed" on the Sabbath! To make sense of this we need to take a closer look at the Hebrew word used here.

The Hebrew word *nephesh* is at the root of the word translated "was refreshed." While the verb form is used here, the noun *nephesh* is the most common way the root appears in Scripture. *Nephesh* is the closest Hebrew equivalent to the "true self." It refers to all that constituted "Life"—with a capital L—for the people of Israel. It can also be translated as "throat" or "life-breath"; one's personality, being, or self; one's soul; even the members of one's household. All that in one word! *Nephesh* is one's essence, shaped by one's body and intimate relationships. Contrasting with the English word "soul," *nephesh* is profoundly embodied. You do not *have* a *nephesh*; you *are* a *nephesh*. It is what the Great Shepherd "restores" in Psalm 23. It is what blesses the Lord in Psalm 103.

The verb used in Exodus 31:17 suggests that Sabbath "re-*nephesh*es" us. One scholar described this as "a fresh infusion of spiritual and physical vigor, the reinvigoration of the totality of one's being."[5] That sounds pretty amazing to me! That is, I think, what we all want deep down, to be fully and completely alive. And yet, our work is costly. We give and we give. Even when our work is meaningful and life-giving, it can often leave us depleted and spent, even frustrated and resentful. How much more so when the work is demeaning or monotonous. Thus, the Sabbath inquires whether our work is the best (or only) place to search for an answer to life's most fundamental question: Who am I? Who is this broken, battered, and beautiful *nephesh*?

We tend to search in vain for external answers to this question. But the only way to truly answer it is to *live* into it, to slowly *become* the answer by slowly growing more fully into ourselves. Sabbath apprentices us along this lifelong journey. It helps clear the fog and noise from all the messaging we receive that attempts to supply answers based on the unsustainable whims of what we do, what we have, and what people say about us. Each of us needs to answer that fundamental question for ourselves. We need each other, of course; no one can do this alone. Yet each person's journey is, ultimately, their own.

There is a Hasidic tale that captures poignantly both the urgency and the paradox of becoming the *nephesh* that we are. In the tale, near the end of his life, Rabbi Zusya says, "In the coming world, they will not ask me: 'Why were you not Moses?' They will ask me: 'Why were you not Zusya?'"[6] Rabbi Zusya's wisdom is echoed in the words of Master Shifu when he reveals his purpose to his puzzled pupil, Po, the Dragon Warrior of *Kung Fu Panda 3*, saying, "I'm not trying to turn you into me; I'm trying to turn you into *you*."[7] The Sabbath is a companion to us on the journey of becoming ourselves, of finding again what T. S. Eliot called "the Life we have lost in living."[8] The hope is that when that fateful day comes, Rabbi Zusya's question won't even need to be asked, since our life—our *nephesh*—will have already lived the answer.

Sabbath Honors Our Bodies and Limits

We live in a time of paradox regarding our bodies. As I discussed in the previous chapter, our current era has increasingly abstracted work from our bodies and physical locations, focusing work more and more on mental activity facilitated by screens instead of sunlight. In an environment like this it is easy to forget that we have bodies and that they have needs and limits. This is especially true when the demands on our time and energy are so high and everything around us tells us to just push through and stop whining, that we can sleep after we retire—or die!

The church doesn't have a great track record on its teaching of the "work" of discipleship and faith either. In many Christian traditions faith is reduced to believing the right ideas, discipleship is diminished to acts of reading and uttering words, and worship and sermons rarely refer to the whole body outside of cautioning us against the temptations of the flesh.

At the same time, in the larger culture, our bodies are the focus of a multibillion-dollar industry, whether it is hair or skin products, workout equipment or gym memberships, diets and cookbooks, fashion and clothing, reality shows and podcasts about health, pharmaceuticals, or food manufacturers. We are living in the tension of a time in which a great deal of attention is directed toward something we are adamantly ignoring.

Whether we sacrifice our bodies to get ahead or get by, deny our passions and desires in search of purity, or obsess over products to improve how we look and feel, our bodies are suffering. They are crying out for rest and attention if we will just slow down long enough to listen.

The weekly break from work on Sabbath gives us an opportunity to do just that: to honor our bodies, to ask whether the pace of our life is sustainable, to listen to what hurts, what is sore, what is begging for our attention. Instead of waiting for sickness to force us to stop, Sabbath invites us to stop and listen every week. But more than just stopping our frantic striving, it's also an opportunity to embrace activities or experiences that bring us delight and connect us to our deepest joy *in our bodies*, whether it's going for walks, snuggling with a child or pet, slowly sipping wine with a friend, or learning the steps to Michael Jackson's "Thriller" or the latest viral dance track. Sometimes we have to assert joy into our lives as an act of protest against the belief that there is no time or space for it. A Sabbath practice is a weekly invitation to do that. A Sabbath posture invites us to bring our joy and delight with us to work and assert it there as well.

Sabbath Is a Gift

Jesus said, "Sabbath was made for humankind, and not humankind for the Sabbath" (Mark 2:27). From this we can learn many things. For example, we are not slaves to Sabbath. The Sabbath was created by God to fulfill God's purpose, just as humans were. But more than anything else this passage reminds us that Sabbath is a gift given to us by God in love. The first humans were created at the end of the sixth day, so their first day of life was Sabbath; they rested before they ever worked.

Sabbath rest is radical because we cannot earn it, nor is it given as a reward. It is a gift.

We are generally more comfortable earning things than receiving things, though. We would rather offer help than receive it, meet a need than express one. We're more comfortable being strong than weak, generous than needy, the counselor than the counseled. We believe that our lives will matter more if we are the ones giving, not receiving. But Sabbath is *always* about receiving. It is *never* about earning or achieving.

We resist the Sabbath because we do not know who we are apart from what we do. And when we are put in a position where there is nothing for us to do except "do nothing," we are terrified. We are terrified because we imagine we will discover that *we* are nothing, that our lives do not matter and that all our striving and rushing around has been in vain.

The Sabbath wants to remind us every week that our lives *already* matter, and more than we could possibly imagine! We are *already* the brightest lights shining in a dark and hurting world. But we don't trust in the goodness or the embrace of God. We don't trust that God already loves us *just as we are*. We don't trust that we deserve delight even if we haven't completed our work. We don't trust that if we stop working the world will remain intact. The gift of the Sabbath is to burst our belief in limiting lies, and to remind us that rest and delight are birthrights we cannot earn. Are we willing to receive this gift?

Sabbath Celebrates Unproductive Time

Mariah and I have been exploring breathing practices lately. Recent research on the importance of breathing has confirmed centuries of indigenous wisdom on the essential connection between healthy breathing and overall well-being, including reduced stress, anxiety, blood pressure, and more. Breathing is also a metaphor for living. When we inhale, we receive life from the world in the form of rest and refreshment. When we exhale, we offer our gifts to the world in the form of work.

What is obvious about breathing is that we must exhale *and* inhale to survive. The same is true regarding work and rest. We are created in the image of the creating God; we are meant to create. Work is *good*; it is native to who we are. But we cannot survive if all we do is exhale. Eventually, we would run out of breath and collapse. And just as we must balance exhaling with inhaling, we must balance working with resting.

What is fascinating about breathing as a metaphor for work and rest is that many breathing techniques give more time to exhaling than inhaling. It is possible to breathe in quickly and sufficiently. It is harder to breathe out quickly and completely. Maintaining a balance between the inhale and exhale does not mean the two are equal in duration. "Six days you shall work," says God in the fourth commandment. "But the seventh day is a Sabbath to the Lord your God" (Exodus 20:9-10). And that ratio is not imbalanced! You exhale for six days and inhale for one.

This establishes a rhythm for life. We are created to create, and many of us will create a lot! But we will only be able to sustain that level of productivity if we also regularly and intentionally do not produce. It is like the tree in Psalm 1 that is a symbol of the ideal disciple. The tree produces its fruit "in season" (Psalm 1:3). The tree does not produce fruit all day every day; it produces *only* in its season. And just as both tree and soil need the inhale of winter before exhaling another harvest come summer or fall, so too we need regular breaks from producing to be able to produce when the season is right.

The six-and-one-day rhythm resonates with a weekly Sabbath practice. But the metaphor of seasonal fruitfulness also resonates with a Sabbath posture. Many of us experience seasons of life that are marked by either great productivity or challenging dormancy. The Sabbath invites us to see those seasons as mutually enriching and necessary. We are tempted to view seasons of dormancy as failure, but the Sabbath invites us to resist that temptation and see fallow seasons as an opportunity to trust and grow in one's capacity to wait.

Part of the Sabbath's work is to disorient and disrupt the ways current work culture has shaped our values, behaviors, and identities. By loosening the vise grip of productivity, achievement, and striving while reconnecting us to our bodies, our limits, and our identities as God's beloved children, Sabbath frees us to live with greater freedom, joy, and delight. But many people today are trapped in unjust economic situations that prevent them from weekly rest. In some cases, Sabbath seems to be a privilege available only to those who can afford it.

Sabbath Is and Is *Not* a Privilege

If you've ever had a severe respiratory infection, have lived near a wildfire, had the air knocked out of you, or woken up gasping in the middle of the night, you understand something of how breathing can be a privilege. "Breathing privilege" is the opportunity some people have to live in an area that does not have contaminated air, or to live without genetic susceptibility to pulmonary diseases or infections. But, of course, breathing is *not* a privilege; it's a fundamental human right. The same is true for Sabbath.

"Sabbath privilege" is the cultural, social, or economic opportunity to *not* work one day a week. The term "privilege" acknowledges that it is not available to everybody. In fact, it implies it is actively withheld from or denied to some.

To say someone has Sabbath privilege is to say that their livelihood does not depend on a schedule that requires them to work seven days a week; they are permitted to and can afford to take a day off each week, if they choose. For someone whose work includes domestic responsibilities such as childcare and home upkeep, it means they have a partner or resources that allow them to take a break for a time each week.

Sabbath privilege refers to the *access* some people have to Sabbath practices in their life. That is to say, they have access to rest and delight, to self-determination, to spending unproductive and inefficient time experiencing play and intentionally doing nothing. It also means they have adequate health-care benefits and are paid a living wage that includes sick days. It means they live close enough to spaces where they can go—alone or with their families or friends—to experience beauty and tranquility and let go of life's worries.

"The single mother who works more than a full-time job in order to keep food on the table does not have ready access to Sabbath," writes author Lauren Winner.[9] The working poor and others who struggle mightily to make ends meet have not been afforded the privilege of a Sabbath-shaped life. Economic inequity is not surprising in an "*avodah* economy" governed by the principles of Egypt in which access to rest and delight and freedom for some is dependent on the denial of those privileges to others. Sadly, Sabbath privilege is a reality in our world today.

And yet, just as breathing is not a privilege, so too Sabbath is not a privilege. Breathing is a human right, and Sabbath rest is our birthright, instituted by God at the dawn of Creation. I came to understand how Sabbath is and is not a privilege in a new way while reading a reflection on gardening by the inimitable poet Ross Gay, whom I call the Poet Laureate of Delight.

Ross Gay *loves* delight. He is an apostle and an ambassador for delight.[10] He believes everyone should be free to delight. He also loves to garden. He is likewise an apostle and ambassador for gardening. For him, gardening is a birthright equal to delight.

In his book *Inciting Joy*, Gay reflects on the inadequacy of the term "privilege" to describe birthrights such as gardening and delight, but also "health or healthcare or potable water or clean air . . . or having 'free time' or *not* being imprisoned or *not* living near a power plant."[11] While it is well intentioned to call these privileges, doing so ultimately obscures the fact that withholding or denying these opportunities is what Gay characterizes as an act of "violence, it is abnormal (even if it is the norm), and it is an imposition of precarity that is not natural."[12] In other words, to call a birthright a privilege flips the script and normalizes injustice while alienating equity. He goes on to say that these absences are not an affliction, "but an infliction. It is on purpose. And the withholding from some of the means of life, of which means there are plenty to go around, is a *disprivilege*. Which is to say: life, though it is a gift, is not a privilege."[13]

So it is with Sabbath. Sabbath is a gift, but it is not a privilege. The withholding of Sabbath is a *disprivilege*. It is the legacy of Egypt expressing itself in structural inequities that prevent some from having access to what has been freely given to all by God. The fact that Sabbath is systematically withheld from some exposes an injustice in the system and puts an asterisk on the Sabbath rest of the rest of us. Recognizing that the Sabbath both is and is not a privilege can help clarify the purpose of our work in the world. The prophet Isaiah reminds us to "call the Sabbath a delight" (Isaiah 58:13). We work, in part, to ensure *all* can call it so. Until then, our Sabbath, and our delight, remain incomplete.

REFLECTION QUESTIONS

- Listed below are words and phrases that characterize the two kinds of work embodied in the Hebrew words *avodah* and *melakhah*. Check the words on both lists that you would use to describe your current experience of work (whether paid or unpaid).

Avodah
- ☐ Unceasing
- ☐ Denies dignity to the worker, the community, and/or the earth
- ☐ Soul-crushing
- ☐ Fueled by anxiety
- ☐ Driven by fear of scarcity
- ☐ Quantity over quality
- ☐ Celebrates only productivity and profit
- ☐ Dehumanizes the worker, damages the community, pollutes the earth

Melakhah
- ☐ Ceases for rest and delight
- ☐ Bestows dignity
- ☐ Glorifies God
- ☐ Fueled by trust in God's abundant sufficiency
- ☐ Animated by abundance
- ☐ Quality over quantity
- ☐ Celebrates craftsmanship, handiwork, and skilled labor
- ☐ Benefits the worker, the community, and the earth

Based on the words you checked above, how would you characterize your experience of work overall? In what ways does it resemble *avodah*, the work Israel did in Egypt, void of Sabbath rest? In what ways does it resemble *melakhah*, work shaped within the limits of Sabbath rest?

- Listed in the chart below is a summary of the four cultural forces that shape how we see our work (from chapter 2) and how Sabbath seeks to disorient that cultural formation.

CULTURAL FORCES THAT SHAPE HOW WE SEE OUR WORK	HOW SABBATH DISORIENTS OUR CULTURAL FORMATION
Our work defines our identity.	Sabbath re-*nephesh*es (or refreshes) us.
Our work is disconnected from body and space.	Sabbath honors our bodies and limits.
Our work teaches us we must earn everything.	Sabbath is a gift.
Our work traps us in a cycle of productivity shame.	Sabbath celebrates unproductive time.

» Which of the four cultural forces are you most aware of in your current experience of work? How does it impact you? For example, consider the internal narratives it prompts, how it leads you to view or treat others, how it undermines your ability to experience rest and delight, etc.

» Which of the four Sabbath disorientations do you feel most drawn to or intrigued by? Why?

- In what ways, if any, have you experienced Sabbath privilege? Sabbath disprivilege?

Sabbath Practice: Ceasing from Work

The word *shabbat* is related to the Hebrew verb "cease, rest." It describes a day given to cessation from work. One of the first steps toward creating a sustainable Sabbath practice is determining what you will cease from on your Sabbath day. What constitutes work for you? Keep in mind that your answer and what you choose to cease from may change over time. For now, you're just establishing a baseline to play with in the future. Different people define work differently, so keep an open mind, resist rigidity, and expect to compromise, especially if you will be practicing Sabbath with others.

Use a journal or pad of paper to define work in response to the following prompts.

- List the actions, behaviors, places, outfits, emotions, or objects you associate with work.

- List the commitments, beliefs, habits, behaviors, people, or places that most commonly separate you from your *nephesh* or contribute to exhaustion or anxiety. These may or may not be related to your "work." Think broadly about the "things done daily" that complicate your ability to rest, and from which you can cease on Sabbath.

- Briefly review your two lists and then circle the items you want to cease from on your next Sabbath. Be realistic. Start small and build your confidence.

- After Sabbath ends, reflect on the experience in your journal. What did you notice? What was easy to cease from? What was challenging?

- Consider circling one or two more items from your list to cease from on your next Sabbath.

4

REORIENTING: WORK, REST, AND DELIGHT

Work is love made visible.
KAHLIL GIBRAN, THE PROPHET

There is something unifying in this annual act of tidying the world. Every day the news is full of all we can't set right. But we can drag the rake through the yard so that we can see the path again.
ROSEMERRY WAHTOLA TROMMER, "Raking the Leaves with Jack"

The prophet Isaiah reminds us that God longs for us to "call the Sabbath a delight" (Isaiah 58:13). *Delight* is such a powerful word, naming an experience that stands at the heart of what it means to be human. I understand delight as that elusive rush of energy and presence experienced by someone who is *fully alive* in a moment. It lives at the intersection of joy, presence, connection, and play. Play opens our hearts to curiosity and new experiences; connection multiplies our delight because it's shared; the present moment is the only threshold to delight; and joy is delight's oldest companion.

But I never heard "Sabbath" and "delight" in the same sentence growing up. Sabbath was about resting, yes. It was about going to church and having a family meal. But if it was about anything, it was about *not* doing things. My immediate family didn't have much of a Sabbath practice, so most of my associations with the word came from stories my mom told of her childhood. All I knew was that Sabbath was synonymous with prohibitions, which were intended to maintain the sanctity of the day. Most forms of play were prohibited: no swimming in the lake or using the boat. No hitting a ball or playing a ball game. No golfing, no games, no riding bikes. Additionally, no yard work, no washing or gassing up the car, no eating out, no shopping, no causing someone else to work. The goal was to prohibit anything that would potentially disrupt the holiness of the day. Approved activities included church twice a day, a family meal, Bible reading, napping, and preparing to teach next week's Sunday school lesson. This isn't the full story of my mom's early Sabbaths, but it's all I knew growing up, and it was enough to plant seeds of negativity in my heart about the Sabbath. I was glad we didn't take Sabbath very seriously as a family because what my mom described sounded boring and restrictive, the furthest thing from delight I could imagine.

And then, a few years ago, as I was reflecting on what Isaiah 58 contributed to the Bible's testimony about the Sabbath, the climactic line "call the Sabbath a delight" kept ringing in my ears as part of the bedrock of Sabbath teaching in Scripture. In fact, I am convinced that delight is both a trailhead for and a signpost along the Sabbath way. If a Sabbath practice is whittled down to its irreducible core, what remains is largely a commitment to making room in one's life to recover a sense of delight. But Isaiah's Sabbath delight is neither escapism nor cheap thrills. It is not a selfish abnegation from responsibility nor a laugh at someone else's expense. It does begin by *not* doing things, however, such as,

> not going your own way,
> > serving your own interests,
> > > or speaking empty words.
>
> ISAIAH 58:13

But it doesn't end there. To understand Isaiah's invitation to delight, we must first understand Isaiah's context, which I refer to as a "delight diaspora."

REORIENTING: WORK, REST, AND DELIGHT

A Delight Diaspora

The first thing to note about Isaiah's context is that the message of Isaiah 58 was given to a community of exiles returning to Israel after decades of devastation in Babylon. They had not only been exiles from their homeland; they had also been what poet Maya Angelou brilliantly called "exiles from delight."[1] They were part of a delight diaspora. While the return from exile was a joyous occasion to be sure, it was also a time of profound uncertainty, and the people were struggling to rebuild their lives back home after losing so much. Isaiah's instinct to reintroduce the Israelites to Sabbath at this critical juncture of their return to their homeland suggests that Sabbath helps guide us home—to our literal homes, but even more so on the metaphorical journey home to ourselves.

The experience of exile, whether physical or metaphorical, is disorienting, lonely, and frightening, full of grief, loss, and uncertainty. It is a vulnerable experience. In Isaiah's time, the people tried to overcome that sense of vulnerability in two ways. First, through an enormous exertion of effort in every area of life. And second, through rigid adherence to spiritual practices such as fasting and Sabbath, believing that by perfecting the practices they could manipulate God into giving them the material and spiritual blessings and security they longed for. But their efforts were unsuccessful. "Why do we fast, and you do not notice? We humble ourselves and you care not!" (Isaiah 58:3). All their striving and strict adherence to the letter of the law was an attempt to exert control in a situation that felt out of control. Along the way, they lost track of the spirit of the Sabbath. They had become enslaved to effort, anxiety, and scarcity. They had re-created Egypt without realizing it.

Isaiah's solution was Sabbath *delight*. Delight is incompatible with control. It is built on trust and turns striving on its head. It naturally reorients our priorities by reminding us of what matters most to us, which we can lose sight of when all we see is scarcity and stress. The people had returned from Babylon, but they had also brought a Babylon mindset home with them.

I wonder if you can relate. Perhaps you have lost the tune of your heart's song or fallen out of step with the Spirit. You may feel buried under an ocean of obligations and regrets, or your life may feel vulnerable, steeped in scarcity. Maybe you are seeking stability through trying to control your life (or someone else's) or through legalistic adherence to practices like Sabbath. If so, the Sabbath asks you this question: *When was the last time you felt genuine delight?*

I suspect the delight diaspora today is a vast and sprawling crowd. And understandably so. As my dear friend Kyle Small often says, "There's a lot of pain in the world." While poet Ross Gay traveled the country promoting his books *Inciting Joy* and *The Book of Delights*, he was asked different versions of the same question over and again: "When all of this is going on . . . why would you write about joy [or delight, or gardens, or flowers]?"[2] The assumption behind the question was that joy and delight are privileges, and that the privilege they represent is the ability to live free from grief, pain, and sorrow. And since grief, pain, and sorrow are unavoidable and ubiquitous, it is at best naive, and at worst offensive, to speak of joy or delight at a time like this. But Gay is adamant that joy and delight are *not* privileges—and they are not separate from pain, but rather "what emerges from how we care for each other *through* those things."[3] Ross Gay's books embody a different approach to the troubles that besiege us: *How can you not write about joy and delight when all this is going on?*

I'm with Ross Gay and Isaiah on this. Now more than ever, we need to pour the light of our souls into the world. We need to gather all the goodness and love and forgiveness and playfulness and joy and gratitude and attention and encouragement and silliness and presence we can and offer it to everyone we meet. We need to reconnect with our own delight, and we need the delight of others—just to survive.

The Sabbath gives us permission to prioritize delight one day every week. It makes room for us to embrace our delights, and so to come back home to ourselves, to return from exile. The hope is that, as our Sabbath practice brings us home to ourselves week after week, our Sabbath posture helps us show up to work and the rest of life with more and more of ourselves as well.

Most of us, like the Israelites before us, face significant barriers to living into that vision. Some of those barriers grow out of our relationship to work. The Sabbath can help us reconnect our work to a sense of God's ongoing activity in the world. It can give us space to explore different ways of showing up to work that dignify us and our coworkers. It can help us redefine our priorities by reorienting our sense of achievement and productivity. Each of these steps along the Sabbath way reconnect us to our *nephesh*, our truest self, and put us in the position to experience delight, that sense of being fully alive. It will take time for the Sabbath to transform our relationship with work. In fact, it took over a decade for my wife and me to negotiate work and rest in a way that honored both of our limits and began to reconnect us to delight.

Negotiating Work and Rest

My day job is demanding and often stressful. As a knowledge worker who lacks clear workday hours, has a to-do list that never ends, and works in a culture that prioritizes achievement and rewards saying yes, it's easy for work to take over my life and extract all my time and energy for its own purposes. When this is paired with a deep anxiety about finances and an unconscious commitment to scarcity, the result is a profound imbalance that looks like over-functioning and feels like exhaustion. For years, it was difficult for me to disconnect, which meant that even when I was present at home, I wasn't always *present* at home. Sabbath, for me, was a chance to physically slow down, even literally sit down—which often resulted in falling asleep!

My wife's situation is the opposite of mine. Mariah is at home every day and splits her time between maintaining our home, creating art and guided journals, and tending to her body, due to the complications of her chronic illness. For her, Sabbath was an opportunity to get out, go places, and do things together since I was around and available.

For years, this contrast between our weekly schedules and our perceived Sabbath needs created conflict in our relationship. But it never occurred to me to contextualize Sabbath to our situation. The Sabbath

I had inherited was about *not* doing things, and that was the Sabbath I made sure we kept—no work, no shopping, no economic activity, no making anyone else work. We kept trying to cut-and-paste a Sabbath of universal prohibitions into our life, and it kept not working. It alienated my wife and created resentment in our relationship. In other words, delight was difficult to find. How marvelous it has been to discover that not every Sabbath practice must be identical!

It was Mariah who helped me to understand Isaiah's call to delight as essential to the Sabbath way. The realization that Sabbath *ceasing* is intended to create opportunities for *delight* transformed our approach to both Sabbath and life. It gave us a North Star by which to orient our practice amid the unpredictable winds of life. It allowed me to loosen my legalistic grip on our Sabbath day and opened me to compromises that honored my wife's needs as well as my own. Connecting our Sabbath practice to a Sabbath posture compelled me to take a hard look at my priorities and how the way I was working prevented me from giving my best to my family. That realization led to some hard but necessary decisions to pull back at work, which have enabled me to be more available—and awake!—when I am at home.

However, just because we've come to an agreement about this doesn't mean we no longer need to negotiate work and rest. It's an ongoing balancing act. For example, just a few weeks ago I was reading one of my favorite authors on a Sabbath afternoon and found myself getting inspired with ideas for this book. This presented me with a dilemma: Do I break my Sabbath to develop an idea for my book about keeping the Sabbath? I slowed down, got quiet, and asked myself this question: *Do I want to work out of exuberance for the idea or out of fear that I won't be able to re-create the inspiration tomorrow?* I discerned it was a mixture of both, so I decided to sketch out the idea on a note card so I wouldn't forget, and then I put the book down and went for a walk. The following day, the inspiration returned, and the chapter is better for it. But even if the inspiration hadn't returned, I would have no regrets. Asking the question I did, and earnestly living into the answer, is a core aspect of honoring the Sabbath.

Reconnecting Our Work to God

Another core aspect of Sabbath is to reconnect the work that we do with the work that God is doing in the world. The Sabbath commandment in the book of Exodus (20:8-11) connects human rest and work with God's rest and work in Creation. We rest because God rested, and we work because God worked. Part of what it means to bear God's image in the world, therefore, is to mimic God's creative pattern of work and rest. And the assumption of the text is that when we engage in these acts of divine mimicry—of working and resting as God worked and rested—we participate with God in God's original work and rest! To work in the world is to partner with God in God's work of redeeming all things. To rest with God is to participate in God's delight and joy in all that God has made.

This sense of our work in the world being a participation in God's work in the world is captured in the Jewish concept known as *tikkun olam* (tee-KOON oh-LAHM), which means something like "repairing the world." The phrase can describe an almost endless array of seemingly insignificant actions, such as straightening a crooked rod, maintaining a roadway, cutting one's fingernails, setting a table, changing a diaper, planting a seed, grading a paper, or raking the leaves. What *tikkun olam* teaches is that when we do these things, we are joining God in repairing the world. Any time we engage in activity that improves the world or helps put things back to rights—changing the oil in our car, bandaging a boo-boo, sitting in silence with a grieving friend, attending a demonstration against injustice—we are swept up into God's action in the world.

Poet Rosemerry Wahtola Trommer has captured something of the spirit of *tikkun olam* in her poem "Raking the Leaves with Jack."

> *I believe that these rhythms of raking and making piles*
> *bring us closer together—all of us rakers, all of us*
> *who step into the slow cadence of pull and reach,*
> *and pull and reach. There is something unifying*

> *in this annual act of tidying the world. Every day the news is full of all we can't set right. But we can drag the rake through the yard so that we can see the path again.*[4]

When the way forward seems lost or covered in the shadow of night or grief or stress, it is often the simple tasks done with new awareness that help us find our way again and enable us to recover a sense of purpose and presence in the larger endeavors of our lives, such as our jobs, our schoolwork, or our parenting.

Poets like Rosemerry and teachings like *tikkun olam* help us reconnect the ordinary elements of our lives to matters of ultimate significance, revealing that our lives are part of a story bigger than ourselves. As a theologian, I call this "sacramental theology," the awareness that God is already at work everywhere, and that our task is to join God in the honorable work of repairing the world, using the gifts and capacities we've been given in our everyday lives. In this way, *tikkun olam* reframes work within a cosmic context that takes seriously God's active and ongoing presence in the world and in our lives. When we lose sight of whether or how anything we do on a day-to-day basis makes any difference whatsoever in the world, *tikkun olam* helps to repair the connections between what we are doing in our little corner of the world and what God is doing in the whole wide world.

Cultivating an awareness of this can help reinfuse our work with a sense of purpose that touches on the deepest part of what it means to be made in God's image. If God is love, then everything we do and all that we are finds its source and end in love, including our work. Writer and artist Kahlil Gibran captured this beautifully in his remarkable book *The Prophet*. When asked about the nature of work, Gibran's prophet replied:

> All work is empty save when there is love;
> And when you work with love you bind yourself to yourself, and to one another, and to God.

And what is it to work with love?

It is to weave the cloth with threads drawn from your heart, even as if your beloved were to wear that cloth.

It is to build a house with affection, even as if your beloved were to dwell in that house.

It is to sow seeds with tenderness and reap the harvest with joy, even as if your beloved were to eat the fruit.

It is to charge all things you fashion with a breath of your own spirit.[5]

Whether we are spinning cloth, building homes, grading papers, emptying the dishwasher, painting canvases, creating apps, changing diapers, managing people, or securing bumpers to a vehicle on a line, *tikkun olam* invites us to engage in that act as an expression of love. Reconnecting our work to God is reconnecting our work to love. Gibran goes so far as to say, "Work is love made visible."[6]

And there are many ways to make love visible at work. One is to recover a sense of purpose in your work beyond its economic benefit. What is the larger story your work contributes to? Who are the people you can love while doing your work? Who benefits from the work you do? Hold them in your heart as you do your work and imagine their gratitude as you go about your day.

Setting an intention is another powerful way to do this. For example, set an intention before every shift to show up with a positive spirit and a commitment to being an encouraging presence. Set an intention to be patient with your children when they get hungry and whine, or to do one thing purely for yourself after your children go to bed or once you can hand them over to your spouse for a while. Set an intention to say yes when you want to say yes, and no when you want to say no. Or set an intention to reorient your relationship with productivity and achievement, to ease the pressure of perfectionism and open yourself to greater possibilities of delighting in your work.

Reorienting Achievement and Productivity

Sabbath is synonymous with nonproductivity. It seeks to decouple our self-worth from our list of achievements—or failures. It invites us to remember who we are apart from what we do and the praise we get for doing it. It isn't opposed to achieving goals. Instead, it wants to create reflective distance between who we are as humans and who we become when we are defined by striving and achievement.

For people who are driven, ambitious, goal-oriented, and susceptible to believing they are what they do, the Sabbath space of *not* doing can be disorienting, raising the uncomfortable question, "Who am I when I'm not achieving or producing?" For people who are driven not by ambition but a deep sense of shame, who use achievement to secure the affirmation they crave and to silence the voices telling them they're not worthy, the Sabbath pause from doing can be similarly unsettling, turning up the volume of the inner critic's question "Who are you when no one is praising you for what you've accomplished?"

Life will eventually prompt these questions for all of us. The Sabbath helps us engage them safely when little is at stake. One way I have found it helpful to begin interrogating my devotion to achievement in a playful and indirect way on Sabbath is by disrupting my daily step goal.

I love my step counter. I find great satisfaction in getting to 10,000 steps. I also get disappointed in myself if I don't reach the goal, sometimes going to great lengths to get the final few thousand steps before sleep—such as walking in place while I brush my teeth (and sometimes going to bed sweating). Because achieving this goal is somewhere between positive and meaningless, it's provided a low-stakes way to explore my relationship with achievement and goals more generally. In short, I've been intentionally *not* achieving my step goal on Sabbath to practice letting go of that felt need, and then paying attention to what that letting go feels like.

Before I got a Fitbit, I counted steps on my phone. During the week, I compulsively brought my phone everywhere to count each step, no matter how short the distance. This meant my phone was always with me. On Sabbath, I would try to break up with my phone in order not to count my steps. I often wasn't successful. One Sabbath evening I took out my phone while I was brushing my teeth (don't judge me). Instinctively, I checked my step counter and noticed I was at 9,959. Like a robot, I began walking in place to reach 10,000. Then I remembered it was Sabbath and I stopped! I placed my phone on the nightstand at 9,976 steps. It happened again a few months later when I ended the day at 9,996!

Stopping short of the goal is just the first step, though. The second step is the most important: paying attention to what it feels like *not* to meet the goal. I have come to realize that not meeting the goal is a deeply humanizing experience. Part of me agonizes over it—just *four* or *twenty-four* more steps! The disappointment is brief and insignificant, but it is important to feel it through. Then I remember it was my choice. I embrace my dignity despite "failing" to reach a goal. Refraining from the instinct to achieve and compete creates perspective and a measure of freedom from which I can consider whether I want to live differently in more substantial ways than just counting steps.

The radical part of Sabbath rest is that it enables us to begin seeing through the facade of achievement and the false hope it holds out for us to earn love or become worthy of it. Sabbath rest is radical because through it we can learn to become less dependent on external factors that we think will help us feel good about ourselves, and instead find ways to feel our intrinsic goodness *in every part of our lives*. Simple practices such as intentionally *not* achieving a goal help us take baby steps toward letting go of crippling perfectionism and incessant productivity shame. They remind us that the Sabbath is not an opportunity to improve ourselves, but to accept ourselves as we are: perfectly imperfect and becoming more whole. They empower us to fill each of our steps with meaning and joy. The Sabbath reminds us that the journey—and not the destination—is the source of our delight and purpose and value. And delight is what the Sabbath longs for us to experience—not just once a week on our Sabbath day, but every day. Reconnecting our work to God's presence and activity and reorienting our relationship with productivity and achievement are a solid foundation on which to build a house of delight where we can dwell throughout the week when we're doing whatever it is we give our time and life-energy to.

Delighting in Our Work

For most of my life I've held an unconscious but deeply influential belief that the only way my work could be meaningful was if it required maximum effort. *Good* work was necessarily *hard*. If I wasn't exhausted at the end of the day, I hadn't done *good* work. This belief has benefited me in some ways, such as having a strong work ethic, taking pride in my work and valuing excellence, and being available to my students outside of class. But it has also cost me dearly. It fed the lies my inner critic told me that I wasn't working hard enough, that I wasn't producing as much as my colleagues or other professors like me were, and that the only remedy was working *harder* (even though it often wasn't clear to me what that meant other than longer hours). This belief also prevented me from experiencing some of the connection and delight I have longed for in my work throughout my career.

I am not suggesting that hard work is bad or in any way conflicts with the Sabbath. Not at all. The Sabbath celebrates hard work that is dignified and dignifying. What I'm suggesting is that the belief that work *must* be hard to be good is bogus and can lead to exhaustion and resentment—of the work we do and of anyone who doesn't seem to be working as hard as us.

The Sabbath is helping me interrogate this belief. I am exploring approaches to work that lead to deeper satisfaction, produce higher-quality work, and are more likely to leave me energized than exhausted. The Sabbath's commitment to delight and its unequivocal affirmation of my goodness and enough-ness apart from what I do and what others think of me helps reorient my priorities away from *doing* toward a certain way of *being* in the world, whether I'm at work or at home. It's helping me cultivate a relationship with work that is less serious and heavy, less encumbered by the belief that work must be hard. Sabbath is inviting me to explore ways of increasing my delight in my work.

REORIENTING: WORK, REST, AND DELIGHT

When the culture tells me that my identity and self-worth are dependent on what I do, what I have, and what others say or think about me, the Sabbath reminds me that my truest self—my *nephesh*—is held fast in the heart of God and is restored to me through rest and re-creation. Although my work may involve only my brain or my voice while the rest of my body and its limits may be ignored or denied, the Sabbath reminds me that my limits are good and natural, that rest is essential and is my birthright. When the culture of work impresses upon me that everything must be earned and nothing is free, the Sabbath reminds me that life itself is a gift, and that rest and delight are freely given to all who will receive them. And when work equates my value with my productivity, trapping me in a cycle of shame and burnout, the Sabbath rejoices in unproductive time and reminds me that I am already enough, just as I am. And this is as true for you as it is for me.

The Sabbath invitation is to delight in our days, which include our work! It also knows that to do this we need a regular break from work to gain the necessary perspective to return to it with a fresh and open spirit, seeking to find ways of reconnecting our work with God's work in the spirit of *tikkun olam*. When we do that, we enable ourselves to rediscover the purpose that drew us to our work in the first place, or perhaps we may find a new purpose in it, maybe even for the first time.

REFLECTION QUESTIONS

- What experiences, if any, did you have with Sabbath as a child? For example, did you associate Sabbath primarily with prohibitions or with delights?
- The teaching of *tikkun olam* means something like "repairing the world," but instead of focusing only on big things, *tikkun olam* also encompasses small or seemingly insignificant things.
  - » Think back over the last day or two and identify two or three small acts of kindness you performed. In what ways, if any, does thinking of them as repairing the world shift your perspective?

- » What connections might you make between these actions in your little corner of the world and the work God is doing in the whole wide world?
- Kahlil Gibran wrote, "All work is empty save when there is love; / And when you work with love you bind yourself to yourself, and to one another, and to God."
  - » In what ways does this statement challenge you? In what ways does it encourage you?
  - » How might imagining work as an act of love in partnership with God shift your relationship with the daily tasks you perform?
- Sabbath is synonymous with nonproductivity. It seeks to decouple our self-worth from our achievements.
  - » To what degree would you say your identity and value are tied to achievement and productivity? A little, a lot, somewhere in between?
  - » What thoughts or emotions are you aware of when you consider the question, "Who am I when I'm not producing or achieving?"

Sabbath Practice: Practicing Tikkun Olam

Rosemerry Wahtola Trommer's poem "Raking the Leaves with Jack" beautifully illustrates the deeper impulses of the ancient Jewish ideal of *tikkun olam* ("repairing the world"), in which every act of healing, tidying, organizing, connecting, repairing, or improving joins us to God and to others, and infuses our actions with cosmic significance. Practicing *tikkun olam* multiplies our potential for fulfillment and expands our opportunities to live with purpose.

Identify the various actions you engage in throughout a typical day. Write down as many actions as you can, paying particular attention to those that have a reparative element to them, no matter how small. For example, changing a diaper, answering the phone, responding to an email, attending a meeting, asking a coworker about their weekend, organizing the pantry, walking your dog, chopping vegetables, filing a report. As you look over the list, select one or two actions to prioritize on your next "typical" day, perhaps tomorrow!

Set an intention. On the morning of your practice day, set an intention to engage in your chosen actions with purpose, remembering that when you do so, God is with you and you are contributing to God's dream of redeeming all things! Write yourself a note and post it where you will see it often or put a few reminders in your phone as prompts to perform your action throughout the day. As you do so, imagine other people around the world—whom you know or don't know—who are doing the same activity, and feel your connection to them. Remember with Rosemerry that "all of us / who step into the slow cadence of pull and reach" are unified through that simple act.

Reflect on your experience. At the end of the day, reflect on how your *tikkun olam* mindset and practice impacted the way you engaged your actions throughout the day. Did you feel more connected—to yourself, to others, or to God? Did you feel uncomfortable, like you weren't sure how to do it? Did you feel a deeper sense of fulfillment? Consider adding more actions from your list in future days or consider dedicating one hour of a day to maintaining a *tikkun olam* mindset about *every* action you take. Reflect on the difference practicing *tikkun olam* makes in how you experience and view your work.

PART 2

SABBATH AND TIME

5

ORIENTING: WHAT IS TIME?

Time is money.
BENJAMIN FRANKLIN

[We live] in a temporally discombobulated society.
JUDITH SHULEVITZ, THE SABBATH WORLD

*Never hurry through the world
but walk slowly, and bow often.*
MARY OLIVER, "When I Am Among the Trees"

One sunny late spring morning several years ago, my wife and I were sitting quietly on the front steps of the seminary housing we were renting while I worked toward my master of divinity degree. It was an unseasonably warm morning for this college town, nestled by the shores of Lake Michigan, which dumped "lake effect" snow all winter and piled up cumulus clouds like so many cotton balls all spring and summer. We were chatting quietly, enjoying the warmth, the breeze, the easy company. Then, out of the blue, my wife started shouting. It took me entirely by surprise; I almost fell off the stairs.

I followed her eyes across the street and my jaw dropped at the sight. A man was running down the sidewalk with a very small puppy on a leash behind him. The man was lean and fit, with chiseled arms, chest, and legs. You could tell in a single glance that he took fitness seriously and his body was accustomed to long runs.

The puppy, however, looked to be no more than a month old. It was all skin rolls, fur, and potential. But on this morning, it was all terror. It was not yet fit for running. But the man didn't seem to care. He was running at *his* pace. The puppy was just dragging behind him, bouncing on the pavement, and yelping uncontrollably. The sight and sound of each tumble was enough to break your heart. And my wife's piercing shout—"Hey! *Hey!* Slow down! You're hurting it!"—shocked me back to reality. But I was too late; he had rounded the corner and was gone. And I did not run after him. We sat in simmering and astonished silence for some time.

In the silence, I tried to take in what had happened. My brain began to compute the utter cruelty of his behavior—his selfishness, his abuse of power, his indifference to the puppy's size and strength, his refusal to accept the puppy's limited capacity. This was compounded by my own guilt for not chasing after him. I had watched in silence, a passive observer—and now I had to live with that.

I don't know what compelled him to abuse his puppy with such indifference. Maybe his headphones were on too loud, and he couldn't hear the puppy's yelps. I want to believe the best, but it's a hard conclusion to justify, all things considered. More likely, he wanted to get his workout in on his terms, and this puppy was going to have to learn how to keep up, even if it had to learn the hard way. The man's willingness to sacrifice his puppy on the altar of speed has become for me a parable of the worst consequences of our current relationship to time. We are so blindly committed to the "more, bigger, stronger, faster" mentality that we are in denial of the consequences of our lifestyle on those around us, whether human, animal, or earth.

To experience the kind of rest and slowness offered by the Sabbath, we need to reconsider our relationship to time. And one way to do that is to focus first on our language and our imaginations. Approaching it from this perspective reveals how some of the common metaphors we use to visualize and speak about time play a significant and sometimes harmful role in how we live in and relate to time.

What Is Time? Three Metaphors

What is time? Is it absolute or relative? Is it a scientific fact or a culturally shaped experience? Does it move fast or slow? Does it move through us, or do we move through it? Is it an economic, political, familial, or theological reality? Does it begin at a certain hour or when everyone shows up? Is it one thing for industry and another thing for agriculture? Is it one thing for young people and another for the aged?[1] The answer to each of these questions is, "Yes!"

Clearly, time is not one single thing. It is complex and varied. Our language reflects the diverse character of time, though it tends to prioritize aspects of time that are beneficial to the marketplace. For example, the metaphors of a line, a block, and money dominate how we speak about and imagine time. Each of these prioritize aspects of time that have considerable consequences for our living.

Time Is a Line

The line is perhaps our most enduring visual metaphor for time. Every history textbook and museum display reinforce this most basic truth: time is a series of sequential moments moving from past to present and on into the future. Implicit in this image is a belief that the past is a series of discrete events laid out on a line. Also implicit is the orientation of time: it is moving toward the future, always progressing toward a goal. This suggests that *we*, too, should always also be moving forward, advancing, progressing, growing, enhancing, producing, achieving.

The problem is that time as a line doesn't accurately reflect the cyclical nature of life. When we lose a job or a loved one, suffer an injury, experience abuse or trauma, struggle with mental health, or we have or develop some form of disability, we are unable to move forward at the speed linear time teaches us we are "supposed" to. We may not even be able to move forward at all. Experiences like this are often labeled as failure, weakness, laziness, or depression.

We would do well to take poet Brad Aaron Modlin's advice and "not confuse movement with progress."[2] Experiences of life slowing down or even stopping in its tracks are universal and can occasion profound learning—if we are willing and able to meet the moment. Sometimes slowing down, standing still, or even moving backward is the way to true progress.

The linear shape and incessant forward-moving direction of time was reinforced in consequential ways through the invention of the clock. One of its effects was to give the impression that time could be broken into tiny bits—hours, minutes, seconds—that are manageable and controllable. Even though the earliest clocks had only hour hands and were invented to regulate prayer practices in Benedictine monasteries, it wouldn't take long for some people to discover that a more precise version of clock time could also be used to regulate and control *people*, and for great profit.

These developments gave rise to what linguist Benjamin Whorf called Standard Average European Time (SAET).[3] As Scottish theologian John Swinton describes it, SAET "separates and compartmentalizes the various aspects of our past, present, and future lives. This mode of time creates the impression that time is fragmented," which transforms time into "a series of dislocated fragmented moments held together by the transient necessities of human desire."[4]

The linear metaphor for time precludes the possibility of a holistic sense in which time is "held together," for a line has no center, no point of orientation, no anchor by which to ground our experience. A line that divides time into fragmented bits connected by the "transient necessities of human desire" is a significantly less compelling vision for what holds time together than that offered in the Bible and sustained through the Sabbath. It is too easy, inevitable even, to get lost in a world defined by the clock and oriented toward a future that does not exist outside of our projections, fears, and hopes.

Time Is a Block

Another pervasive image for time is the block. The most common way we encounter time as a block is on our calendars. I use the calendar on my phone, but it's the same for a physical calendar or a daily planner.

ORIENTING: WHAT IS TIME?

When I open my phone's calendar app, I see a day, laid out in a column, partitioned into a series of one-hour blocks. My job is to "block off" my time commitments in bright colors to indicate that I will be busy during that time. Most days, just about every minute of the calendar is covered in colored blocks.

Seeing time as a sequence of multicolored blocks suggests that time is a commodity over which we exert control. Here, time is not abstract and disembodied as with a line. Time blocks are resources we can manipulate and use to achieve our goals. On the one hand, I am immensely grateful for my calendar. It helps me remember appointments, sends me reminder notifications, and helps me visualize my day so I know how to prepare for each moment. It also helps me avoid double-booking myself, which helps me respect the people with whom I commit to spending time.

But on the other hand, block time also has a more sinister side. When time is reduced to a commodity we can control for our own ends, it can become an object we seek to dominate and exploit. This commodification of time cannot be separated from the larger economic forces that dictate the purpose of time—greater productivity and increased efficiency, all in the service of higher profit margins. The more things we can squeeze into our schedule, the fewer blocks of time we leave unfilled, the more we can accomplish in each day, the better we can feel about ourselves.

Block time also reinforces one of our society's greatest values: *busyness*. We wear busyness like a badge of honor. We fret over blank blocks of time on our calendar and scurry around trying to *look* busy so others won't think we're lazy. The message is that when we're busy, we're important. So we pour more and more into our days, dividing our time into smaller and smaller bits, trying to squeeze out more efficiency to force ourselves into greater productivity. But this simply sets us on a path of self-diminishment. As the guru of gratefulness Brother David Steindl-Rast reminds us, "The Chinese pictograph for 'busy' is composed of two characters: *heart* and *killing*."[5] How true that is.

This pattern of self-diminishment recalls the conversation about productivity shame addressed in chapter 2. Productivity shame is the habit of "setting unrealistic expectations for what you can accomplish, and then beating yourself up when you fall short."[6] We tend to expect too much of ourselves because we've allowed the terms of our expectations to be set by the marketplace.

Productivity shame isn't just restricted to the workplace; it infiltrates our homes and personal lives as well. For example, we may see the curated presentation of our friends' lives on social media and assume they are juggling their various responsibilities while still having time for fun with their family and friends. We feel shame about not being able to do that ourselves. We listen to the voice of productivity shame when it tells us we are not good enough, efficient enough, or productive enough. So we cram our calendars in a futile effort to find that elusive sense of worthiness, contentment, and *enough-ness*.

When our productivity shame, block time, and obsessive busyness converge, they form a three-headed monster running amok in our lives, robbing us of our ability to be present or content, keeping us looking over our shoulder, wondering when it's going to jump out and consume another hour, another day, another year. Rabbi Abraham Joshua Heschel imagined time as a monster as well, "with a jaw like a furnace incinerating every moment of our lives."[7] It's a terrifying image, and yet I relate to it instinctively. I have felt its heat. I have held the ashes of my good intentions and wondered where the time went. The Sabbath reminds us that time is bigger than our metaphors and that neither the block, the monster, nor the shame are the end of the story. But before we can appreciate how Sabbath transforms our relationship to time there is one more contemporary metaphor to explore.

Time Is Money

The metaphors of time as a line and time as a block describe how we *see* time. But how do we *speak* and *think* about time? In speech, our metaphors are often economic and reinforce all the dangers inherent in time as a line and a block. We *spend* time, *save* time, *use* time, *waste* time, *borrow* time, *can't afford* the time, wonder if it's *worth* the time, *invest* time, *give* time, *set aside* time, *run out of* time. Benjamin Franklin's claim continues to echo in our everyday speech and behavior: "Time is money."

One obvious way to understand the view that time is money is in relation to the compensation received for hours worked. In this context the phrase is not a metaphor since time literally translates into money when a worker clocks in and clocks out. Since most everyone desires to have more money, and since rising costs make it feel like our money is always losing its value, it takes very little effort to justify sacrificing more and more time on the altar of productivity to transform that time into cash. This creates a cycle of scarcity thinking that reinforces the dangers inherent in the *metaphor* of time as money.

Equating time with money impacts our living in ways far beyond the reach of hourly-wage jobs. In fact, we are all impacted by a time-is-money approach to life, whether we have a job or are a student, a stay-at-home parent, or a retiree.[8] "Time is money" is shorthand for a way of relating to time defined by our economy's values of productivity and profit by way of efficiency. It is doing over being, productivity over presence, speed over stillness. A time-is-money approach tells us our value is dependent on how fast we move, how much we produce, and how much we make. In this way, it amplifies the damaging implications of *both* the "time is a line" and "time is a block" metaphors. In fact, I understand "time is money" as a kind of umbrella term under which the other two metaphors fit.

"Time is money" is a linguistic reflection of how we have conflated our relationship with both time and money into a singular experience of lack. We never have enough money; therefore, we never have enough time. And our fear of scarcity drives our commitment to speed. "When time is money, speed equals more of it,"[9] observes author Judith Shulevitz. And the commitment is hard to break.

Ironically, though, our attempts to hurry up only slow us down, a truth playfully captured in the phrase, "The hurrier I go the behinder I get." Have you ever felt the weight of this truth press down on you? Like when you leave late and in your hurry misread the signs, take the wrong exit, and end up even further behind? Or in your rush out the door, you drop the keys under the car and get your pants dirty reaching for them and then have to change your outfit? Or in your sprint to send a few more emails before leaving work, you hit "Reply All" and send that snarky response about your boss to everyone rather than just to your coworker?

Prioritizing speed and efficiency in response to the various and complex challenges we face in life can do more than make us late or force an awkward apology to the boss. When we try to resolve life's complexities by increasing our velocity, we distort the world and threaten to lose sight of what truly matters. Poet David Whyte articulates this powerfully:

> The trouble with velocity as an answer to complexity is, after a while, you cannot perceive anything or anyone that isn't traveling at the same speed as you are. . . . And things that move according to a slower wave form actually seem to become enemies to you, enemies to your way of life. And you get quite disturbed by people who are easy with themselves, and easy with life, and aren't charging around like you do.[10]

I find Whyte's description both relatable and tragic. When time is money, we begin to view each other as competition, or threats, even enemies, instead of as neighbors or fellow humans trying to make our way in the world. Speed and competition eliminate curiosity and we forget that each person's life is as complex as our own. We forget that before anything else, our responsibility as humans is to love God and love neighbor. When we move with velocity through our days, as David Whyte says, our vision narrows until it eliminates everything that is moving slower than us. And it is hard to love what we do not see.

Clearly, our dominant metaphors for time are inadequate to foster the kind of life that leads to love, contentment, connection, and joy. When time is a line, a block, or money, we are compelled to speed up our lives, to master and control our days, and to equate our value with our busyness and the figure on our paycheck. Or, conversely, we receive the message that if we don't make money and are not busy our life is less valuable than another's. All this is to say that how we conceive of and therefore relate to time is not neutral; it has a powerful ethical dimension.

The Ethics of Time

In 1973, social psychologists John Darley and Daniel Batson conducted an experiment that revealed a meaningful connection between one's relationship to time and one's ability or willingness to respond to—or even see—someone in distress. They called it the Good Samaritan study.[11]

Darley and Batson went to Princeton Theological Seminary to conduct the experiment with those who, ostensibly, would have been the most likely to have devoted their lives to upholding the message and values of Jesus' parable of the Good Samaritan (see Luke 10:25-37). The study involved determining the personality type of each participant and then assigning the group one of two tasks. Half the group was told to write a sermon on the Good Samaritan; the other half was told to prepare a talk about the kinds of jobs seminary had prepared them for.

Participants were then sent to a different building on campus to present their prepared remarks. One-third of the participants were told they had plenty of time to get to the other building, one-third were told they weren't late but that they shouldn't dawdle, and one-third were told that they were late, and they should hurry.

The *real* experiment took place along the path between the buildings where an actor was planted, unbeknownst to the participants. The man was in visible distress, slumped over in a doorway. He would cough twice, loudly, and then moan as each person approached. The researchers wanted to see who would stop to offer help, and to discover why people do or do not stop to offer help to strangers who appear to be in distress. Is it related to an aspect of their personality (specifically, religious convictions), cultural conditioning (familiarity with the parable of the Good Samaritan), or something more contextual?

What they found was remarkable and ironic, though likely unsurprising due to how deeply relatable the findings were. *The only meaningful variable that impacted whether participants stopped to help was how big of a hurry they were in.* Those who were not in a hurry were much more likely to stop and help than those who thought they were late or almost late.[12] Knowledge of the Good Samaritan story, or even preparing a message on it, did not substantially impact their ability to live out the story. Ironically, some participants literally stepped over the man on their way to preach on the Good Samaritan, just as the priest and Levite do in the parable. The researchers concluded that "ethics becomes a luxury as the speed of our daily lives increases."[13]

Darley and Batson reported that participants who hurried because they were told they were late acknowledged having seen the man but not noticing he was in distress. I wonder how many times I am moving so quickly that I don't even notice people around me who are hurting, grieving, suffering, or in some sort of crisis. How often do I choose to avert my eyes and just keep moving because I don't have time to engage?

In her book *Restless Devices,* sociologist Felicia Wu Song describes the results of a different study that found how deep our lack of truly seeing each other goes. The study was conducted by social theorist Zygmunt Bauman, who found that a common strategy for dealing with time scarcity is avoiding eye contact. Bauman's study found that acknowledging the living presence of another human being "spells waste: it portends the necessity of spending a portion of precious yet loathsomely scarce time on deep diving"[14] into what Song calls "embodied interaction." Embodied interaction is a way of talking about presence, of offering one's full attention to another person.

And presence is a form of love. We cannot love someone if we do not give them our full attention. If we are distracted, if our attention is divided, if we are with them in body but not in mind or spirit, our ability to love them diminishes significantly. To love in this way takes time. But when we view our time and attention as scarce commodities, precious resources we must hoard to survive, what suffers most is our capacity to love.

Beyond the metaphors for time we've already discussed, there is another reason why our time and attention feel so scarce. We are alive during an era in which our ability to pay attention is under greater and greater threat. In fact, our attention has become the singular product that multiple multibillion-dollar companies are selling to the highest bidder. Many of us—myself included—are addicted to the technologies these companies create, which are massively profitable and are fundamentally shifting our relationship with time.

Time and Technology

Felicia Wu Song explores how the "digital ecology of social media, texting, gaming, and endless streaming of video content"[15] form us by dictating the terms by which our relationships and economic life are structured. The companies that generate and maintain the digital ecology hold immense power to the extent that we may very well experience real costs—socially, economically, professionally, and otherwise—if we fail to conform to their terms.

Over the past several years, some of the very people who helped create the "digital ecology" have begun to speak out about its dangers, and about how companies knowingly designed their products to create the effects we are experiencing today. Song quotes Sean Parker, who founded Napster and was Facebook's first president. Parker said their primary design objective was to "consume as much of your time and conscious attention as possible," and that their business model is built on "exploiting a vulnerability in human psychology"—namely, the human need for connection.[16] These companies create addictive processes with intermittent feedback loops ("likes" and "shares," etc.) that give us dopamine hits, but on an inconsistent schedule, which keeps us coming back time and again.[17] What they have designed is a mechanism for infinite cycles of mutual consumption. The apps consume our time and attention, and we consume their product. Back and forth it goes—wash, rinse, repeat.

When consumed in moderation and with intention and limits, social media can be immensely life-giving, facilitating connections with friends and family and reconnections with old friends and acquaintances, as well as fostering delight in random videos of stupid human tricks, inspiring stories, whimsical insights, and adorable dog memes. But intentional, moderate engagement with social media is not sufficiently profitable, so apps such as Facebook, Instagram, TikTok, and YouTube are designed to create addictive behavior that overrides our instincts to stop scrolling and start living our lives. And young people are particularly susceptible to these designs.

Shortly before Song's book was released in 2021, Jeff Orlowski-Yang, Larissa Rhodes, and other former industry insiders released a bombshell documentary called *The Social Dilemma* in which several former high-level executives, designers, and engineers of social media companies spoke honestly and passionately about the vision and values they built into the digital ecology.

As I watched the documentary it struck me that they were describing the next stage of the evolution of time. The prior stage was about commodifying, controlling, and monetizing time itself, which the three metaphors explored earlier demonstrate. In the current stage the pursuit is to commodify, control, and monetize *how people use their time*. Now *we* are the product; *our* attention is what they package and sell to advertisers for billions of dollars a year.

Jaron Lanier, a computer scientist considered one of the founders of virtual reality, put an even finer point on it: the product is "the gradual, slight, imperceptible change in your own behavior and perception." This is their only product; the only thing for them to make money on is "changing what you do, how you think, who you are."[18] These companies have a vested interest in our distraction. Their business model is dependent upon us remaining half-awake and inattentive. Judith Shulevitz was right: we live in "a temporally discombobulated society."[19]

Walk Slowly, and Bow Often

The metaphors we use for time set us up for failure by prioritizing excessive productivity, busyness, efficiency, and speed. The digital ecology designed to colonize our attention is as effective as it's ever been. Time feels as scarce as money and it seems like the only way to get more of either is to work harder, cram more into each day, and never stop long enough to consider if there might be another way.

But in those chance moments when we do stop long enough to take a breath, to sit in the quiet of a peaceful sunset, to sip a slow cup of coffee or meander through the woods, we have the chance to imagine—as poet Mary Oliver once did—what it would take to,

never hurry through the world
but walk slowly, and bow often.[20]

When Mary Oliver speaks of walking slowly and bowing often, she's not talking about prostrating ourselves before all we see in an act of worship. Instead, she invites us to take an internal bow that is the offering of our full attention, the deep acknowledgment of another presence, whose life is as beautiful and complex as our own. It is the opposite of avoiding eye contact. It is the first step toward another way of being in the world that resists the formative influence of social media and the digital ecology, what artist and writer Jenny Odell calls "the attention economy,"[21] in favor of paying meaningful attention to life. To bow before the monarch caterpillar, the weeping willow, or the chatty neighbor is to say, "I see you and I honor you. You have a right to be here; you, too, are the beloved of God."

In other words, walking slowly gets us only halfway. We must also slow down internally so we have attention to offer the world, which is to say, the capacity to fully love the world. The invitation and permission to slow down is one of the Sabbath's first and essential gifts. When we do so, we position ourselves to perceive more clearly how fast we've been moving and how exhausted and isolated we've become. That's when we are likely to discover that we "have traveled too fast over false ground,"[22] as the late Irish poet and priest John O'Donohue put it. Our current relationship with time forms the rickety foundation holding up the false ground on which our lives are traveling. Facilitated by metaphors that commodify time, speed up our lives, and incentivize busyness and distraction, we need new metaphors to help us reimagine what time is and how we can relate to it in ways that foster abundance, presence, and love.

REFLECTION QUESTIONS

- Which of the three metaphors for time—a line, a block, or money—resonate most with your experience of time? What recent examples come to mind that demonstrate how this view of time influences your thoughts or actions?

- If presence is a form of love, we cannot love someone well if we do not give them our full attention. Briefly recall an interaction you had with someone in the previous twenty-four hours. Overall, how would you assess the degree to which you were present to that person? Circle the number on the continuum that best describes your response.

  0   1   2   3   4   5   6   7   8   9   10

  Not at All Present   **Completely Present**

  I was unable to love well   *I was able to love well*
  and did not give this person   *by giving this person*
  my full attention.   *my full attention.*

  » What factors influenced the degree to which you were able to be present?

  » What, if anything, do you wish you had done differently?

- The conclusion of the Good Samaritan research project at Princeton Theological Seminary was that "ethics becomes a luxury as the speed of our daily lives increases." When have you experienced this dynamic? In other words, how do hurry and busyness undermine your ability to be your best self or to live fully aligned with your values?

- If the digital ecology is eroding our capacity to be present and pay attention—to love—what might be at stake, personally and collectively, in the relationship we have with our devices and their apps?

- How do you understand the significance of Mary Oliver's invitation to "walk slowly, and bow often" for your own life? If you were to try it for the next twenty-four hours, what might it require of you?

Sabbath Practice: Create a Timeless Day

One of the gifts Sabbath offers is a weekly opportunity to relate to time differently. A simple yet powerful way to do this is to cover all the clocks in your house for the duration of your Sabbath day.

Covering the clocks creates something akin to a timeless day. This gives you an opportunity to both explore your relationship with time and to develop your ability to pay attention to your body. For example, instead of relying on the clock to tell you when to eat, eat when you feel hungry. If you feel antsy, go for a walk. If you feel drowsy, take a nap. If you feel bored, pay attention to it—don't just rush to fill the space with a meaningless distraction.

In addition to covering your clocks, put away your phone and other electronic devices. Set them to airplane mode or turn them off entirely and put them in a drawer. If it's necessary for people to be able to reach you, designate one or two times throughout the day to briefly check messages or make a phone call, so long as it's done purposefully and for a limited period of time. Before putting your phone in the drawer, consider thanking it for all the good it offers you, such as connecting to loved ones and giving you access to learning more about the world.

Throughout your Sabbath day, pay attention to what happens inside you when you don't know what time it is and/or don't have your phone. Note how often you look at the clock to check the time and allow the covering to remind you that it's Sabbath and the time is simply "now."

Afterward, use the following prompts to reflect on your timeless day.

- How often did you look at a clock to try to check the time? How did you respond when you saw the covering and couldn't tell the time?

- Why did you want to know what time it was? What difference, if any, would knowing the time have made to what you were thinking about or doing?

- What was it like to go a day without your phone? How often did you reach for it throughout the day?

- What was going on inside you when you wanted to use your phone? (For example, boredom, anxiety, loneliness.) Why do you think you connect that emotion to your phone use?

6

DISORIENTING CLOCK TIME[1]

The higher goal of spiritual living is not to amass a wealth of information, but to face sacred moments.
ABRAHAM JOSHUA HESCHEL, THE SABBATH

In chapter 5, we explored the ways we have been oriented to relate to and think about time. We considered the metaphors that shape our understanding of time and influence our habits and behaviors within time. Specifically, how the tyranny of clock time pushes us away from presence, contentment, wholeheartedness, and joy; and how we are trained to reduce time to a commodity we can control and manipulate to our own ends, stripping it of its sacred dimension and wringing it for profit—while wringing ourselves of life.

Here, we explore other ways of imagining time, metaphors that present a very different picture of time. Rooted in a biblical worldview and modeled on the template of Sabbath, these metaphors offer an alternative to linear, economic, and commodified views of time. They are counter-stories enabling a posture of protest against living half-lives of anxiety and busyness, of endless production and distraction.

These alternative metaphors demonstrate that time does not have to be a slack-jawed monster incinerating our days in its white-hot mouth-furnace! Instead of a line, what if time were a flower? Instead of a block, what if it were a labyrinth? And instead of money, what if time were a rowboat? While these metaphors may initially seem counterintuitive, I believe they offer a generous and generative alternative to the three metaphors currently dominating our view of time.

What Is Time? Three Alternative Metaphors

The fullness of life is available to us only during one "time"—the present moment. It cannot be found in the past or the future, where the time-shapers of our day want us to live. Only in the present can we experience joy and rest, gratitude and connection, belonging and delight. The Sabbath is a practice deeply rooted in the present. One of its gifts is a sacramental framework that invites us to dwell in the present moment—not because it's better for our overall health (which it is) or because we're exhausted from the busyness and need to pause now and then (which we are, and we do), but because that is where God dwells. When we abide there, we can encounter God's life-giving power, hear God's life-affirming voice, and be re-membered back to ourselves. To do that, though, we need to unlearn some of the habits developed in our long immersion in linear, commodified, and monetized views of time. Our relationship to time needs to be disoriented before it can be reoriented. Our unlearning begins by steeping ourselves in alternative metaphors for time.

Time Is a Flower

How might our relationship with time change if we imagined it as a daisy instead of a line? Can you picture a daisy, with its bright yellow center around which beautiful interlacing petals grow? Trace the edge of a petal with a finger and watch as it proceeds out from the center and then returns to it. Together, the petals frame the entire center of the flower in a continuous flow of color, life, and beauty.

This is essentially what time "looks" like when its template is the Sabbath. Unlike linear time, Sabbath time is centered time. The bright-yellow center is the Sabbath, where God dwells. The petals are the weekdays between Sabbaths. The center nourishes the petals and holds them all together. The vitality of the petals is dependent upon staying connected to the center, which enables them to contribute to and participate in the abundance and beauty of the flower. Each petal, then, represents the flow of time. The basic unit of time is a week, symbolized in the first Creation account. One side of the petal is akin to the first three days of the week, the other side the second three days.

The Sabbath day is not the only center, however. And the week is not the only petal-shaped time period. For example, in ancient Israel, annual festivals such as Passover, Sukkot, and Yom Kippur, which reenacted seminal stories of Israel's sacred history, were also centers that ushered them into encounters with the presence and holiness of God. Here, each petal is a year, stretching from Passover to Passover or Yom Kippur to Yom Kippur. In my own life, this would be Easter to Easter, birthday to birthday, or each year when my wedding anniversary or ordination anniversary comes around.

Petal-shaped time does not require standardized time spans, such as a week or a year, though. The center represents any encounter with the presence of God, which could happen at any moment. A sunset, an exchange with a neighbor, summer's first juicy bite of fig, belly laughs at a perfectly timed joke, or sitting in sacred silence with a grieving friend. In the Hebraic reckoning, we are never far from the center. But, crucially, each return to the center is an echo of the Sabbath.

When a weekly Sabbath is the point around which our life is oriented, the Sabbath nourishes our living on the other days of the week just as the center nourishes a petal. Establishing a weekly pattern of slowing down one day to process and appreciate one's life and relationships makes it easier to pause during the week when something significant— whether terrific or terrible—takes place.

I'm struck by how Australian pastor Simon Carey Holt describes the invitation the Sabbath offers to us to experience all of time differently.

> [Sabbath is] about moving from one experience of time to another; from time that is linear and sequential, purposeful and progressive, directed toward a goal, to a time that is not

directional in shape, but a spherical whole that draws the pieces of yesterday, today and tomorrow together.[2]

This is what the Sabbath cultivates in us when we orient our lives around it. When we make room at the *end* of each week to be present to our lives in all their complexity, it becomes easier to make room *during* the week to do the same. When we rehearse the act of pausing work to reorient our priorities back to presence and connection, it becomes instinctive to do that throughout the week as well. When we do so, our lives take on a distinctly floral shape, adding beauty and richness and peace to a world desperately needing more of each.

Time Is a Labyrinth

Traveling a labyrinth is an ancient spiritual practice of intentional, meditative movement (usually walking, but there are finger labyrinths as well) in which a person is invited to move slowly and intentionally along a path toward a center, perhaps releasing their concerns and worries along the way, and then slowly progressing back outward where they return to the world, refreshed and recentered.

If you look at a labyrinth from above, it might appear to be a maze. But labyrinths differ from mazes in several important ways. The intention of a labyrinth is not to confuse you, but to free you of the need to find your own way. In a maze there might be many entrances and multiple routes to the center, but labyrinths have but one path, which gently guides you toward the center and back out again. That there is only one path eliminates the need to make choices, which fosters submission and trust. To walk a labyrinth is to celebrate unproductive time. It is to be present to the process, to feel each foot on the ground, to listen to the sounds around you and the voices within you, in order to offer them all up to God in prayer.

The path you follow, however, is not direct. Many paths reverse back on themselves, so you feel like you're walking the same path but in the opposite direction. Ideas of moving forward or backward—and the related ideas of progress and failure—lose all meaning. After a while you let go of those categories and settle into simply *being* as you go. Most labyrinths are circular, so the path makes successively smaller arcs from the outside toward the center, and then, upon reversing, makes successively larger arcs before releasing you back into the world. Others are designed so that you very quickly find yourself near the center but are unable to enter it. Then, just as quickly, you are back out near the edge. Over the course of walking, you approach the center several times before actually entering it.

Some seasons of life feel full of progress and momentum, as if we've hit our stride and have all kinds of energy to sustain our endless lists of tasks and meetings and opportunities. In other seasons we feel overwhelmed by everything, like we are doing our best simply to have made it to the end of the day without a major crisis: we are alive, the kids are alive, thank God, let's go to bed. The labyrinth teaches us that each of these paths are part of the journey to the center, where the Sabbath dwells, where God dwells. A Sabbath sensibility does not view our busy seasons as fundamentally bad. Instead, the Sabbath is equally our companion through seasons of speed and busyness as it is through seasons of slowness and ease. But the Sabbath makes room to explore *why* a season of life is so busy, and what values are being expressed through the choices that have led to the busyness. It also encourages us to redefine "progress," and to perceive seasons of slowness or stagnancy, when we may feel far from our center, not as seasons of failure but as gifts, opportunities to reevaluate and reconnect to who we are and how we want to live.

Time Is a Rowboat

This may seem like an unusual metaphor for Sabbath-infused time, but bear with me. When you are rowing a boat, you are facing away from the direction you are going. You start out facing the shoreline and row backward toward your destination. You get your bearings from what you are looking at, which is what you are moving away from. This is a remarkably accurate image of ancient Israel's orientation to time.

What the rowboat image suggests is that ancient Israel faced the past and *backed into the future*. This time orientation is expressed in some of the time-related words in biblical Hebrew. For instance, the word *qedem* (KEH-dem) is one of the words for "ancient past" and "primordial history." But it is also the word for "before" and "in front," as well as the word for "east." Kind of remarkable, right? But consider the connections within this range of meaning. The east is where the sun comes up; it evokes the time of origins and beginnings. Ancient maps were turned ninety degrees from modern maps and took the east, rather than the north, as their point of orientation. Geographically, Israel was oriented toward the east; chronologically, they were oriented toward the past.

Similarly, *acharit* (a-ha-REET) is the Hebrew word for "behind" and "after" as well as the word for "future." In the spiritual geography of ancient Israel, the past is before you and the future is behind you! You don't go out and "make a future" for yourself. In a continual act of trust, you back into the future, trusting that it is held by the one who "will not let your foot slip" (Psalm 121:3).

Old Testament scholar Hans Walter Wolff first offered the image of the rowboat for how Israel moved within time.[3] He pointed to Jeremiah 29:11 as a helpful example. It is a favorite verse for many Christians searching for hope in chaos and suffering.

> "For I know the plans I have for you," declares the LORD.
> "Plans of peace, not of pain,
>   to give you hope and a future [*acharit*]."

God promises us an *acharit*, but it is not up to us to make it happen. Our responsibility is to trust the process, be present, and to "listen to the voice behind you saying: 'This is the way, walk in it'" (Isaiah 30:21). It is the voice of God guiding and directing our backward-stumbling steps into the unknown.

I find great comfort in this view of time. And it resonates deeply with the Sabbath's weekly invitation to let go of our need to control our lives, to dictate the future, to strive until we collapse, to earn our way to grace. When we orient ourselves toward the past, we can see the times in our lives when God was present and working in ways we could not see in the moment. And we can also look beyond our own lives to see how God has worked in the lives of our friends and family, in the lives of our ancestors, and throughout the pages of Scripture. To orient ourselves in this way within time is to remember that God is God, and we are not. And when life's storms rise, when the waves crash over the edge of the boat, when our arms get tired from rowing and we are filled with fear, we can remember that the God who made the wind and the water is with us, giving us the courage to trust that the waves will eventually return to the still waters that quiet the soul.[4]

The metaphors of a flower, a labyrinth, and a rowboat offer a diverse yet consistent depiction of time that is generous and generative, playful and purposeful. Together, they offer a stark contrast to the metaphors of a line, a block, and money, which seek to control time by fragmenting it into bits, reducing it to commodities to manage or a series of ticks and tocks that translate into dollars and cents on a spreadsheet or paycheck. While aspects of those metaphors may be necessary for contemporary life, and even useful in certain conditions or seasons, these alternative metaphors offer more compassionate and life-affirming ways of relating to time that are rooted in abundance and make room for the messiness and unpredictability of life.

The real question, though, is how do we live into the vision presented by these alternative metaphors when the world we inhabit day in and day out is ruled by the other ones? How do we cultivate a relationship with time shaped by abundance rather than scarcity? Do we even believe such a thing is possible? It's important to name that doing so is not easy. The currents of culture and the inertia of our lives flow in the opposite direction of this kind of shift. However, if we do nothing, nothing will change. The Sabbath makes room for us to explore ways of leaning into the kinds of changes the three alternative metaphors represent. And one simple way to begin is to pay attention to our language and fast from using the words *busy* and *hurry*.

Fasting from Busyness and Hurry

I tend to rush from thing to thing and move fast through the world. I am an athlete and quite tall, so I like to walk quickly and often bound up and down the stairs. When I go for a walk, I use a step tracker that tracks my pace per mile, and I often choose to keep moving to avoid a dip in my pace rather than to pause and bear witness to some mini delight calling for my attention along the way. Probing a bit deeper, though, I also tend to be perennially late. Because my basic assumption about life is that there isn't enough time, it is easy to convince myself to bang out a few more emails in the thirty seconds before I have to leave, or to stack too many appointments too close together in my calendar, which means that if one goes long or something unexpected comes up I am behind the eight ball for the rest of the day.

A few years ago, I began feeling convicted about all this senseless rushing around as I started taking the Sabbath more seriously as a lifestyle and not just a weekly pit stop. So I tried an experiment. I gave up the words *busy* and *hurry* for Lent. Since our words express the overflow of our hearts, I wanted to eradicate these words from my vocabulary as part of eradicating the experience from my life.

It sort of worked. The mind is a tricky thing. Along the way, I discovered loopholes, such as saying life was "full" instead of "busy," while I kept racing through my days. I eventually learned that if I wanted to take this slowing-down thing seriously, just eliminating the words was insufficient. I had to find a way to pair slowing down *externally* with the much harder task of slowing down *internally*. I needed an embodied practice that would help me nurture the desire behind my fast to fruition in my life. So I also committed to walking slower between meetings and to letting myself amble on a walk sometimes instead of always speed-walking. I committed to not hovering anxiously next to my wife if she

DISORIENTING CLOCK TIME

wasn't ready to leave when I was. I committed to driving the speed limit *every time I drove*. These embodied practices reinforced the practice of watching my words and regularly brought to my attention how easy it is to fall into old habits of rushing and racing through life.

After Easter that year, I extended my Lenten practice indefinitely. I still work hard to avoid the words *busy* and *hurry*. When people ask, "How you doing? Staying busy?" I like to respond with some version of, "I'm trying *not* to stay busy, actually. It's hard!" I also still drive the speed limit. Of all the commitments I made, this was probably the hardest at first. But now, several years out, it has been by far the most transformative.

For most of my life I've been a habitual speeder. Absolutely no less than five miles over the limit, usually eight to ten. And that was when I *wasn't* in a hurry (and I usually was)! But over the past few years that I've been religiously driving the speed limit, I've discovered that when I resist the temptation to rush by leaning into the belief that there is enough time, my experience confirms that belief. When I resist the temptation to weave through cars and get irritated by long traffic lights and slow drivers, I tend to show up wherever I'm going much calmer and more present than I used to when my habit was hurrying.

The commitment to driving slower has also taught me to leave earlier and to resist overstuffing my schedule with appointments. Now I schedule in transition time and try to overestimate how long a meeting will go to create buffers or space for the spontaneous. Inevitably, sometimes I don't leave enough time and I am late. But even then, when I notify the person and apologize, letting them know when I will arrive, almost every time they either tell me it is no big deal or that *they are also running late*. When this happens, my effort not to rush gives them permission to do the same.

Driving the speed limit has been a formative spiritual practice and central to cultivating a Sabbath posture in my life. I am calmer, less anxious, more present, more grateful, more attentive, and less likely to arrive at my destination agitated or irritable, blaming this or that for why I was late and bringing all that anxiety into the room with me. I am beginning to wonder, with poet and life coach Michelle Wiegers, whether driving slower

> *is the only way*
> *to live my best life,*
> *to keep from running so fast*
>
> *that I go right past myself?*[5]

When I race through life, I don't just run the risk of going right past myself, I run the risk of going right past a lot of things I really care about. I imagine you can relate. How many times have you rushed from thing to thing throughout the day and forgot to call your siblings on their birthday, or overlooked that meeting with your boss, or shouted at your child to stop bothering you when all they want to do is spend time with you? The Sabbath invitation to slow down prompts us to reflect on the values that inform the pace of our lives and how we relate to time each day. It also helps strip away the layers we've added onto time to reveal its deeper purposes. One central purpose of time is to enable encounter.

The Purpose of Time: Encounter

We have explored various ways of imagining time and some of the implications of each metaphor but have not yet explored its purpose. While there are no doubt many legitimate answers to the question "What is the purpose of time?," perhaps the most compelling answer from a Sabbath perspective is demonstrated by a significant Hebrew word for "time," *mo'ed* (moh-ED). *Mo'ed* suggests that the purpose of time is encounter.

Mo'ed is a very specific word for "time." It refers to a special sort of elevated time, something more like "appointed time," as in a particular season, feast, or festival. And the purpose of Israel's festivals, beyond an opportunity to eat meat (from the sacrifice) and gather as a community, was to encounter the living God in worship. This was the destination toward which the rhythms of Israel's life were oriented.

Mo'ed means more than just "appointed time," however. Biblical Hebrew seems to anticipate the space-time paradox of the theory of general relativity by a few millennia, for *mo'ed* can also refer to a *place*—the "gathering place" where the Hebrew people came to encounter God in the festivals. The Tabernacle is often called the Tent of *Mo'ed*, translated as the "Tent of Meeting" or "Tent of Encounter." Whether *mo'ed* refers to a place (the Tabernacle) or an appointed time (Passover or Yom Kippur), its function was to facilitate encounters between God and the people, the people and each other, as well as the people and creation, as the festivals incorporated many aspects of the created world into their rituals.

The Tabernacle, like the Temple that came after it, was God's earthly house. It was the incarnation before the Incarnation. It was the bottom rung of Jacob's ladder, the point at which heaven and earth kissed, akin to what the Celtic spiritual tradition calls a thin place. The ancients called such a place a "navel of the earth," a remnant of the earth's metaphorical umbilical cord from which its power and vitality were sustained by God's presence, power, and love. It was the center of the center of the world.

While the Tabernacle was a *mo'ed* in space, the Sabbath is a *mo'ed* in time.[6] Rabbi Abraham Joshua Heschel saw in the Sabbath a blueprint for an architecture of time built on the foundation of God's holiness. Mixing metaphors of time and space in the spirit of *mo'ed*, Heschel declared that "the Sabbaths are our great cathedrals."[7] Each Sabbath invites us to encounter God's presence.

According to Heschel, the Sabbath reveals to us that "the higher goal of spiritual living is not to amass a wealth of information, *but to face sacred moments*."[8] The Sabbath apprentices us in encountering sacred moments. In fact, it teaches us that *every moment* has the potential for sacredness. Every moment is holy.[9] All of life is encounter. We are never far from the center.

Of course, life doesn't always *feel* like encounters with the sacred. We often forget there even *is* a center. Many days our only true encounter is with our mattress when we collapse into bed at the end of a long day. And even those encounters are too often too short. The Sabbath offers us an alternative by making space in our lives to experience time slowing down, even as it encourages us to give ourselves and others grace, because it's hard to slow down in a world addicted to speed. The Sabbath's orientation toward encounter invites us to explore how we can reconnect our experiences of time with the essence of God and the greatest of all commandments: love. Sabbath invites us to explore what it could look like, in the warp and woof of our daily lives, to expect encounter and pursue love.

REFLECTION QUESTIONS

- Briefly review the descriptions of the three metaphors for time—a flower, a labyrinth, and a rowboat.
    - » Which of the metaphors do you find most compelling or meaningful? Why?
    - » Which of the metaphors do you find most helpful for understanding the events and experiences of your past?
    - » Which of the metaphors do you find most helpful for reframing your concerns in the present or your worries about the future?
- Looking ahead to your plans for the next twenty-four hours, what changes would you have to make to fast from busyness and hurry? Consider changes to your patterns of thought, speech, and behavior.
- Rabbi Heschel said, "The higher goal of spiritual living is . . . to face sacred moments." How do you interpret what he's describing? What do you think it might mean in practical terms to live as if the purpose of time is to encounter God?

Sabbath Practice: Bless God for Life's Encounters

The Jewish tradition of blessing God is both ancient and powerful. Over the years, different Jewish traditions have developed dozens of blessings that are memorized and offered, by Jews who practice this tradition, at many points throughout the day. Each blessing is tailored to a different type of encounter, such as seeing a rainbow, beginning or ending the study of Torah, taking the day's first breath, or receiving good (or bad) news. Part of the purpose of this tradition is to impress upon those who practice it that God is present and active in the world, and any and every experience we have is an opportunity to encounter God.

One blessing stands out as being especially relevant for a broad range of experiences. It is recited at the beginning of each annual festival, and at moments when something good happens that hasn't happened in a while, such as seeing an old friend or eating the summer's first fresh strawberry. It's called the *Shehecheyanu* (sheh-heh-He-YAH-nu) blessing, which roughly translates to "who gives us life." Here is my translation of the blessing in full.

> *Blessed are you, O Lord our God, King of the universe.*
> *You are the one who gives us life.*
> *You are the one who sustains us.*
> *You have caused us to touch this moment in time.*

Lines two through four each identify a different way in which God is present and active in our lives. Line two names God as the source of our life-giving experiences, when we feel fully alive and experience delight. Line three acknowledges that God is with us in challenging moments and sustains us through them. The final line reminds us that everything we've experienced throughout the day has brought us to this moment—caused us to touch or encounter it.

On your Sabbath day, write down this blessing on a card or sticky note and keep it in your pocket or post it where you will see it often. You might even consider memorizing it. When something delightful or meaningful happens, offer it as a short responsive prayer, acknowledging God's presence in your day. Then, at the end of the day, use it as a practice of reflection, praying slowly through each line as a prompt to remember how God showed up in that way throughout the day.

7

REORIENTING: TIME IS LOVE

Time is love.
JOHN SWINTON, *BECOMING FRIENDS OF TIME*

Love is patient.
ST. PAUL, 1 CORINTHIANS 13:4

Is this the path of love?
ROSEMERRY WAHTOLA TROMMER, "The Question"

In his 1946 novel *Zorba the Greek*, Nikos Kazantzakis describes a poignant scene that illustrates the dangers lurking in any approach to life that prioritizes speed, productivity, efficiency, and control above all else. Zorba is a man of indefatigable passion. He is a steward of life's pleasures, living every moment to the absolute fullest. But he is also a man whose relationship to time once distorted his passion for life, resulting in devastation. It happened one day as Zorba walked through a forest and chanced upon a butterfly just as it began to emerge from its chrysalis.

> I waited a while, but it was too long appearing, and I was impatient. I bent over it and breathed on it to warm it. I warmed it as quickly as I could, and the miracle began to happen before my very eyes, faster than life. The case opened. The butterfly started slowly crawling out. And I shall never forget my horror when I saw how its wings were folded back

and crumpled. The wretched butterfly tried, with its whole trembling body, to unfold them. Bending over it I tried to help it with my breath, in vain. It needed to be hatched out patiently, and the unfolding of the wings should be a gradual process in the sun. Now it was too late. My breath had forced the butterfly to appear all crumpled before its time. It struggled desperately and, a few seconds later, died in the palm of my hand. That little body is, I do believe, the greatest weight I have on my conscience.[1]

Did you notice how Zorba's relationship to time was the critical factor that caused his fascination with the butterfly's transformation to devolve into a scene from an entomological horror film? It was not malice or rage that killed the butterfly, but hurry and impatience. A blindness to his own power enabled Zorba to do what he did. And while his intentions were pure, his longing for the butterfly to flourish dissolved in the face of his impatience. His intention had no bearing on the impact of his actions.

I'm guessing I'm not the only one who finds this story convicting. We all know that rushing makes messes of things, but we still do it all the time. While it's unlikely our rushing in the routines of life will lead to the kind of catastrophic outcome that befell Zorba's butterfly, we nevertheless inflict little deaths on situations when we force them to acquiesce to our anxious timelines. We rush conversations by speaking over each other and not listening; we rush while driving and put ourselves and others at risk; we rush intimacy and end up feeling disconnected and lonely; we rush to make a big purchase and end up with regret or in debt; we rush to advance at work and end up missing our children's growing up; we rush through our very lives and end up never truly living them.

I don't think the point of Zorba's story is that going fast or being impatient inevitably causes death and destruction. But it does invite us into careful and intentional reflection on our relationship with time— why we move at the pace we do, what motivates us to do so, and why we get so anxious and uncomfortable with things unfolding at their own pace. Instead of prompting us to ask ourselves how productive we are with our time, it encourages us to wrestle with a different set of questions. How can we live in such a way that helps those around us flourish? How can our actions bring life instead of death? What would it look like for our relationship with time to be shaped by the abundant and life-giving love of God, as opposed to the scarcity mindset of a consumerist society?

I believe the Sabbath is a practice that can help us live our way into the answers to these questions. The Sabbath's invitation to slow down, be present, take stock of our lives and our living, extend grace to others and ourselves, and actively cultivate delight offers gentle guidance, week after week, for how to live beyond the diminishment of a time-is-money approach so we can embrace the subversive truth that time is love.

Time Is Love

In his award-winning book *In Praise of Slowness*, journalist Carl Honoré compares the terms "Fast" and "Slow," which for him are a "shorthand for ways of being, or philosophies of life."[2] His descriptions are almost perfect analogs to how I understand the differences between "time is money" and "time is love."

> Fast is busy, controlling, aggressive, hurried, analytical, stressed, superficial, impatient, active, quantity-over-quality. Slow is the opposite: calm, careful, receptive, still, intuitive, unhurried, patient, reflective, quality-over-quantity. [Slow] is about making real and meaningful connections—with people, culture, work, food, everything.[3]

Within a time-is-money mindset, time feels hard, combative, oppositional. Time is *against* us, and we must strain with all our energy and strength to survive. Sometimes our metaphors even suggest a level of malice, when time is a thief, a monster, or an enemy we must defeat.

By contrast, a time-is-love approach flips the script from hard to soft, from enemy to friend, from thief to something more like a doting grandparent. It is slow instead of fast, at ease instead of hurried, abundant instead of scarce, kind instead of cruel. "Time is love" is invitational, personal; it seeks and prioritizes connection. Love is inherently abundant; it has all the time in the world.

Where the time-is-love rubber hits the time-is-money road, though, is in this thorny question: How do we inhabit a time-is-love posture in the midst of days filled with meetings and deadlines and rehearsals and diapers and obligations and unexpected interruptions, when there's more to do than time to do it, when the only way to get everything done—or even some things done—is to go faster and carry more? Or perhaps you're in the opposite situation—you are retired, just lost your job, or had an accident and are in recovery, and now you have more time than you know what to do with. How can you meet your days with a sense of presence and purpose? What does a time-is-love posture actually look like in real life?

These are *the* questions we need to ask—not with an air of incredulity and cynicism, but with genuine curiosity. If we ask them honestly, they can become mirrors, helping us to see our patterns and habits more clearly. These questions can even become lamps illuminating paths we can explore to live beyond the limitations we assume. Such questions help clarify what's at stake for us each day we are alive in this blessed and broken world. Namely, that "how we spend our days is, of course, how we spend our lives," as author Annie Dillard put it.[4] For many of us, spending our days with the mindset that time is money is no longer sustainable; if we continue to do so, we will one day look back at how we spent our life and not like what we see.

These questions—all of which are some form of *But how can I live differently?*—are just a starting point. Their objective is to prepare us to ask the *real* question—a question that can become a compass, reorienting us back to the Sabbath way. In her poem, aptly titled "The Question," poet, teacher, and kindness-spreader Rosemerry Wahtola Trommer reveals what the real question is.

REORIENTING: TIME IS LOVE

THE QUESTION
for Jude Jordan Kalush, who asked the question

All day, I replay these words:
Is this the path of love?
I think of them as I rise,
as I wake my children,
as I wash dishes,
as I drive too close
behind the slow blue Subaru,
Is this the path of love?
Think of these words as I stand in line
at the grocery store,
think of them as I sit on the couch
with my daughter.
Amazing how quickly six words
become compass, the new lens
through which to see myself in the world.
I notice what the question is not.
Not, "Is this right?"
Not, "Is this wrong?"
It just longs to know
how the action of existence
links us to the path of love.
And is it this? *Is it* this?
All day, I let myself be led by the question.
All day I let myself not be too certain
of the answer. Is it this?
Is this the path of love? I ask
as I wait for the next word to come.[5]

This is the best way I know to live into a time-is-love posture. Ask yourself at any given moment, *Is this the path of love?* Ask it every day, multiple times a day. When you're scanning Instagram during a colleague's presentation at work, ask yourself, *Is this the path of love?* When your child is once again daydreaming instead of getting ready to leave and you once again respond in ways that escalate the tension, ask yourself, *Is this the path of love?* When you feel the conflict between getting more work done and being present to your family, your friends, or yourself, ask yourself, *Is this the path of love?* When you say yes when you want to say no, ask yourself, *Is this the path of love?* When you say no when you want to say yes, ask yourself, *Is this the path of love?* When you are exhausted but feel guilty resting instead of being productive, ask yourself, *Is this the path of love?*

As the poem makes clear, the ultimate question is not *Is this right or wrong?* That question won't get us very far in exploring the path of love. The answer to the ultimate question may be "no," as in, "The direction I am going is *not* the path of love." But that is different than saying it's "wrong," which is a moral judgment void of curiosity and nuance. The right/wrong framework is native to a time-is-money mindset. It is possible that we may feel shame or anger at ourselves upon realizing we have chosen a path other than the path of love. But even that is an opportunity to ask ourselves, *Is this the path of love?* Is beating myself up over this or that choice the path of love? Is cutting myself off from participating in the life happening around me the path of love? Is telling myself the same old story about not being good enough or always making the wrong decision putting me on the path of love?

When Jesus said the two greatest commandments were to love God and "love your neighbor as yourself" (Matthew 22:37-39), part of what he meant was, "If you don't truly love yourself, you cannot truly love your neighbor." Walking the path of loving ourselves is the foundation for walking the path of loving each other.

Walking the Path of Love

There are myriad ways we can spend our days—and thus our lives—walking the path of love. Some may be more obvious than others, such as living with compassion, offering people grace, pursuing justice, being kind, or seeking another person's best interests. Or we could search the Bible for every passage on love and try to identify the patterns and practices they suggest. While all of those are likely to bear fruit, when Sabbath and time are overlaid onto love, they serve as a clarifying filter, reducing the unlimited number of options down to size. While there are still many things that could be named, when I look at love through the lens of Sabbath and time, three aspects of love stand out as especially helpful for walking the path of love in everyday life: presence, patience, and play.

Love Is Presence

My maternal grandparents taught me the power of presence from an early age. I learned from them that the first and most important step in loving someone is showing up. Whether it was them making the ninety-minute drive to attend a soccer or basketball game, a school play, or a birthday party, my grandparents were committed to being there for our family. Similarly, they felt our love when we showed up, especially for the family gatherings they hosted multiple times throughout the year. They were never more joyful or content than when family was around. This same principle of the power of one's physical presence informs the approach used by many service professionals, such as pastors, chaplains, teachers, social workers, and health-care workers. But showing up is only the first step toward showing love, and being in close proximity to someone is only half of being present.

Beyond physical presence, the kind of love-as-presence the Sabbath cultivates in us—which is profoundly impacted by our relationship to time—is about paying attention, which means being present internally. You know you're practicing love as presence when you listen without judgment; are fully where you are—in body, mind, and spirit; when you resist distraction; when you look at and *really see* the people and places around you; when you are unhurried; or when you offer someone your undivided attention. You know you're *not* practicing presence when you react instead of respond; when you cut someone off instead of listening to what they say; when you think about the game or the grocery list while pretending to listen to the sermon or your child; or when you have your face glued to your phone to avoid interacting with the people around you.

My wife and I have had a yearslong discussion about my habit of being on my phone in the evening during the time we've set aside to connect. Typically, as soon as there was a lull in our conversation, or if she left for three minutes to use the bathroom, I'd pick up my phone. This made her feel like she had to compete with the entire digital universe for my attention. I was present externally, but she had no idea where I was internally and would naturally conclude that whatever I was doing was more important to me than she was.

The answer we have found is to have agreed-upon boundaries that prioritize our value of connection. For example, we (try to) put our phones in a drawer in the evenings. If we want or need to check something, we simply say, "I'm going to look something up," or "I have to respond to a text," so the other person isn't left wondering, on the outside looking in. We practice this on our Sabbath days and extend the practice into our week to change our posture from distracted to attentive. This helps us be present to each other in the ways we want to be. A simple practice such as this can also help parents model to their children healthy ways of relating to each other and to technology.

Our attention can be divided by more than technology, of course. For example, the burdens we carry—worries or regrets from the day about things we said or did or didn't say or do—can gnaw at us and divide us in our spirit. What is the path of love in these situations? One path is to be honest and vulnerable—with ourselves and the people we are with—about what is weighing us down. This prevents those we care about from having to draw their own conclusions about why we seem distracted or irritable. It builds empathy and understanding, enabling connection and sharing of burdens.

Love Is Patience

Have you ever considered why *patient* sits atop the list of words the apostle Paul used to describe love, the most powerful force in the universe?

REORIENTING: TIME IS LOVE

> *Love is patient*, love is kind. It does not envy, it does not boast, it is not proud. It does not dishonor others, it is not self-seeking, it is not easily angered, it keeps no record of wrongs. Love does not delight in evil but rejoices with the truth. It always protects, always trusts, always hopes, always perseveres.
>
> I CORINTHIANS 13:4-7, NIV (EMPHASIS ADDED)

Paul knew that patience is foundational to love, an essential way we image God to our neighbors, and a central virtue by which, as Jesus put it, "everyone will know that you are my disciples" (John 13:35).

And patience is 100 percent an expression of our relationship to time. The difference between patience and impatience is not how long we wait, but *how* we wait. It's about how we relate to time while we wait. Impatience looks like hurry, anxiety, rushing, nagging, irritation, reactivity; it exerts force to get what it wants, which is to speed things up. Impatience can blind us to the consequences of our actions—just as it did to Zorba with the butterfly. While generally having no effect on wait time, impatience cuts us off from joy and compassion while we wait.

Patience, on the other hand, is the capacity to wait well. It looks like ease, trust, stillness, contentment, presence, attentiveness. It is not passive, but it allows life to flow on its course and at its pace. Patience would have been Zorba noticing his instinct to hurry the butterfly's emergence but choosing instead to stand in wonder and bear witness as the transformation unfolded on its own timeline. Patience is a doorway we can walk through to experience joy, connection, and comfort even when we don't yet have what we want.

When you were a kid, did you ever experience, as I did, an adult trying to instill patience in you by singing Herbert the Snail's chorus from the *Music Machine*? "Have patience, have patience. Don't be in such a hurry"?[6] Despite what I'm sure were good intentions, this chorus didn't teach me much about patience—and never helped me develop it. Ironically, all it ever did was feed my irritated impatience! And that has continued into adulthood. Even today, hearing it sung is a surefire way to undercut my ability to wait well.

While Herbert the Snail was never very helpful in teaching me about patience or cultivating it in me, the Psalms have been. In Psalm 130, for example, two synonymous verbs, *qivah* (key-VAH) and *yachel* (ya-HEHL) are translated "to wait" and "to hope," which are both central aspects of patience. Psalm 130 is a lament psalm that begins in the darkness of dread and grief and ends with the hope of light coming with the rising sun. The psalmist compares Israel waiting on the Lord to watchmen on the city walls waiting for dawn to break (see Psalm 130:6). Since the sun rises on its own schedule, night watchmen learned to wait patiently and expectantly. This suggests that waiting well is not a posture of passive indifference, but of active hope, bearing witness in expectation of what the Spirit will do in any given situation. Patience is rooted in trust, and, like trust, grows over time. We can learn patience only by waiting, just as we can learn trust only when we feel vulnerable. In waiting, we learn to wait. In trusting, we learn to trust.[7]

Sabbath has a reciprocal relationship with trust. It requires trust to practice Sabbath, and practicing Sabbath develops trust. It can feel vulnerable to stop producing, stop racing, stop working, or stop striving, even when doing so makes room for us to slow down, to listen to our life, to connect with loved ones, or to remember what brings us delight and makes us feel alive. A Sabbath practice is a slow apprenticeship in trusting the abundance of God.

As our trust grows and our comfort in slowing down increases, our ability to wait well grows too. And when we wait well, we lavish those around us with love. Our children are less likely to feel like inconveniences, interruptions in our day are less likely to derail us, and people will *feel* Christ in us, whether or not they can articulate why.

Love Is Play

Making room in our lives to play is one of the Sabbath's greatest gifts. Play refers to any activity that is inherently unproductive, void of obvious utility. But it is also a posture we take toward life that is marked by ease, presence, levity, and engagement. Play prioritizes connection over production and ease over force. It is loose as opposed to tight. Instead of caring solely about getting things done, its concern is spreading life and light. Its only goal is joy. Its purpose in time is for us to *lose track of time*. In a world of adulting, play is often seen as childish. But play is not childish; it is childlike. It is animated by curiosity, wonder, and delight. Play wonders, "What if?" when others see a dead end. Play says, "yes, and" instead of "no, because."[8] Play is an effective if underappreciated way of practicing presence, of training our hearts to love.

Although play involves ease, it is not easy. In fact, it can be quite costly. Because it eschews productivity and resists utility, playfulness may be one of the greatest threats to the supremacy of a time-is-money mindset. This can make playfulness feel dangerous or threatening, especially to very serious, (self-)important, powerful people. And if those people have power over you, being playful can feel vulnerable. You might not be taken seriously if you inhabit a playful spirit, are quick to laugh, or are interested in things outside of work or the topics of breezy conversation.

Whether at the workplace, on the ball field, or in the kitchen, when the *modus operandi* is productivity and efficiency above all else, play becomes an act of protest. In a time-is-money world, play must always yield to work—"You can't play unless your work is done!" or "You have to *earn* the right to play!" But in a Sabbath-shaped world where time is love, work yields to play *every week*. The Sabbath is a coronation ceremony crowning delight and connection as king and queen.

There are a million-and-one ways to inhabit a playful spirit in your life, and you'll need to take stock of your personality, your preferences, and what does or does not feel comfortable to you. But to stimulate your imagination, here are a few ways I try to be playful, whether at home, at work, or out in the world. One way to prioritize connection at work is to ask a coworker about their life outside of work, or to bring in treats to share and celebrate a "just for the heck of it" holiday. It could also mean walking to someone's office or calling them instead of writing an email. Sometimes I take being childlike literally and pack my lunch in a Spider-Man lunch box that I put in the common fridge. I might bring extra fruit snacks to share with my coworkers and students or write a goofy (or encouraging) note and put it on someone's desk while they're away.

I have been exploring small but meaningful ways of connecting to strangers by intentionally telling people that I like their shirt, pants, hair, or accessory. It brings a smile to their face—and to mine—every time. At home, Mariah and I have recently tried a new and playful way of working through the conflict that always seems to rise when we cook together. We have started saying aloud an intention before we begin cooking. For example, my intention might be "to bring a good attitude, to listen to Mariah's instructions carefully, to truly see her, and to dance to at least one song on the playlist."

Walking the path of love by being present, patient, and playful often involves very small acts, but their impact is big. They can help us get out of our heads and our fears and get back into our bodies. They can help the people around us feel seen and included, like they belong, aren't a burden, and that their presence matters. Walking the path of love is about increasing our joy and the joy of others. It's about pursuing "what makes for peace and for mutual upbuilding," as the apostle Paul put it (Romans 14:19). It is about helping us become more childlike—more forgiving, more imaginative, more curious, more alive, more connected. And there's a lot at stake in our becoming more childlike. It was Jesus who said, "Truly I tell you, unless you change and become like children, you will never enter the kingdom of heaven" (Matthew 18:3).

It's also important to note, however, that walking the path of love does not mean a wholesale abandoning of the way of "time is money." To become like children is not to abandon adulthood. Rather, it is to become child*like* without becoming child*ish*. Similarly, walking the Sabbath way is to be discerning of how we engage the diversity of time-related mindsets throughout our lives.

Time Is Love—and Money

The various metaphors for time we've explored make clear that time is complex and multilayered, a diamond with many facets (to add yet another metaphor!). Qohelet, the speaker in the book of Ecclesiastes, knew this well, saying, "There is a time for everything" (Ecclesiastes 3:1, NIV). This

REORIENTING: TIME IS LOVE

suggests that living wisely *in time* involves embracing the complexity of time and learning to navigate between different orders of time.

While it may seem as if I've been advocating for a singular approach to time (that the only way we should see time is through the lens of love), that is not my intention. Nevertheless, the time has come to dethrone the time-is-money mindset from its near-total dominance over our lives. Even so, I am not suggesting we replace one dictator with another, however benevolent a time-is-love dictatorship might be!

I want to put the time-is-money mindset in its place *alongside* the time-is-love mindset of the Sabbath. As Qohelet reminded us, there is a time for moving fast, for prioritizing productivity, efficiency, and getting stuff done. Sometimes *doing* has to lead. Sometimes we can't say yes to our children when they want to play if we have work that needs doing. But we can't say no every time either.

The Sabbath invitation is to be very clear about what our values are in relation to time, so that when we feel the tug between fast and slow, distraction and presence, work and play, productivity and the people we love, the choice we make aligns with our values and the way we want to show up to our lives. The Sabbath reminds us that, if we truly want to know the fullness of life, we must stop marginalizing experiences of delight, joy, and connection; and we must stop diminishing capacities such as presence, patience, and playfulness. Actively cultivating these experiences and capacities in our Sabbath practice, and intentionally incorporating them into our Sabbath posture throughout the week—whether in the grocery store, the doctor's office, the boss's office, or our own kitchen—will put us in the position to receive more of the goodness life has to offer each day.

Walking the path of love is being present to the moment in a way that moves us toward gratitude. It's being patient with life's unfolding in a way that allows us to bear witness to our own and others' transformation. It is beholding the tender wings as they unfold—not with the impatience of Zorba, but with the awe and wonder of a participant in the mystery of being and becoming. It is leaning into playfulness, which opens us to join with life wherever it is happening, connecting us to our own delight and that of others.

REFLECTION QUESTIONS

- Reflect on your response to the story of Zorba and the butterfly.
  - In what ways, if any, did it feel convicting?
  - What memories did it bring to mind? For example, times you behaved as Zorba did or experienced being rushed as the butterfly did.
  - When are you most likely to become impatient with life and tempted to speed up life's unfolding, as Zorba did with the butterfly?

- Journalist Carl Honoré uses the terms "Fast" and "Slow" as shorthand for two ways of being in the world. Based on his descriptions, how would you characterize your way of being in the world—your experience of time—in this season of life? Circle the number on the continuum that best describes your response.

  0   1   2   3   4   5   6   7   8   9   10

  Fast   **Slow**

  Busy, controlling, aggressive, hurried, analytical, stressed, superficial, impatient, active, quantity over quality   *Calm, careful, receptive, still, intuitive, unhurried, patient, reflective, quality over quantity*

  Overall, how comfortable are you with your response? How sustainable is this way of being in the world and experiencing time?

- We walk the path of love in everyday life when we choose *presence* over distraction, *patience* over hurry, and *play* over productivity (pages 116–122).
  - Briefly recall the events of the previous twenty-four hours—what you did, whom you encountered, your state of mind and heart. In what ways, if any, were your activities, interactions, or mindset marked by distraction, hurry, or productivity?

» In the same activities, interactions, or mindset you just identified, what might choosing a posture of presence, patience, or play have required of you? What would you have lost and/or gained by making this choice instead?

Sabbath Practice: Walking the Path of Love

Just as we can train our minds and bodies to learn a new skill with practice and repetition over time, we can train our hearts to love by the choices we make in everyday life.

- Choose one of the three practices for walking the path of love in everyday life—presence, patience, or play—as your focus for the next seven days.

- Identify the activities and/or relationships in which you most want to shift your choices or mindset by practicing presence, patience, or play each day. For example, your daily commute, work meetings or daily tasks, interactions with a family member, friend, or colleague.

- In addition to looking for spontaneous ways to practice your chosen path of love, identify one or two actions you will be intentional about following through on. For example, "I will not exceed the speed limit," "I will listen and ask follow-up questions," "I will choose the longest line," "I will invite someone to lunch," "I will engage in at least one playful act a day at work/school/home by . . ."

- At the end of seven days, briefly reflect on your daily experiences of practicing presence, patience, or play. What did practicing your chosen path of love require of you? What, if anything, shifted in you or your relationships as a result?

PART 3

SABBATH AND COMMUNITY

8

ORIENTING: WHAT PREVENTS COMMUNITY?

*Disconnection in all its guises . . .
is becoming our culture's most plentiful product.*
GABOR MATÉ, THE MYTH OF NORMAL

*We find belonging by making enemies. We belong
to each other by dividing others from us.*
DAVID STUBBS, professor of ethics and theology, Western Theological Seminary

The quirky film *Lars and the Real Girl* tells the painful and inspiring tale of twenty-seven-year-old Lars Lindstrom during one monumental Minnesota winter. Lars's life has been marked mostly by loss. His mother died giving birth to him, leaving a wake of grief from which his father never emerged. In a sense, Lars lost both of his parents before he was born. His older brother, Gus, overwhelmed by the deafening silence of their collective sadness, left home as soon as he could and never looked back. This left Lars alone and abandoned. He spent his life in isolation, rejecting every invitation to connection. He was literally untouchable, wearing layers of clothing like armor to protect himself from human touch, which caused him severe physical pain.

The title of the film comes from the unusual strategy Lars develops to avoid processing the memories of his childhood trauma that are triggered when Gus and his wife, Karin, move back home and discover that

Karin is pregnant. Her pregnancy awakens Lars's fear that a whole new generation might live in the iron grip of loss as he had. Without healthy ways of processing his pain and isolation, without real connections to lean on, and without models of healthy vulnerability, he has to invent a connection he can control. To do this, he orders a life-size doll from the internet and pretends she is real. He even makes up a backstory for Bianca, which includes a recent accident that left her paralyzed to explain why none of her limbs work and she can't feed herself. No one knows what to do with Lars's delusion, least of all Gus and Karin.

The film gets *really* interesting when the local psychologist, Dr. Dagmar, suggests that the only way to help Lars heal is to *go along with his delusion*—to see Bianca as Lars sees her, as *real*. Gus cannot abide this idea and rejects it out of hand. He just wants Dr. Dagmar to "fix" Lars. He refuses to see the world from Lars's perspective or enter his experience.

"Everyone's going to laugh at him," Gus complains.

"And you," Dr. Dagmar replies, gently reminding Gus of his pattern of choosing his own comfort over Lars's.[1] This moment marks a turning point for Gus. While it's extraordinarily difficult at first, over time the act of loving Lars the way Lars needs to be loved helps bring about a transformation in Gus's life just as it does for Lars.

While the premise might sound absurd, *Lars and the Real Girl* is a poignant meditation on loneliness and grief, the costs of disconnection, and the consequences of cutting ourselves off from others because we're too afraid to risk the connection our souls crave—whether we're "healthy" like Gus or lost in a delusion like Lars. It's relatable because loneliness is a universal human experience that is endemic to our modern, globalized, consumerist, and hyper-individualist society. Indeed, loneliness and its effects are one of the primary barriers we face to experiencing true community and belonging today.

Exclusion is another barrier to community explored through Lars's story. It is hinted at in Gus's gut response to Dr. Dagmar. It's also seen in the way the filmmaker plays with the audience's expectations. We expect people to reject Bianca and exclude Lars for being weird, for making people uncomfortable, or for being emotionally unstable. Indeed, the leaders of Lars's small church seriously consider that option as they're embarrassed by the idea of him bringing a sex doll into the sanctuary, even if he's not using Bianca for that purpose. The film explores these layered tensions in very interesting and poignant ways, which ultimately point toward hope.

I found myself surprised by how relatable Lars's character was, despite our wildly different life experiences—and our very different strategies for processing pain! I realized that most of us are not so different from him. He was oblivious to how his ways of coping with loneliness and grief—of pushing people away, resisting the sadness even as he was absorbed by it, and externalizing his grief by inventing alternate realities—were influenced by larger structures and cultural values.

While the particularities of our lives are likely quite different—different from Lars's, but different from each other's as well—we, too, have been shaped by cultural forces invisible to us whose values influence our experience of community and connection, from the internal longings we feel to the ways we express (or repress) those longings with each other. Therefore, our exploration of Sabbath and community begins where *Lars and the Real Girl* begins, by considering some of the cultural barriers we each face in experiencing community and connection.

Cultural Barriers to Community

While the Sabbath is deeply personal, it is not individualistic. The Sabbath longs for the *whole* "community of creation" to flourish.[2] Hence, the focus of our Sabbath explorations now shifts from the personal to the communal. Specifically, to considering the countercultural ways the Sabbath makes room for us to experience meaningful connection and redefines what it means to belong in a cultural context that produces isolation, division, suspicion, and dissatisfaction.

While the number of cultural forces shaping our view of community are legion, two are particularly impactful—the first is economic, the second philosophical. More specifically, the first is capitalism and the second is dualism. I believe these two cultural forces are barriers that play an outsized role in defining how we in the twenty-first-century West experience community, seek connection, and understand what it means to belong.

Barrier 1: American Corporate Capitalism

Economic systems have an enormous influence on shaping the values we live by and how we view and relate to each other—whether we are aware of that influence or not. In fact, the influence is often greater the less we're aware of it. This is true regardless of what the economic system may be. I'm calling attention to what renowned psychologist Tim Kasser and his colleagues refer to as "American corporate capitalism" (ACC)[3] for two reasons: because it is the form of capitalism that has shaped the culture within the US, where I live, and because it's arguably the most influential economic system in the world today.[4] ACC does what every economic system is designed to do: incentivize behaviors that reinforce its goals, as well as "define the role of participants, and determine rules for many human interactions and exchanges."[5] ACC's goals are driven by the corporate agenda of maximal profits through unlimited growth, too often by any means necessary.

The problem, as we will see, is that the success of ACC is dependent upon the suppression of values and behaviors central to the Sabbath way. This suggests that keeping the Sabbath is inherently an act of resistance against the economic forces driving contemporary culture. In fact, this is a big part of why practicing the Sabbath is *so hard*—like trying to sleep on the beach in a hurricane or do yoga next to a NASCAR track. Neither the cultural nor the economic climate in which we live are conducive to rhythm or rest, to connection or belonging. In fact, according to author and psychologist Gabor Maté, the exact opposite is true: "Disconnection in all its guises—*alienation, loneliness, loss of meaning,* and *dislocation*—is becoming our culture's most plentiful product."[6]

ORIENTING: WHAT PREVENTS COMMUNITY?

To understand this, we need to explore the values that drive ACC, which is to say, the economic values that shape our attitudes, behaviors, and choices every day. Kasser and his colleagues identified four primary values that govern how institutions operating within ACC function:

1. Self-interest
2. A strong desire for financial success
3. High levels of consumption
4. Interpersonal styles based on competition[7]

The gospel ACC preaches is that what people truly want—what fosters happiness and fulfillment—is money, affordable products to consume, and a sense of having "won" at life through achievement and financial success. In other words, fulfilling the "American Dream." ACC's message is that the way to get what we want is by competing with others, each person serving their own interests. If everyone works "together" by competing against everyone else in pursuit of self-interest, ACC promises that society will improve.

There is no question that ACC has benefited the marketplace and has increased our standard of living beyond the wildest dreams of our ancestors. But when it comes to building community, ACC builds only barriers. It promotes a strategy for collective enhancement that boils down to the paper-thin gospel of selfishness, competition, and having enough money to consume whatever we want. This is how it defines the good life. And if we are successful in each of those areas, it will feel good, for a time. But this vision is missing life's most precious and ultimate components. Chief among them is a sense of belonging.

It is no wonder, then, that our society is experiencing an epidemic of loneliness and isolation built on the cracked foundation of dissatisfaction and dislocation. And I don't use "epidemic" as a metaphor. US Surgeon General Dr. Vivek Murthy recently declared loneliness an epidemic, not only because it is so widespread, but also because of the devastating physical and emotional consequences it inflicts.[8]

Barrier 2: Dualism

A second barrier to our experience of community and connection is equally as pervasive as ACC but is less visible and probably less familiar. I'm referring to the philosophical ideology known as dualism, what indigenous theologian Randy Woodley calls "the founding fallacy of the Western worldview."[9] With its roots in ancient Greek philosophy, a dualistic approach to life divides the world into binaries (*dual* meaning "two") or opposing pairs, which are then invested with figurative and/or moral significance as either superior or inferior. Typical expressions of dualism are the dichotomy between mind and body, spirit and flesh, reason and emotion, light and dark, sacred and secular.

Every dualism has two emphases. The first is to draw a hard line between each half of the pair: light/dark, church/world, us/them. The efficacy of the framework depends on how clearly the dividing line is drawn and maintained. The second emphasis is on creating a hierarchy between the two halves. In moral terms, one half is good; the other is bad. In religious terms, one is close to God; the other is far from God. In social terms, one belongs; the other is excluded. To look at the world through a dualistic lens is to view it in either/or terms: white or black, right or wrong, friend or foe, in or out. Dualistic frameworks have no patience for nuance or mystery. Their pursuit is control and power, and their strategy is division and exclusion.

The consequences of this are visible everywhere we look. Our polarized political climate has become an extreme form of dualism in which to belong to one party necessarily means to oppose the other. Loyalty is more important than the common good, and compromise is tantamount to betrayal. The either/or posture of dualism is visible in social media threads in which people label and judge each other based on a few words they've said, and then proceed to reject them, tear them apart, make fun of them, excommunicate them, and so on. It is visible in approaches to Christian discipleship that prioritize the mind and exclude the body, reducing faith to believing the right things and failing to dignify the body, celebrate its desires, or take seriously matters of abuse or injustice, which always have physical consequences. It is visible in approaches to the Bible that take every word literally and view interpretation as a matter of black-and-white, ignoring the role of genre, historical context, the complexities of translation, or the ways in which ancient debates about matters of faith and theology are present and sometimes unresolved in Scripture.

Dualism is visible in the long history of racism within the US and around the world in which lighter skin is viewed as superior and darker skin inferior. This dualistic dehumanization has justified everything from chattel slavery to the genocide of Native Americans to Jim Crow laws to mass incarceration to anti-immigrant sentiments.

Dualism entrenches an us/them mentality into our definitions of community and what it means to belong. So often we answer the question "Who belongs?" by answering a different question instead: "Who *doesn't* belong?" We answer the first question by answering the second. My colleague and friend, the ethicist David Stubbs, articulated this poignantly: "We find belonging by making enemies. We belong to each other by dividing others from us."[10] Belonging to a group based on the exclusion of others is a false belonging. It doesn't just diminish those who are excluded; it's self-diminishment as well.

Yet it is this commitment to exclusion as a strategy for belonging that makes dualism so desirable and so devastating. This is one place where the consequences of dualism and ACC converge to undermine true community and belonging. Many of us are so lonely and isolated that any taste of connection feels like a cup of cold water in the desert, even when our belonging is dependent on another's exclusion. And in a time when so much feels outside of our control—with so much pain and suffering in the world and so many things to be anxious about—the prospect of a framework that provides a sense of certainty and control is profoundly appealing. But the costs of dualism far outweigh its facade of simplicity. Our unwitting apprenticeship in ACC and dualism has fostered a culture of loneliness and exclusion in which none of us feel as if we truly belong.

The Consequences of Capitalism and Dualism on Community

Loneliness and exclusion are not only barriers to our experience of community, they are also consequences of how our contemporary world has been constructed. They aren't accidental and have not happened by chance. They are the inevitable outcomes of the economic and philosophical foundations of the modern Western world. And they make experiencing true community *really* hard. Finding and living in community is difficult enough on its own, without the influence of global forces beyond our comprehension complicating it all!

Finding ways of living beyond these barriers involves more than acknowledging their existence and learning about their origins, however. To move toward deeper experiences of connection and belonging, we must also understand how they operate and impact us. Doing so will make it clearer how the Sabbath can help us address the sour fruit they have produced: an epidemic of loneliness and a plague of exclusion.

An Epidemic of Loneliness

In his beautiful book *Together*, Surgeon General Vivek Murthy explores the contours of the epidemic of loneliness affecting not just the US, but many places around the world. Loneliness is not the same as being alone. It's possible to be surrounded by people but still feel disconnected from everyone and everything. And that's the difference. According to Murthy, "Loneliness is the subjective feeling that you're lacking the social connections you need."[11] It's about *feeling* disconnected, not necessarily being isolated. Loneliness breeds shame, spawning a "self-perpetuating condition, triggering self-doubt, which in turn lowers self-esteem and discourages us" from reaching out to others to get the connection we crave.[12] Loneliness feeds the lie that we are the only ones who are lonely.

And this vulnerability is exploited and monetized by ACC. As Gabor Maté has observed, "Qualities like love, trust, caring, social conscience, and engagement are inevitable casualties . . . of a culture that prizes acquisition above all else."[13] By celebrating consumption and preaching competition, our culture "fails to value communality—our need to belong, to care for one another, and to feel caring energy flowing toward us." A society so constructed denies "the essence of what it means to be human."[14]

This truth is reflected in the opening pages of Scripture. The Bible's second account of Creation (Genesis 2) has a single human created at the beginning of the account, as opposed to a pair—or group—of humans created in community at the end of the account (Genesis 1). In the first account, everything God created was *tov* ("good"). By the end of the second account, however, the human remains alone without a suitable partner with whom to belong. God's recognition of the human's desperate condition is the first thing in all of creation—in all of history—to be described as *lo tov* ("not good," Genesis 2:18).

God's declaration that the human's isolation is *lo tov* is a purposeful contrast to God's repeated delight in the *tov*-ness of creation in Genesis 1, where seven times God "saw that it was *tov*."[15] Reading Genesis 1 and 2 together suggests that the *tov*-ness in Genesis 1 does not just describe God's pleasure in what was made or the expertise of God's craftsmanship. It describes the goodness of each element *and the goodness of their intrinsic interdependence*. Connection is inherent to creation's goodness. It's what we were made for—and not just humans, but all of creation. This suggests that the disconnection we experience in loneliness is not just *lo tov* in that it's unfortunate, but that it goes against the very fabric and purpose of creation. Loneliness has cosmic consequences.

And those consequences are being felt in communities across the country and around the world. A recent study found that 22 percent of US adults "often or always" felt lonely or socially isolated.[16] Another study found that one in three US adults over age forty-five report feeling lonely.[17] And the severity is only worsening. A *New York Times* study found that the percentage of Americans identifying themselves as lonely doubled between the 1980s and 2016.[18]

The consequences of loneliness are not just emotional and psychological; they are physical as well. It turns out that loneliness is a matter of life and death. A recent groundbreaking study, guided by an international panel of experts and led by professor of psychology and neuroscience Julianne Holt-Lundstadt, asked the simple question: "Do social relationships reduce our risk of dying early?"[19] The research, which spanned more than a year, surveyed 148 different studies, and involved more than 300,000 participants from all over the world, found that the answer was a resounding "yes." Dr. Holt-Lundstadt and her team found that people with strong social relationships are 50 percent less likely to die prematurely than those with weak connections. Even more surprising, persistent loneliness negatively impacts someone's lifespan *as much as* smoking fifteen cigarettes a day, and it is also more dangerous than obesity, excess alcohol, or a sedentary lifestyle.[20]

All of this is to say that the experience of loneliness is profoundly challenging. And it is nearly universal. The tragic irony is that this common experience could be a powerful way to find real connection and healing with each other, since we all know something of what each other is experiencing. Yet so many suffer in isolation. This isolation is compounded by the ways in which cultural ideals such as rugged individualism and the lie that vulnerability is weakness conspire to stigmatize loneliness, keeping us from risking the connections that could foster healing.

The deeper problem this points to is that these symptoms are neither random nor surprising. Gabor Maté describes them as "the concrete manifestation of a particular socioeconomic system, a distinct worldview, and a way of life."[21] Which means that any solution that same system offers is just going to perpetuate the problem. Any effective remedy that facilitates meaningful connection and belonging must therefore come from outside of the system. It must be the expression of a different set of values and an alternative worldview, one that is embedded in a different way of life.

A Plague of Exclusion

Exclusion is as pervasive an experience as loneliness, and its effects are equally as devastating. Recall how dualism reframes the world in binary terms as a strategy to simplify complexity, eliminate nuance, and consolidate control and power for whichever half of the binary is determined to be superior. While the word *exclusion* can refer to many experiences—from rejection by a love interest to denial of an application to being the one person not invited to the party—the kind of exclusion I am referring to as a consequence of dualism manifests in broader structural and systemic ways that are nevertheless felt profoundly at the personal level.

For example, consider how our language both expresses and reinforces exclusion by examining the term *normal*. In his profoundly insightful book *Becoming Friends of Time*, theologian of disability John Swinton speaks to the dangers—and even violence—that lurk in the term "normal."[22] Etymologically, the word comes from both Latin and Greek and is related to the practice of building. The Latin root refers to an instrument called a T square, which a builder used to construct walls and corners at a right angle. The adjective *right* refers both to the type of angle *and to the preferences of the builder*. A T square's value is found both in its utility to the builder's vision and its conformity to the builder's expectations. T squares that did both were right or normal. Those that did not were worthless and discardable. And those were the only two options—normal or worthless.

This makes perfect sense within the context of construction, since failure to build a wall at the correct angle could end in disaster. The problem began to creep in during the early nineteenth century when medical science adopted the term *normal* to express its understanding of health. *Normal* was diagnostically paired with its binary opposite term, *pathological*.[23] If a patient was not healthy in the normal way, they were considered pathological. As you might imagine, the definition of *normal* here raises some profoundly significant questions. Who was empowered to define the term? What cultural values informed that definition? Who had the power to enforce the consequences of a pathological diagnosis? Such a diagnosis could justify all manner of inhumane treatment of someone—even if that person was healthy, just not in a way that aligned with the assumptions of those who defined the terms. Indeed, medical history is littered with the consequences of the abuses this dualistic framing introduced and the power dynamics that supported it. Marginalized groups have been the victims of precisely this kind of medical mistreatment, whether African Americans who were denied health care or were victims of involuntary experimentation during slavery and Jim Crow, or Mexicans and Native Americans who were involuntarily sterilized during the 1960s and 1970s, to name but a few tragic examples.[24]

According to philosophy of science professor Ian Hacking, the term *normal* quickly grew beyond medicine and was applied to "almost everything. People, behaviour, states of affairs, diplomatic relations, molecules. . . . [It] became indispensable because it created a way to be 'objective' about human beings."[25] This objectivity was, however, deeply *subjective*, ambiguous, and contextual. Nevertheless, the term *normal* became endowed with the power to determine what was right and good and desirable. Clearly, normal is not neutral.

Sociologist Lisa Wade distinguishes the terms *norm*, *normal*, and *normative* from the perspective of sociology.[26] A *norm* is what is common or frequent, the statistical majority, such as building walls at ninety-degree angles or being right-handed. *Normal* is understood in contrast with *abnormal*. Since being right-handed is the norm, being left-handed is abnormal and therefore undesirable. Or a more generous take would be that while left-handedness may be normal, right-handedness is the norm.

Normative, on the other hand, refers to a "morally-endorsed ideal."[27] Normative is the norm calcified and coupled with power. Right-handed normativity would say that everybody *should* be right-handed, and left-handers are inferior, morally suspect, and untrustworthy.[28] As with the abuses in medical history, norms can easily be invested with cultural values and become normative, which is to say, norms that are *enforced*. Try offering your left hand to someone you meet on the street in the Middle East and see how they react.[29]

What the terms *norm*, *normal*, and especially *normative* reveal is how a dualistic framework can justify violence and exclusion when the terms are invested with social, cultural, political, religious, or judicial power. And while the idea of legislating right-handedness as the normative way to use one's hands—and punishing left-handedness with the full force of the law—is undoubtedly farcical, it is only a thinly veiled analogy for historical and contemporary examples of systematic exclusion built on the rickety foundation of dualism. It is not difficult to see how the same normative principle when applied to other expressions more central to one's body, identity, or personhood—whether height, weight, gender, race, ethnicity, physical or cognitive ability, or sexual orientation—can have a soul-crushing impact on one's ability to experience joy, connection, affirmation, and fullness of life in a world that will not accept them as they are.

Healing from Loneliness and Exclusion: Sabbath and Self-Compassion

Experiences of loneliness and exclusion can be extremely painful and disorienting, causing us to question our value and worth, diminishing our confidence, and preventing us from offering our full, beautiful selves to the world. These experiences tend to increase our stress and amplify the voices of our inner critics, who blame us for our suffering, telling us we should have acted differently, that we are unlikable, that we are too much, too awkward, too different, and will never belong. The practice of self-compassion is one powerful way to respond to this habitual internalized messaging—what journalist Judith Shulevitz memorably called the "eternal inner murmur of self-reproach."[30]

Self-compassion is especially well-suited to partner with the Sabbath to help us heal from the consequences of the cultural and economic climate in which we live, because the teachings of self-compassion confirm two fundamental Sabbath truths: we are beloved, and we are enough. These truths are central to a fruitful and abundant life. They are also central to the experience of community, which the Sabbath and self-compassion both prepare us for and compel us toward. Self-compassion is not self-absorption; rather, it is offering oneself grace in order to inhabit that grace with others. As Christian education professor James Wilhoit describes it, "The gospel calls us to be people who 'clothe yourselves with compassion, kindness, humility, gentleness and patience' (Col 3:12, NIV). And that stance of compassion and kindness should be directed both inward (self-compassion) and outward (compassion)."[31]

Author and psychologist Kristin Neff is regarded as the pioneering researcher in self-compassion. In a TEDx talk on self-compassion, she defines it this way: "Self-compassion is not a way of judging ourselves positively. Self-compassion is a way of relating to ourselves kindly, embracing ourselves as we are, flaws and all."[32] To offer ourselves compassion is not to wallow in sorrow or to nurse bad memories. It is to recognize we are human, flawed, and imperfect. It is to acknowledge that whatever emotion we are feeling is real, and to give ourselves permission to feel it. This positions us to heal from it and move toward what we value and long for. Sometimes we may not even be aware that we are suffering. We become so accustomed to the inner critic's voice that it becomes normalized, and we identify with it. Self-compassion offers us a gentle way to break that cycle and begin to heal.

So, too, the Sabbath is a way of gently breaking cycles of isolation and exclusion. To practice Sabbath is to resist the formative influence of ACC and dualism and forge new paths that lead to real connection, meaning, and belonging. It is to learn to see the world through a lens of wholeness and interdependence instead of division and competition. It is to cultivate a way of being nourished by God's delight in creation instead of gorging ourselves on the empty calories of acquisition and profit. The Sabbath way is a path that reorients us from disconnection to connection, from loneliness to community, from exclusion to belonging, and from anxiety to peace.

In *Lars and the Real Girl*, once Lars's community came to see that his delusion was his own unique way of processing his pain and loneliness, they began to surround him *in his delusion* with warmth and kindness. They played along, dignifying him by treating Bianca as real, even going so far as to take her on excursions without Lars! The community fell in love with Bianca, which is to say, they fell in love with Lars. And that love became the taproot of his healing—and theirs. I find Lars's story profoundly hopeful. In the face of epidemic levels of loneliness and exclusion in our world today, the depiction of community presented in *Lars and the Real Girl* offers a glimmer of hope that while connection and belonging can feel like enormous risks, when love is taken seriously, they are worth it.

REFLECTION QUESTIONS

- How would you describe what it means to experience community and belonging today? What personal experiences have shaped your understanding?

- How do you respond to the idea that the values of economic systems such as capitalism routinely shape our attitudes, behaviors, and choices?

- In what ways, if any, have you witnessed values such as self-interest, a strong desire for achievement and financial success, or high levels of consumption or competition in the context of Christian community?

- Dualism is an either/or mindset that creates a hierarchy in which one half is good and the other bad. What kind of dualisms are you aware of within your own Christian community, especially in terms of what defines who belongs or does not belong?

- In what ways, if any, have you experienced what it's like to be on the outside of what's considered normal? What insights might that experience provide about what it means to create a community of belonging and acceptance?

Sabbath Practice: An Invitation to Self-Compassion

On a Sabbath day (or any day), set aside time to intentionally offer yourself compassion. Follow the steps below, an adaptation of the practice outlined by Kristin Neff.[33]

- Give yourself permission to treat yourself kindly.

- Take a deep breath in and let it out slowly. Invite God to be present with you and to help you experience the compassion God has for you.

- Offer yourself intentional, gentle touch. You might place your hands over your heart, cradle your face, hold your hands together, or give yourself a hug. Gentle touch soothes the nervous system and opens it to healing.

- Identify an area in your life in which you treat yourself harshly, are overly critical of yourself, are embarrassed about, or generally feel negative about.

- Acknowledge to yourself—silently, verbally, or in a journal—what you are feeling as you recall this area of your life. Focus on "feeling" words or emotions to express what you're experiencing. For example, instead of saying, "I feel bad," or "I feel good," consider, "I feel sad," or angry, or betrayed, or lonely, or encouraged, and so on.

- If you can, name the sensations you feel in your body related to that emotion. For example, tight shoulders or sick to your stomach.

- Offer yourself compassion as if you were speaking to a beloved friend who just shared all of that with you. You can say it out loud or write it in a letter or journal, then read it to yourself. For example, "I'm so sorry you are experiencing this right now. That sounds really hard. You are not alone. I am right here with you. I love you. It's going to be okay."

- Reflect on how you feel now that you have offered yourself compassion. Do you feel lighter? Freer? More grounded? Something else?

9

DISORIENTING DUALISM AND DISCONNECTION

So all you outcasts, come!
The City of God is your home.
And the Lord will greet you, rejoicing to sing:
"You belong, you belong, you belong with me."

WENDELL KIMBROUGH, "You Belong"

We are made to tell the world that there are no outsiders.

ARCHBISHOP DESMOND TUTU, FORGIVENESS AND RECONCILIATION

Have you ever wondered what it might have been like to watch the events of Genesis 1 unfold as if you were an audience member and Creation was performed on a stage the size of the universe? Have you wondered what God's first experience of *shabbat* along with all of creation might have felt like, sounded like, or looked like on the seventh day? Here's what I see when I slow down and imagine each stanza in the Creation poem.

After the curtain rises there is nothing but darkness, a slight wind, the sound of lapping water. Then, into the darkness emerges a Voice of incandescent joy that, as it meets the darkness, transforms into pure illumination. The brilliance is not opposed to the darkness; it is somehow interlaced with it. With the whole audience, I am caught up in the divine gaze, a sense of giddy delight rising within me. We all marvel together: "Wow! This is *good*!"

The Voice speaks again, and the light and darkness separate, each to their own domains. Yet between them a space of overlap persists where light and dark dance together, which the Voice calls "evening" and "morning." The frame zooms out as the waters recede and the sky appears. Then the waters pool and dry ground emerges from the depths. The Voice, now singing, beckons the earth to join the song. As it begins to sing, the frame zooms in to reveal the earth's voice transforming into plants, flowers, and fruit trees, all exploding in exultation as creation and Creator harmonize.

Zooming out from seeds to galaxies, we watch, mouths agape, as the sun and moon are born and the Creator sets each star in place. Zooming back in again, we see the waters teem with schools of fish, and above them, birds take flight through the skies. Their delight in swimming and soaring is matched only by God's glee in watching them swoop and dive. Again, the knowing wells up within us: This is *good*!

The stage rotates to reveal the land once again joining God in the song of Creation. Now animals of all shapes and sizes emerge from the soil. God takes in the whole sweep of creation and then concentrates attention on one last creative effort: humankind.

When this is done, everything slows down. God stops working, steps back, and appreciates the indefatigable goodness of creation. With a gentle sweep of the hand, God welcomes all creation into God's Sabbath joy, a spacious pause of rest, connection, and delight. This shared rest galvanizes what had been clear all along: everyone and everything belongs in the community of creation.

As the curtain descends, we in the audience find ourselves on the stage, having been drawn in by the gravitational pull of God's generosity. Just before the curtain falls, in the vision's final frame, God's laughter erupts and washes over all like a cool breeze on a summer evening. A deep knowing arises within us: *All shall be well.*

It's a beautiful vision, isn't it? I love imagining God's ebullient joy in creation, both in the process and the result. And how the centripetal force of God's love and delight poured into the Sabbath draws all of creation to itself—even the audience! God's love includes all of creation in its embrace.

This idyllic vision of *shalom* among the community of creation did not last, though. By just the third and fourth chapters of Genesis, trust had been broken and murder was introduced into human history. And the rest of the Bible is, in one sense, a record of the attempts made by the people of Israel, the early church, and the triune God to grapple with the fallout. How can we restore a sense of what was lost from God's initial Creation vision? What does it look like to belong to each other when trust is broken and violence is real? The Bible presents the Sabbath as one answer to these questions.

Sabbath as the Foundation of Community

During an especially critical moment in Israel's history, these questions of connection, community, and belonging became fraught with existential urgency. When the captives returned from Babylonian exile and attempted to re-create their community, they did so alongside the Israelites who had remained in the land—from whom they had grown estranged in both cultural and religious identity—as well as the Canaanites still living in the land.

As you might imagine, this created a difficult context in which to re-create the community of Israel, when it wasn't clear who should or shouldn't be able to claim that identity. Suspicion took root. The people divided into camps of *us* and *them*. Some leaders were duplicitous and abused their power and influence. They took advantage of the crisis and exploited the vulnerable. Sound familiar?

As a leader during this time of crisis and transition, the prophet Isaiah[1] knew he needed to intervene. And that's when he did something extraordinary: he identified the Sabbath as the foundation on which to build this new community.[2] In his understanding, the Sabbath both exposed and corrected Israel's habitual sins of dualistic exclusion and economic exploitation that resulted in disconnection and dislocation—the very things we explored in the previous chapter, the very things we need help exposing and correcting today.

Isaiah used the Sabbath to challenge the very premises by which Israel's leaders justified practices of exclusion and economic injustice. And, as we might expect, not everyone agreed with him. Some embraced his radical vision of a community defined by Sabbath values while others resisted how it threatened their status, influence, comfort, or traditions. I believe the overall message of the Bible supports Isaiah's prophetic instincts. And yet, the cultural forces that resisted the Sabbath in Isaiah's day remain active today. This suggests that Isaiah's prophetic vision of a Sabbath-shaped community is likely to be as subversive and even controversial now as it was then. Understanding why and how Isaiah drew on the Sabbath to disorient and disrupt patterns of exclusion and disconnection during his time may help us face similar challenges today.

Disorienting Exclusion: Identity and Belonging in Biblical History

Every community throughout history, including those in the Bible, has had to engage the question, "Who belongs?" In the Bible, different generations offered different answers. The result is a debate threaded throughout its pages. Old Testament scholar Walter Brueggemann writes that, in general, in the Old Testament, belonging to God's covenant community was reserved for those who "keep Torah, who obey the commandments of Sinai, and who swear allegiance to these commandments."[3] But *how* that obedience was understood and the implications of that understanding for membership varied widely.

While the debate is complex and layered, one thread of the debate is particularly relevant for us today. This thread begins in the wilderness as the recently liberated slaves attempt to answer, for the first time in their history, "Who are we?" and "Who belongs with us?"

Belonging in the Wilderness
The question of community membership became urgent in the wilderness. As Israel's leaders grappled with what it meant to be in covenant with a holy God and anticipated the looming threat of paganism in Canaan, Israel's leaders prioritized ritual purity as the essential filter for community membership.[4] This drew clear lines between who belonged

and who did not, which is to say, who had access to worship God—in the Tabernacle and later the Temple—and who did not.

It was a dualistic framework whose categories were absolute. For example (and to oversimplify it), if you ate the right foods, were born without a disability, avoided contact with the wrong things (such as carcasses), and were a circumcised male, you basically had full access to worship God, which was the epitome of belonging. Socially, for those who were excluded, the law essentially said: *You can live with us, but you will never truly belong to us.* Theologically, it said: *We don't want you with us when we worship, and neither does God.*

A portion of Deuteronomy 23 represents an early voice in this ancient debate. It excludes three groups from the worshiping life of Israel: eunuchs, those born out of wedlock, and foreigners (see Deuteronomy 23:1-8). The first two verses delineate the exclusion of eunuchs and those born out of wedlock:

> No one whose testicles are crushed or whose member is cut off shall enter the assembly of the LORD. No one born of an illicit union[5] shall enter the assembly of the LORD. Even to the tenth generation, none of them shall enter the assembly of the LORD.
> DEUTERONOMY 23:1-2

In this context, the term *eunuch* would have included men who had been castrated as well as those with distorted genitalia who were unable to impregnate or conceive new life. Some were born this way, others became eunuchs as punishment, and others submitted to it voluntarily. Regardless of the cause, eunuchs were excluded from fully belonging to the covenant community. They were the epitome of the "other," not fitting any clearly defined category.[6]

Additional categories of those deemed "other" in Deuteronomy 23 included children of illicit birth and foreigners. The very existence of illicit children called into question the purity of their parentage. And foreigners or immigrants living among the Israelites were excluded based on ancient grievances. For example, although Egyptians and Edomites could *potentially* be eligible for membership, Ammonites and Moabites were banned *for ten generations* "because they did not come to greet you with food and water on your way out of Egypt" (Deuteronomy 23:4). The result of the laws laid out in Deuteronomy 23 was a clearly delineated, if not altogether consistent, line in the sand, excluding groups of people from full participation in worship based on the circumstances of their birth or the actions of their ancestors.

Belonging in the Wake of Exile

Several generations later, as the Babylonian exile ended and the captives were returning home to Palestine, the community was confronted with a crisis of belonging that forced them to rethink their traditions regarding membership and exclusion. The exile had fundamentally changed the cultural foundations of the Israelite community. For example, Jeremiah had encouraged the captives to marry and have children in Babylon. While it is unclear if he meant for them to marry and multiply only among themselves, the result of the exile was that some of the returnees, as well as many of those who stayed in Canaan, had married non-Israelite wives and had children of mixed ancestry (see Jeremiah 29:6). Given this situation, after a couple generations, who is an Israelite and who is a foreigner? The post-exilic leaders Ezra and Nehemiah felt this ambiguity threatened their ethnic and religious identity. Guided by the Torah's tradition of exclusivity expressed in Deuteronomy 23:1-8,[7] they sought to protect their identity by "establishing rigorous religious boundaries between themselves and their neighbors."[8]

But Isaiah took a different approach marked by pastoral sensitivity and an improvisational spirit. Instead of appealing to Deuteronomy 23 or the Torah more broadly, Isaiah appealed to two interrelated traditions to determine membership in the beloved community: the blessing tradition and the Sabbath.

The blessing tradition reconnected community membership to creation and prioritized the essential *tov*-ness of each person as created in God's image. Sabbath resulted in a radical reorientation of the law, essentially eliminating the dualistic foundation on which the exclusions were built. Notice how Isaiah, speaking on God's behalf, combines the blessing tradition and Sabbath in this passage:

> *Blessed* is the one who does this,
>> the child of Adam who holds it fast—
>
> who safeguards my *Sabbath* and does not profane it,
>> who safeguards their hands from doing evil.
>
> ISAIAH 56:2, EMPHASIS ADDED

Isaiah then rewrites the stipulations in Deuteronomy 23 regarding eunuchs and foreigners and offers a more expansive vision of a community in which those who were marginalized are not only welcomed and included, but in which they wholly belong.

> Do not let the *foreigner* joined to the LORD say:
>> "The LORD will surely divide me from his people!"
>
> And do not let the *eunuch* say:
>> "I am a dried-up tree, a withered branch."
>
> For thus says the LORD:
>
> "To the *eunuchs* who safeguard my *Sabbaths*,
>> and choose what pleases me,
>> and hold fast to my covenant,
>
> I will give to them, within my house and my walls,
>> a monument and a name
>> better than sons and daughters.
>
> An everlasting name I will give them,
>> which cannot be cut off."
>
> ISAIAH 56:3-5, EMPHASIS ADDED

Can you feel the tenderness and pastoral compassion of Isaiah as he speaks these words to those who had been excluded from belonging? What is remarkable, as Brueggemann notes, is that "there is only one condition spelled out . . . keep Sabbath! This is the single, solitary mark of membership."[9] As if this weren't enough, God, who self-identifies as *"the one who gathers the outcasts of Israel,"* goes on to proclaim, "I will gather yet others, besides those already gathered" (Isaiah 56:8, emphasis added). Apparently, God was just getting started by welcoming eunuchs and foreigners into his house and including them in the covenant inheritance. *All the outcasts* will belong as well, including those of illicit birth mentioned in Deuteronomy 23.

These are profound and radical declarations. Yet when we consider them in light of the Sabbath's core message—which anticipates the core message of the gospel—they seem obvious. The fundamental message of the Sabbath is that you are loved *as you are*; you are enough *as you are*; you belong *as you are*. You don't need to earn rest or delight. Rest and delight are your birthrights. You don't need to change and become someone new to fit a dualistic paradigm to belong. You belong *as you are*.

In God's eyes, the eunuchs don't need to be healed and the foreigners don't need to somehow become native-born to belong. Isaiah 56 makes it clear that *the rules governing who belongs needed to change to include them*. And God seems comfortable not spelling out all the details of how this would work. Apparently, both the Lord and the prophet trusted in the power of Sabbath-keeping—not as an add-on to life, but as life's core defining practice—to cultivate the kind of character, connection, and mutuality that empowers people to live in *shalom* amid difference and to "choose what pleases me and hold fast to my covenant" (Isaiah 56:3).

Radical messages like Isaiah's are controversial. While preaching good news to those who have been excluded, they tend to violate a sense of fairness and propriety held by those who *already* belong. Perhaps you know something of what it feels like to be excluded, on the outside looking in, and you greet Isaiah's message with enthusiasm. Isaiah's message is good news for you. And you are not alone. Conversely, perhaps you feel some discomfort with the implications of Isaiah's vision. Perhaps it feels too radical, too generous, too exploitative, or too threatening to the stability of tradition. If so, that's understandable. You are not alone, either. In fact, Israel also struggled to live into the Sabbath-infused vision

Isaiah presented. Israel's leaders, beginning with Ezra and Nehemiah, resisted making the changes Isaiah's reforms required, and the exclusions of Deuteronomy remained until the time of Jesus.

Belonging in the Early Church

New Testament writers had to reengage the debate about identity and belonging in light of Jesus of Nazareth. One of the most compelling examples of this is described in Acts 8, when the Holy Spirit sends Philip to the chariot of a God-fearing Jew (a non-Jewish convert to Judaism) who was returning to Ethiopia after celebrating Pentecost in Jerusalem. This Ethiopian—a foreigner—was also a eunuch. In other words, he was the singular embodiment of the Deuteronomy 23 exclusion: a "withered branch" who was "joined to the Lord" but "divided from God's people" (Isaiah 56:3). When Philip arrives at the chariot, he discovers the eunuch is reading—get this—*the scroll of Isaiah!*

Philip explains the gospel, connecting Isaiah's message with that of Jesus. You can almost hear the tension between exultation and trepidation in the Ethiopian eunuch's voice when he asks, "What is to prevent me from being baptized?" (Acts 8:36). In other words, "What are the practical implications of Jesus' radical love for me? How does the life, death, resurrection, and ascension of Jesus resolve the debate between Deuteronomy 23 and Isaiah 56 about whether I belong?"

Philip's verbal response is not recorded, but his actions leave no doubt about the answer: The Ethiopian eunuch is baptized, becomes a full member of the people of God, and receives, in the words of Isaiah, "a monument and a name *better than sons and daughters*" (Isaiah 56:5, emphasis added).

Philip's response to the Ethiopian eunuch resonates with Paul's declaration that in Christ, "There is no longer Jew or Greek; there is no longer slave or free; there is no longer male and female, for all of you are one in Christ Jesus" (Galatians 3:28). Paul's message is *not* that distinctions of ethnicity, socioeconomic status, or gender no longer exist, but that *those distinctions no longer separate someone from belonging to God in Christ.*

The story told in Acts 8 is not just the fulfillment of Isaiah 56 but of myriad texts that depict God's dream of a Sabbath community as a place where all belong and where external distinctions are no longer grounds for exclusion but are celebrated as part of the rich diversity that makes all things *tov*. Like the vision presented in Psalm 87, lyrically captured in Wendell Kimbrough's gorgeous song titled "You Belong," in which those from East and West and even "God's sworn enemies" receive this radical invitation:

> *So all you outcasts, come!*
> *The City of God is your home.*
> *And the Lord will greet you, rejoicing to sing:*
> *"You belong, you belong, you belong with me."*[10]

Sabbath is the ultimate leveler. Socioeconomic status, pedigree, gender, age, none of these matter on the Sabbath. On the Sabbath, all are equal. *No qualifications necessary.* To breathe is to belong to the Sabbath community. With one voice the Sabbath and the gospel say: *You belong.*

Belonging Today

The implications of this biblical debate about belonging remain as urgent in our contemporary context as they were for God's people thousands of years ago. We, too, are steeped in a world of "us and them" in which dualistic definitions of membership define the terms of the debate. While the specifics may be different and we don't talk as much about "foreigners" and "eunuchs" today, topics such as immigration and the LGBTQ+ community are hot-button issues that still cause division, suspicion, and exclusion in local, regional, and national contexts both within the church and the broader society.

Walter Brueggemann summarizes the implications of the Sabbath for our current debates:

> We have so many requirements that are as old as Moses. But here [in Isaiah 56] is only one requirement. It is Sabbath, work stoppage, an ordinance everyone can honor—gay or straight,

woman or man, Black or White, "American" or Hispanic—anybody can keep it and be gathered to the meeting of all of God's people.[11]

In short, Brueggemann states, Sabbath disorients and "deconstructs the notion of being 'qualified' for membership."[12] This is echoed in the late Archbishop Desmond Tutu's claim: "We are made to tell the world that there are no outsiders."[13]

These issues about community and belonging are exceedingly complex. And the Sabbath certainly can't resolve them on its own. The role it played in the ancient biblical debate, however, can help guide our current debates. For example, we could begin by affirming the resonance between the core message of the Sabbath and the core message of the gospel—that everyone is created in God's image and beloved of God, that no one can earn God's love or grace, and that delight, rest, abundance, and joy are birthrights of every single person. How might the tenor of our debates shift if we began not by drawing lines in the sand, but by affirming what we can all agree on, and building from there?

We could build on that foundation with a collective confession that we are, like the prophet Jonah, more comfortable *receiving* "amazing grace" than we are *offering* it to those we believe don't deserve it, for whatever reason. Perhaps then we could agree that the experience of exclusion is profoundly disruptive to one's well-being, and that if we wouldn't want that for ourselves or our grandchildren, why would we inflict it on anyone else? Maybe *then* we could embrace our common humanity, despite our differences, and bring that communality with us as we consider, with open hearts and open minds, what we might learn from biblical texts such as Isaiah 56 and Acts 8.

Disorienting Disconnection: Sabbath and ACC

We are today confronted continually by cultural forces that glorify competition, financial success, self-interest, and incessant consumption. In short, by the unfortunate consequences of American corporate capitalism (ACC). From offices to neighborhoods, from classrooms to boardrooms, from the halls of Congress to the algorithms of social media, behaviors rooted in ACC's values are rewarded with power, influence, affirmation, and wealth.

In many ways, it feels like we're in an unprecedented time—that no society before ours has faced such a complex and daunting situation and we don't have a clue how to fix it. And yet, the fundamental issues—of economic inequality, division, disconnection, and spiritual abuse—remain remarkably like those Isaiah and the Israelites faced 2,500 years ago.

In Isaiah 58, the prophet finds himself in a different situation than in Isaiah 56, yet the Sabbath similarly provides a path for his community to move from competition and exploitation to connection and mutual delight—if they are willing to receive its critique of their hypocrisy and submit to its vision of justice and *shalom*.

Isaiah Calls Out Israel's Hypocrisy

As the people of Israel returned from exile and attempted to put their lives back together, they searched for spiritual practices that could anchor them to God's presence and open them to abundance. One practice many of them turned to was fasting. But some of the returnees misunderstood the nature of fasting. Apparently, they felt it was a tit-for-tat transaction through which they secured spiritual blessings regardless of their behavior the rest of the time. And, not getting the response they expected, they cried out to God: "Why do we fast, when you do not take notice?" (Isaiah 58:3). The prophet perceived that those in power were using their fasting as a facade, which they hoped would distract heaven's watchful gaze from their shady business practices and incessant infighting. God responds through the prophet:

> Look, your fast days serve *your own interests*,
>   and you *exploit* all your workers.
> Look, you fast only to *quarrel* and *fight*,
>   and to strike each other with wicked fists.

> Fasting such as this
> will not make your voice heard on high.
>
> ISAIAH 58:3-4, EMPHASIS ADDED

Later in the chapter, Isaiah shifts seamlessly to speaking about the Sabbath in the same vein as he did about fasting: "If you refrain from trampling the Sabbath, from doing whatever you please on my holy day" (verse 13). Isaiah's connection implies a deep resonance between the two practices. And the connection makes sense. Both require ceasing, from food or toil, for a designated time for the purpose of deepening one's hunger for God's presence.

The connection runs even deeper, however. Isaiah also calls out how the Israelite leaders used legalistic adherence to fasting and Sabbath as a pretense to hide their exploitative business practices. The Israelite leaders saw no connection between their spiritual performances and their economic abuses. For Isaiah, their behavior represents an erosion of the true heart and purpose of both fasting and Sabbath, which is to cultivate the character of God and deepen one's capacity to love God and neighbor.

Isaiah Offers His Sabbath Vision

Isaiah teaches that true fasting—and by extension, true Sabbath—bears the fruit of liberation, generosity, hospitality, and genuine community (see Isaiah 58:6-7, 9). Speaking on behalf of God, Isaiah writes,

> Is not this the fast that I choose:
>> to unlock the bonds of injustice,
>> to tear off the straps of the yoke,
> to let the oppressed go free,
>> and to shatter every yoke?
>
> ISAIAH 58:6

Fasting is practicing justice in a culture that incentivizes injustice. It is an act of resistance against a culture of mindless consumption, blind complicity, endless comparison, and inhospitality.

And this is the central overlap between Sabbath and fasting. Both practices are acts of resistance against cultures of excess and exploitation, of scarcity and self-interest. In Isaiah's vision, the Sabbath disrupts our learned human behaviors to compete, control, and exploit—whether we do this to the detriment of ourselves or someone else. For Isaiah, the Sabbath is a vision and a paradigm in which yokes are broken, wrongs are righted, those on the outside are brought in, and each person feels connected to the community as a whole. In a word, Sabbath enables *shalom*.

In Isaiah 58, speaking through the prophet, God offers a delight-filled vision of flourishing that echoes God's original Sabbath vision recounted in Genesis 1. God's promise is:

> Oh, that you would call the Sabbath a delight . . .
>   then you would take delight in the Lord,
>   and I would make you ride upon the heights of the earth;
>   and I would feed you with the bounty of your ancestor Jacob,
>   for the mouth of the Lord has spoken.
>
> ISAIAH 58:13-14

The real challenge, of course, is translating vision into reality and paradigm into practice. Clearly, this won't happen by accident. It didn't in Isaiah's time, and it won't today either. But Isaiah's insight is that when a community orients its life toward the Sabbath way, it opens itself to the possibility of living its way into Isaiah's Sabbath vision, which is to say, God's vision.

REFLECTION QUESTIONS

- How do you respond to the fact that the people of Israel struggled with the same sorts of challenges to community, connection, and belonging as we do today? Do you find it comforting? Disconcerting? Something else?

- Isaiah's vision of Sabbath went beyond a mere day of rest for individuals; it was a vision of inclusion and justice for the entire community. In what ways does Isaiah's vision resemble or differ from what you have been taught about the practice and purpose of Sabbath? How does Isaiah's vision challenge or expand your view of Sabbath?

- Throughout biblical history, God's people defined belonging socially and theologically in various ways (see Deuteronomy 23; Psalm 87; Isaiah 56, 58; Acts 8). Some definitions sought to narrow the realm of belonging and others to expand it.

    » In what ways do you recognize this same dynamic among God's people today? In other words, how are those within the Christian community seeking to narrow or expand the definition of belonging?

    » Knowing that the very act of defining belonging can be divisive, what do you think it means to cultivate the kind of character, connection, and mutuality that enables people to live in *shalom* amid difference? When or how have you seen that modeled well?

Sabbath Practice: Lectio Divina

Lectio divina is a Latin phrase that simply means "divine reading." It is an ancient spiritual practice of Scripture reading that resonates with the Sabbath invitation to presence, slowness, stillness, and listening. It prioritizes focusing our attention on encountering God in the words of Scripture over defining the text's exact meaning or interpretation. Through repeated readings of a passage, it invites the Spirit to illumine the Scriptures in our hearts and makes room for the slow process by which this happens.

On a Sabbath day, choose one of the two Isaiah passages from the chapter as the focus for your reading—either Isaiah 56:1-8 or Isaiah 58:6-14. In both passages, Isaiah identifies the Sabbath as a way forward—through difficult and tense situations—that is marked by grace, generosity, and justice, instead of rigidity, greed, and injustice.

The *lectio divina* process is simple.

- Read the passage once, slowly. Consider reading it aloud, if you're able. Pause for a few minutes to reflect on what you read.

- Read the passage a second time. Pause again, but this time note a few words or phrases that stood out to you. Reflect on them. Consider writing them down in a journal.

- Read the passage a third and final time. Pause and reflect once more, but this time consider, and write in your journal, what you feel the Spirit is calling you to do or who the Spirit is calling you to be in response to what you read.

10

REORIENTING: BECOMING THE BELOVED COMMUNITY

> *Out beyond ideas of wrongdoing and rightdoing,*
> *there is a field. I'll meet you there.*
>
> RUMI, "Great Wagon," THE ESSENTIAL RUMI
>
> *Justice is what love looks like in public.*
>
> CORNEL WEST, Askwith Forum, Harvard Graduate School of Education

Under the *Code Noir* of Louisiana—the "Black Code" established by the French Empire in 1724 to govern and control the Black population of New Orleans, both freed and enslaved—enslavers were prevented from forcing enslaved persons to work on the Sabbath.[1] On the outskirts of the French Quarter was a grassy area designated for them to gather, which came to be known as Congo Square. Every Sunday they gathered to dance, sing, drum, trade, tell stories, reconnect with family members from whom they'd been separated, and sustain their cultural traditions from throughout West Africa and the Caribbean.[2] Amid the dehumanization of America's "peculiar institution,"[3] Congo Square became a groundswell of humanization where gatherers remembered who they were even as they were re-membered as a people and as human beings.

Despite the heresy and contradictions inherent in any form of Christianity that enables empire and enslavement, the Sabbath was preserved and upheld under *Code Noir*. While it did not free the enslaved from the shackles of oppression, and while even their gatherings happened under the watchful eyes of armed guards, on Sabbath afternoons in Congo Square the disenfranchised members of New Orleans met to commune with people who *knew, celebrated,* and *saw* them, and in that recognition *dignified* them. Their gatherings were an act of resistance by which they asserted their dignity—in the form of joyful celebration, movement, and creativity—amid the indignity of enslavement.

Today, Congo Square is recognized as the birthplace of such iconic American cultural institutions as jazz and funk;[4] some suggest the drumbeats and dances also helped shape the rhythms in blues, R&B, even rock and roll.[5] In fact, the first known instance of the word *rock* being used as both a verb and a metaphor was in reference to Congo Square! When the author H. C. Knight visited New Orleans in 1819, he recalled, "On Sabbath evening the African slaves meet on the green, by the swamp, and *rock the city* with their Congo dances."[6]

I was sad (though not surprised) that I'd never heard the story of Congo Square before some friends visited on a pilgrimage and posted about it on Facebook.[7] But I was immediately captivated by the joy and energy of their gatherings and the immense gifts their passion and creativity left the world. I was also struck by the contradictions—their pleasure in gathering, tempered by the presence of armed guards, and that these gatherings were their one opportunity to assert their humanity without being punished for it. And it is these two interwoven Sabbath threads that also stand out to me as having particular relevance for us today—specifically, the role of community and the necessity of justice in our practice of Sabbath.

Sabbath and Community

An essential part of the transformative power of the Congo Square Sabbaths was their communal character. Life grew out of the soil of their *communion*. If the people had practiced Sabbath individually rather than communally, their lives—and our music—would have been greatly diminished. This is relevant for us today because the cultural Christianity that enabled—or enforced—their collective Sabbath observance no longer exists. In some ways this change is good, since obligatory

Sabbath has its own challenges. Without a community to normalize and sustain it, though, Sabbath is extremely hard to maintain.

I feel the force of this dynamic in my own life. If it weren't for the two summers Mariah and I spent near Jerusalem in the mid-2000s, where Sabbath observance is still part of the cultural climate (although this is changing), I don't know that we otherwise would have started practicing Sabbath at home. In Jerusalem, every Friday evening through Saturday the buses shut down, the Jewish shops close, and the people disappear to their homes for rest and fellowship. We began practicing Sabbath there simply because there were no other options! Doing so changed our lives forever.

It's hard to imagine this happening anywhere in the US, inside or outside the church. We have far too few models showing us what Sabbath living can look like and inspiring us—even pressuring us—to try it on for size. I ask my seminary students to do this, but the competition for their time is fierce. And churches are often the last place to look for help. As author and professor A. J. Swoboda noted in reflecting on his time as a pastor, of all the Ten Commandments, he would have lost his job if he'd broken nine of them. "But if I did not keep a Sabbath day, I would probably get a raise."[8] I feel the weight of that truth in the pit of my stomach and have seen it replayed in the lives of clergy friends and former students a hundred times over. Today, many of those friends and students are no longer pastors. I think this is partly due to a failure to appreciate the Sabbath—by both the pastors and their congregations.

I long for every pastor to receive the same guidance Pastor Peter Scazzero gave Rich Villodas as Rich prepared to replace him as lead pastor of New Life Fellowship in Queens. Scazzero had one message for him: *The only way you will lose this job is if you* don't *develop a Sabbath practice!*[9] The logic is that sustainable ministry requires sustainable rhythms of work and rest. As pastor, Rich needed the support of his congregation to do this. And they needed him to model it and teach it so they could explore similar rhythms in their own lives. In my experience, the message Rich Villodas received is way less common than the one A. J. Swoboda received.

While having a community to sustain a Sabbath practice significantly increases its chances of sustainability, it likely won't resolve the aching loneliness so many of us feel. But Sabbath can help us reorient our loneliness toward the connection we crave. That's because the intentional framing a Sabbath practice provides helps us distinguish between two very different ways of being alone: loneliness and solitude. As we saw in chapter 8, "Loneliness is the subjective feeling that you're lacking the social connections you need."[10] It does not matter if you're around people or by yourself; to be lonely is to *feel* disconnected from the life happening around you and to wonder if you have a place in it.

Solitude, by contrast, is *intentional* aloneness. Not the aloneness of anger or defensiveness that shuts people out, but a way of being alone that, ironically, *deepens* our sense of connection—with ourselves, the Spirit, others, and all of creation. Solitude is the ancient practice of entering the silence and listening to it, befriending it, and moving through it to the recognition of our inherent connection to all things.

The late priest Henri Nouwen described solitude as "the furnace of transformation" in which our false self—the fragile and fearful ego-self within each of us that fuels our competition, disconnection, and self-sabotage—burns up and is reborn.[11] Through solitude we come to belong to ourselves. In this way, solitude is, paradoxically, a prerequisite for community since we must belong to ourselves before we can truly belong to another. A Sabbath practice gives us room to experiment with solitude. A Sabbath posture integrates it into the fabric of our lives.

Neither Sabbath nor solitude are likely to eliminate the pain of loneliness from our lives. But they do remind us of a fundamental truth about reality: whether we feel it or perceive it in the moment, we are never alone; we are connected to all that lives. This connection is critical not only for sustaining Sabbath practices, but for experiencing a sense of *shalom* in one's life as well. But that *shalom* and sense of connection with all that lives can be shattered by more than loneliness. The Sabbath also exposes injustice in places where systems exclude and exploit for the enrichment of some. To return to the story of Congo Square, while the enslaved experienced connection on Sunday afternoons, the rest of their lives were marked by exclusion and exploitation. To understand the full measure of the Sabbath we must understand its relationship with justice.

The Holy Triptych: *Shalom*, Justice, and Sabbath

Biblically speaking, Sabbath rest is a birthright, which means withholding it is an *in*justice—what poet Ross Gay called a *dis*privilege.[12] In the case of Congo Square, allowing communal gatherings in one place each week, under police supervision, was not justice, though we might understand it as a first step *toward* justice. The men in power—and they were all men—fulfilled the letter of the Sabbath commandment while rejecting its spirit. They preserved the shell of a Sabbath practice but spurned a Sabbath posture. When Sabbath ended, those who had gathered at Congo Square returned to a life marked by physical, spiritual, sexual, and economic exploitation at the hands of those same powerful men—a situation akin to the injustices the prophet Isaiah decried in Isaiah 58, discussed in the previous chapter. The disparities between life at Congo Square on Sunday afternoons and life during the week for the Black population of New Orleans exposed structural inequities where the work of justice could begin.

To better understand the relationship between Sabbath and justice, we first need to consider how the Bible understands justice overall. In Scripture, justice is not a lone cowboy, a one-person army dispensing revenge on its own terms, as so many Hollywood movies have portrayed it. Instead, justice operates within a matrix of shared concerns, or, to change the metaphor, it is but one panel of what I call the "holy triptych" of *shalom*, justice, and Sabbath. A triptych is a single work of art displayed on three panels. If you take one away, the painting is incomplete. It is the same with the holy triptych—*shalom*, justice, and Sabbath are all necessary and work together to depict the beauty of God's dream for creation. To begin to understand how this is so, we begin with the first two panels: *shalom*, one of the Bible's most important words, and its indivisibility from justice.

Triptych Panels One and Two: Shalom and Justice

Traditionally translated "peace," *shalom* is a word of central importance in the biblical imagination. According to Old Testament scholar Walter Brueggemann, it is a word that "bears tremendous freight—the freight of a dream of God that resists all our tendencies to division, hostility, fear, drivenness, and misery."[13] The word describes a sense of wholeness or completeness in which relationships are restored and every heart is content.

This vision is not an idyllic fantasyland disconnected from the hard realities of life east of Eden. It acknowledges the existence of injustice and identifies pathways for justice to be restored. For example, the related verb *shillem* (shee-LEHM) means to repay a debt, make restitution, or restore something that is broken. Another related verb, *shalem* (shah-LEHM), describes the state of socioeconomic equality achieved by debts being paid or the equilibrium found when one is healthy and at peace within oneself.[14]

Clearly, *shalom* means much more than the absence of conflict. It is the active presence of wholeness and well-being, a life marked by integration and flourishing, a community marked by equity and forgiveness. *Shalom* is also deeply paradoxical, fundamentally non-dual; it dwells in a both/and world. It is both here and not here. It is both accessible and beyond our reach. It is both a tree and a seed. It is Jesus teaching that in him the Kingdom of Heaven has come, and then teaching us to pray, "May your kingdom come" (Matthew 6:10). It is what theologians call the already and the not-yet.

In the biblical imagination *shalom* is indivisible from justice. *Shalom* is the wholeness found on the *other side* of justice. We cannot have *shalom* without first having justice. Because of this, injustice anywhere compromises *shalom* everywhere, to adapt Dr. King's famous phrase.[15]

Therefore, justice begins by identifying the places where *shalom* has been stifled, resisted, squandered, and stolen. This happens not at the centers of power, but on its margins. Indigenous theologian Randy Woodley teaches that *shalom* is "tested on the margins of a society and revealed by how the poor, oppressed, disempowered, and needy are treated."[16] How a community or a nation treats those on its margins is indicative of the quality of *shalom* that exists there. And the work of justice begins by addressing the structural inequities that lead to and sustain the gap between the center and the margin.

But so often today justice is seen only in caricature through a dualistic lens of right/wrong. The justice in our justice system is too often divorced from *shalom*. It is an end in itself rather than the means to a greater end. Instead of prioritizing restoration, growth, and healing, justice is often punitive or vengeful—a mechanism of disenfranchisement rather than rehabilitation.[17]

This dualistic framework is also the lens we tend to bring to understanding justice in the Bible, which is often misunderstood as the opposite of mercy. This is connected to the age-old dualism defining the God of the Old Testament as a God of justice and wrath, contrasting with the God incarnated in Jesus in the New Testament as the God of grace and love. While engaging that debate is beyond the purview of this book, it is important to note that the inherent link between justice and *shalom* in the Bible is critical for understanding justice beyond the limitations of dualism, both then and now. In the Bible, *shalom* is the destination and justice is the vehicle.

Triptych Panel Three: Sabbath

Justice and *shalom* are essential, but two panels a triptych do not make! What role does the Sabbath play? The clearest biblical expression of the holy triptych rooted in the Sabbath is found in Leviticus 25, which describes the Year of Jubilee. The Year of Jubilee is commonly understood as the Old Testament equivalent of the gospel—it provided the foundational vision on which Jesus established his public ministry.

Far beyond an individual day of rest, Jubilee was the radical reorganization of society for the purpose of restoring *shalom*. Celebrated every fifty years (one year after a "week" of sabbatical years—seven cycles of seven years), it forgave debts, restored ancestral property, liberated the enslaved, instituted economic practices that prevented exploitation, and allowed the land to rest while its wild produce was reserved for the vulnerable. The Year of Jubilee was the application of the Sabbath's core message to the social, economic, political, and religious structures of Israelite society. To quote Jesus quoting Isaiah, the Year of Jubilee was "good news to the poor" (Isaiah 61:1; Luke 4:18).

But it wasn't good news to the powerful. For those who benefited from social and economic inequities, the Year of Jubilee required *letting go* of power and wealth and adjusting to a life in which your neighbor's vulnerability did not translate into your enrichment. Brueggemann is certainly right that "it is difficult to imagine a more radical social possibility than the sabbatic principle, particularly as it leads to the Jubilee year."[18]

Given the radical nature of this Sabbath vision, what are we to make of the likelihood that Israel never actually practiced the Year of Jubilee?[19] Can you imagine what would happen if we attempted to do so today? This level of radical grace being extended to the disenfranchised would be hard for many to swallow because the prevailing story is that they deserve justice, not grace. And not the justice that leads to *shalom*, but the punitive sort that says, "You made your bed, now lie in it." Of course, the thing about grace is that it exists only where it isn't deserved.

Implementing the Year of Jubilee would have been just as impossible to imagine 2,500 years ago as it is today. But just because something is impossible to imagine doesn't mean we resign ourselves to the status quo. It probably means we need to exercise our imagination more often! We cannot abandon God's dream simply because it seems unrealistic. Hope is audacious. Somehow, in God's infinite and mysterious wisdom, God invites us to participate in bringing this dream to reality. The Sabbath teaches us to bring what we have and to offer it, then to trust the Spirit to do the rest.

When Jesus inaugurated his public ministry, he did so by rooting it in the soil of Isaiah's interpretation of the Year of Jubilee. Quoting parts of Isaiah 61, Jesus proclaimed:

> The Spirit of the Lord is upon me,
>   because [God] has anointed me

> to bring good news to the poor.
> [God] has sent me to proclaim release to the captives
> and recovery of sight to the blind,
> to set free those who are oppressed,
> to proclaim the year of the Lord's favor.
> LUKE 4:18-19[20]

What is Jesus getting at here? Well, in the first place, Jesus is reprioritizing the holy triptych of *shalom*, justice, and Sabbath as the heart of the gospel. In other words, Jesus is saying, "Everything I do is in service of the vision built on the intersection of these three things." And we cannot comprehend this without also hearing Jesus tell the parable of the Good Samaritan (see Luke 10:25-37), in which he teaches that the radical love of God demonstrated through radical acts of mercy and kindness is the foundation of the new reality breaking into the world in Jesus.

The love depicted in Jesus' parable is captured in the Hebrew word *hesed*. Translated as steadfast love, loving-kindness, loyalty, or mercy, *hesed* is the enduring love of God that forms the foundation of the covenant; it is the force that sustains all of creation. Perhaps the best translation comes from Bible scholar Ellen Davis, who suggested "love-in-action."[21] If *shalom*, justice, and Sabbath are the three panels of the holy triptych, *hesed* is the canvas and the paint. And there is no painting without a canvas or paint!

During Jesus' lifetime, the three panels had been separated and painted over, resulting in exclusion and exploitation of the poor and marginalized. This is part of why Jesus was so intentional about healing people *on* the Sabbath: it was essential to reconnect the Sabbath with justice. During the time of Jesus, those with disabilities were in marginalized social, economic, and religious situations similar to that of eunuchs and foreigners discussed in the previous chapter. Healing them restored them to the community and gave them the possibility of financial independence.

The Sabbath was the perfect setting for Jesus to reassemble the three panels of the triptych because it allowed him to demonstrate the truth activist theologian Cornel West so potently captured when he said, "Justice is what love looks like in public."[22] There is no separation between love and justice; a commitment to one is necessarily a commitment to the other. I love how author, poet, and cultural critic bell hooks says it:

> The moment we choose to love we begin to move against domination, against oppression. The moment we choose to love we begin to move towards freedom, to act in ways that liberate ourselves and others.[23]

When Jesus reconnected justice with Sabbath, he offered a glimpse of *shalom* in which the love of God was manifested in the marginalized being centered, the oppressed being liberated, and the broken being healed, but also in which oppressors repent, seek forgiveness, and find reconciliation with God and their neighbors. In short, he offered a glimpse of the path toward re-creating what, two thousand years later, Martin Luther King Jr. called "the beloved community."[24]

Putting the Holy Triptych into Practice

What else can we learn from the connection between *shalom*, justice, and Sabbath as it appears in the Year of Jubilee and in the ministry of Jesus? One takeaway is the reminder that Sabbath and justice are an inseparable pair of mutually reinforcing commitments. The deeper our appreciation for the gift of Sabbath rest, the more committed we become to preserving that gift for everyone—human, animal, and earth. In other words, Sabbath helps expose inequities, and justice is the work of putting them back to rights.

Another takeaway is the comfort we can find in the "not-yet-ness" of each panel of the holy triptych. The fact that these realities are fundamentally incomplete gives us permission to not have "perfect" Sabbaths every week. It frees us from the crushing pressure of assuming the work of justice is up to us alone—and the disappointment we experience when justice work moves so slowly and sometimes seems to make such little difference. The North Star of *shalom* reminds us that both the work of justice and the rest of Sabbath are *for the sake of life*—they are both most effective when accompanied by joy, connection, and mutual flourishing.

A third takeaway lives in a healthy tension with the second takeaway. While the "not-yet-ness" takes the pressure off, the "already-ness" puts some of it back on. We are expected to participate in and contribute to collapsing the distance between the already and the not yet. We tend to think this happens primarily through dramatic acts of public disruption such as marches and boycotts and demonstrations. While they are essential to the work of justice, it's also helpful to remember the ancient Buddhist adage, "The way you do one thing is the way you do everything." There is power in the little things we do every day to show up to our neighborhoods and workplaces and intimate relationships with love and compassion and curiosity. These, too, can transform us and the world around us.

We put the triptych into practice every time we remember the Sabbath! Every time we embrace our enough-ness and assert our dignity. Every time we honor another's dignity. Every time we slow down our lives to observe how we are living and why we are living that way. Every time we leverage our resources to enable others to slow down their lives. Every time we pay attention to and challenge the role of dualism in our thinking and acting. Every time we deescalate a conversation on social media by acknowledging the humanity of the person(s) we're engaging. Every time we find delight in the seemingly insignificant moments of life: the laugh of a child, the way the sun reflects off a building, the courage of the crocus to bloom in a snowstorm. Every time we are self-reflective, listen in order to understand (rather than respond), don't take our lives too seriously, apologize instead of being defensive, embrace our delights, resist multitasking, practice presence, laugh until we cry, choose kindness over judgment, thank someone and mean it.

It doesn't matter whether we are scientists or security guards, teachers or translators, bus drivers or beauticians—every moment is an opportunity to contribute to the goodness in the world, to see the best in someone, to offer an encouraging word or gentle smile, to give the benefit of the doubt. When we do this, we add color to the canvas.

To lean into such commitments throughout the week is to adopt a Sabbath posture toward our lives. Can you imagine a world in which everybody lived with this kind of intentionality? In the words of the inimitable Sam Cooke, "What a wonderful world this would be."[25] To me, this seems like a pursuit worthy of a life.

And the stakes are high. As I type, bombs are dropping on cities and villages where innocent people are dying, and children are losing relatives, limbs, and even their own lives. Hundreds of millions of people around the world face acute food insecurities.[26] Global powers vie for dominance in the international marketplace and care little about the costs involved in winning—for their competitors, employees, or the earth. The polar ice caps are melting. Species are going extinct every day. Every hurricane season is worse than the previous one.

Against such a global backdrop of terror and threat, we might wonder what a simple act of kindness could mean in the overall scheme of things. I believe it can mean more than we could ever comprehend. They say, under ideal conditions, you can see a candle flame in the dark from over seventeen miles away.[27] I take this to mean that any act of goodness shines a light into the darkness, and enough candle flames lit together can light up the world. Sunday afternoons at Congo Square lit up the world. And the brightness of that candle is still visible.

How will you offer the candle of your life to the world? How will you translate these ideas from theory into practice? I believe the only way to do this is to slow down and make room for self-reflection and joy and delight, to experience what makes you come alive. It is nearly impossible to live into this vision, for example, if all you do is stress about time or money or your family's approval. A weekly pause for rest, for play, for reflective conversation, for a break from whatever sustains your anxiety is critical to making this vision a reality. A slower-paced, more thoughtful, contemplative, and playful posture could light up your life, and through it the world.

REFLECTION QUESTIONS

- In the State of Israel today, Sabbath observance is a communal experience—Jewish businesses and public transportation cease operations and people gather for rest and fellowship. Imagine for a moment that the same were true where you live. What, if anything, might you lose or need to give up on such a Sabbath? What might you gain?

- What expectations does your church have for your pastor(s), ministry leaders, and members when it comes to observing the Sabbath? In what ways, if any, is Sabbath rest encouraged and modeled? Are leaders encouraged to rest or expected to be available 24-7?

- In what ways does the indivisibility of *shalom*, justice, and Sabbath challenge you? In what ways does it encourage or empower you?

- Briefly identify a social ill or injustice that concerns you most. For example, poverty, mass incarceration, or lack of affordable housing or medical care. Who do you imagine might be both positively and negatively impacted in that context if a Year of Jubilee were fully implemented?

- What aspects of the holy triptych—*shalom*, justice, and Sabbath—do you feel most drawn to exploring more and practicing in your own life?

Sabbath Practice: "5-for-5 Connection Challenge"

US Surgeon General Dr. Vivek Murthy suggests a simple yet powerful practice for overcoming our experiences of loneliness and disconnection by establishing new habits of connection and courage. He calls it the "5-for-5 Connection Challenge." The commitment is to engage in one intentional act of connection each day for five days. The challenge involves three simple steps:[28]

- *Step One: Commit to Connect.* Choose five consecutive days and five specific actions to help you connect with people in your life.

These actions can be expressing gratitude, offering support, or asking for help.

- *Step Two: Connect Each Day for Five Days.* Each day select one action and do it. See what happens!

- *Step Three: Reflect and Share.* Consider: How did connecting in this way make you feel? What did you learn about how you're wired, or the kinds of connections you need the most? Can you commit to another five days? Can you commit to *every* day?

PART 4

SABBATH AND CREATION

11

ORIENTING: WHAT HAS THE LAND TO DO WITH SABBATH?

Eating is an agricultural act.
WENDELL BERRY, *WHAT ARE PEOPLE FOR?*

We eat with unprecedented ignorance.
NORMAN WIRZBA, *LIVING THE SABBATH*

I don't remember the moment I realized that the turkey we ate as a family for Thanksgiving had once been a living, breathing, squawking, and periodically flying thing. But my dear friend Tom certainly remembers the day his son first had his eyes opened to the ethical complexities of carnivory and the biological fact that something must die for us to live.

Jeremy was in grade school when his mom set a whole roasted chicken on the table for dinner one day. Up to this point his only association with the edible side of chicken was in nugget form, in which the resemblance between the bird and the food is restricted mostly to the name. But here was an object that kind of *looked* like a bird, with legs and thighs and breasts. Suddenly, the word *chicken* describing this meal connected with the word *chicken* describing the clucking hens he'd chased around at the petting zoo. It was more than his young heart could handle.

"Sick!" he suddenly shouted. "Sick!"

"What's sick, honey?" asked Tom and Judy, taken aback by his unusual behavior.

"Sick!" he repeated, staring at the carcass and pushing away from the table.

His mouth agape, Jeremy pointed at the murdered bird, but he couldn't find any other words to say. What his parents had done to this innocent life cut him to the core. The only word he could find spoke both to his assessment of the situation and the way his stomach felt in light of it. He'd lost his appetite.

A few years ago, I wrestled with a different layer of the ethical complexities of food as I stood in the checkout aisle at a local grocery store with a Christmas tree Reese's Peanut Butter Cup in my hand. I had picked it up, almost unconsciously, from an endcap display as a little surprise for my wife. As I awaited my turn to pay, I suddenly remembered a harrowing news story I had read about big-brand chocolate companies such as Hershey, Nestlé, and Mars that were turning a blind eye to child labor being used to harvest cocoa throughout West Africa, where 70 percent of the world's cocoa supply originates from—including the chocolate in my hand. Adult harvesters are paid a wage below the poverty line—less than one dollar a day[1]—which means that survival requires more family members to work. According to a 2019 study, children as young as five have been found harvesting in Ivory Coast and Ghana, using big machetes to open pods of cocoa held in their own small hands.[2] Even after news outlets broke the story in the early 2000s, very little pressure was applied to the companies to change their practices, so they have dragged their feet to keep their profit margins high.

Remembering this while standing in line, I asked myself if I could knowingly purchase chocolate picked by the small hands of hungry children forced by circumstances to work instead of go to school. Could I justify supporting this business model with my purchase just to get a sugar rush or score a brownie point with my wife? Could my gratitude for this sweet treat survive my knowledge of the human costs created by its existence? I put it back on the shelf.

As I thought about the 79 cents I would save by not buying the Reese's, I was reminded of a fight Mariah and I once had in a grocery store early in our marriage. We were *just* beginning to learn about the impact of industrial agriculture on the environment and were trying to incorporate more organic products into our life. The problem was that I was a full-time grad student, and she was unable to work due to a chronic illness, so we were broke.

These two realities—a growing commitment to sustainable products and our financial situation—collided as we fought over whether to buy regular French's mustard or the organic mustard. Despite the cost difference being mere cents, it felt like a really big decision at the time! She wanted the organic, to honor the earth and to consume the cleanest food possible. I loved that idea, but I was brought up to *always buy the cheapest product*. And I was already concerned that we were overspending our food budget. We went back and forth. Surprisingly, we both felt a lot of emotions. It wasn't our best moment. Today, I can't even recall which mustard we bought, just that we fought about it.

These anecdotes illustrate some of the complex and contradictory challenges we all face every time we buy groceries or sit down to eat a meal. Limited by budgets as well as available time and energy, many of us base our eating choices on what is cheapest and easiest to prepare. This often means prepackaged meals made at an industrial scale from a list of ingredients gathered from the four winds, at least half of which are not immediately recognizable as food. And this is to say nothing of the conditions in which the animals we eat were raised or slaughtered, nor of the chemical fertilizers and fossil fuels burned in the process of raising, harvesting, processing, packaging, and distributing the grains, fruits, and vegetables we eat. In our globalized and interconnected world, eating is fraught with moral quandaries.

And while we rarely think about it this way, farmer and poet Wendell Berry is undoubtedly right that "eating is an agricultural act."[3] As food consumers we stand at the end of a line that begins with sowing and reaping, of calves being born and hens laying eggs. Our participation in agriculture is mostly monetary as we cast our votes by purchasing certain foods and raising the demand for those products. Our choices have real-life consequences about how the land and animals our lives depend on get used and how those who tend them are treated. This is why our eating habits and choices are of central concern when considering the Sabbath.

Sabbath Is for *All* of Creation

Every meal we eat has implications for how the land is used and how animals—and the humans who care for them—are treated. And this concern over the treatment of the land and its animals is not only relevant for conscious eaters. It is a consistent and central aspect of Sabbath teaching throughout the Bible, which means it is relevant for all who would seek to follow the way of Jesus. This led author and professor A. J. Swoboda to conclude that, "Sabbath is, at its core, an ecological principle."[4]

For example, the sabbatical year, described in Exodus 23 and Leviticus 25, applies the Sabbath principle of rhythmic rest to the land, restricting cultivation to a six-year cycle so that the land—including fields, vineyards, and orchards—could rest every seventh year. Leviticus 25 also outlines the Year of Jubilee, which was a Sabbath of Sabbaths that lasted a whole year![5] Celebrated every fifty years, it prioritized the land's need to rest and other matters of ecological justice as central to Israel's worshiping life. The Sabbath isn't just concerned with the land, however. Exodus 23 and Leviticus 25, along with both versions of the Ten Commandments and several other passages, also prioritize the right of animals to rest from the labors that humans use them for.

The first Creation account makes clear that Sabbath rest is not only for humans, but is the climax of *all* creation, the purpose for which it was created. In God's eyes, the nonhuman parts of creation are just as worthy of rest and delight as humans are.

The extent of God's concern over creation's rest and delight is made uncomfortably clear in several passages that connect Israel's exile in Babylon to Israel's *failure to give the land its Sabbaths*. God's concern was not that the Israelites hadn't rested from their labors, but they hadn't allowed the land to rest from its labors. One such passage, which is found among the final verses in the Hebrew Bible,[6] claims that God brought Israel into exile in Babylon:

> to fulfill the word of the LORD from the mouth of Jeremiah
>   until the earth had made amends for its Sabbaths.
> All the days it lay desolate it kept Sabbath,
>   to the fullness of seventy years.
> 2 CHRONICLES 36:21

Think about that for a minute. It is an extraordinary claim. The Hebrew Bible's parting thought justifies the Exile on the grounds that Israel failed to honor its Sabbath commitments to the land, so God simply took the land away from them to give it and the animals their rest.[7]

Passages like this are cautionary tales the Bible speaks *directly to us*. No other generation in human history has so thoroughly ignored and overrun the inherent limits of both land and animals by denying their birthright to Sabbath rest. It makes me wonder how long God will allow *us* to desecrate the land and rob it of Sabbath joy.

And yet, most of us today don't spend a lot of time thinking about the land at all. We are so disconnected from it, separated by concrete, glass, and neon lights that we experience it directly only when we're on vacation to the beach or the mountains. We often forget that every time we eat or drink, we consume the gifts of the earth; every time we breathe, we inhale air the earth has filtered; every time we turn on the lights or fill up our car with gas, we draw on resources the earth has given—or that have been taken from it, often at great cost to its well-being. Whether we recognize it or not, our lives are inextricably linked to the earth. And whether we want to be or not, we are complicit in its degradation simply by living our lives and going about our business.

One of the clearest examples of the complex relationship we have with the land today is demonstrated in our eating practices. Eating is so basic and "normal" that we don't often step back to observe how complicated and fraught it is. Philosopher and agrarian author Norman Wirzba encourages us to take a closer look: "If we were to examine further, we would quickly discover that our food industry bears all the marks of an anti-Sabbath mentality: sacrilege and ingratitude, obsessive control and profiteering, insensitivity and destruction."[8]

This anti-Sabbath mentality is inherent to our economy, and it impacts more than just our food choices, of course. I will focus this chapter on eating because it is something we all do daily, because it is both profoundly simple and profoundly complex, because it has real and meaningful consequences for how animals are treated and land is used, and because eating food together has been associated with Sabbath celebrations since manna in the wilderness.

Eating is also a practice where the themes we've explored throughout this book intersect—from our sense of our identity to our overwhelming busyness and disconnection, to the role of the economy, to our relationship with time, to our sense of being or having "enough," to our feelings of loneliness and exclusion. Food plays a role in each of these areas, and each of these areas, in turn, impacts the choices we make regarding the food we eat.

To understand how this is so, we need to understand two cultural values that train us to see and treat the world in anti-Sabbath ways. Those two values are greed and scarcity, which are mutually reinforcing ways of seeing the world. Greed sees only its cravings for more and grasps at all the wrong things to satisfy its unattended hungers. Scarcity sees only lack and tries to take whatever it can in a vain attempt to soothe its sense of inevitable insufficiency. Greed fools itself by saying, "I need more, because nothing is enough to satisfy me." Scarcity does the same by saying, "I need to *take* more, because there isn't enough for me."

Training in Greed

I recently came across a striking phrase in the book of 2 Peter. Speaking of false prophets who will come to lead the faithful astray, Peter describes them as being "trained in greed" (2 Peter 2:14, NLT). It occurred to me that while Peter was speaking to a unique situation in his own time, the phrase applies just as well to our context today. We live and move and have our being in a culture rooted in and shaped by greed in which the false prophets of corporate profit margins are leading the people down a perishing path. Celtic priest and poet John O'Donohue called greed "one of the powerful forces in the modern Western world."[9] Our blind participation in it is tantamount to training in greed.

What does it mean to be trained in greed? As O'Donohue sees it, greed begins in the eyes. To be trained in greed is to be given lenses that warp our view of the world. "To the greedy eye, everything can be *possessed*," says O'Donohue.[10] Thus, greed reduces the world and its contents to *things*, commodities without inherent value beyond their utility for human possession or self-enrichment. "Possession is ever restless," he continues. "It has an inner insatiable hunger. Greed is poignant because it is always haunted and emptied by future possibility; it can never engage presence."[11] Presence presumes fullness and abundance, which greed cannot abide.

Windigo Economics

O'Donohue's hunger metaphor echoes an ancient indigenous tale told by Native American tribes to teach their children the dangers of greed. The Windigo is a monster born of greed. It was once a human, but ravenous consumption deformed it. No longer able to see itself or the world as it is, the Windigo eats anything it sees—even other humans—in its futile search for satiety. And its disease is contagious. A bite from a Windigo turns you into a Windigo too!

As indigenous poet and botanist Robin Wall Kimmerer describes it in her beautiful book *Braiding Sweetgrass*, Windigo "is the name for that within us which cares more for its own survival than for anything else."[12] And its tracks are everywhere. They are visible "in oil-slick footprints on the beaches of the Gulf of Mexico. A square mile of industrial soybeans. A diamond mine in Rwanda. A closet stuffed with clothes."[13]

As Dr. Kimmerer sees it, we live in a time of "Windigo economics."[14] The very things the Windigo taught native children to avoid, we "are now asked to unleash in a systematic policy of sanctioned greed."[15] To be trained in greed, then, is to be apprenticed in dissatisfaction. It is to believe the gospel of more, bigger, faster; and that "enough" is an unreachable horizon. It is to reject contentment and embrace entitlement. It is to get what we want with no regard for the consequences. It is to be tricked into believing that "belongings will fill our hunger, when it is belonging that we crave."[16]

To be trained in greed is to lose sight of the world as the beloved creation of the loving Creator. It is to see the world not as the "theater of God's glory," as John Calvin saw it;[17] not as the "narrator of God's glory," as the psalmist saw it (Psalm 19:1); but as a commodity—raw material to be controlled, (ab)used, extracted, exploited, and despoiled in the service of possession, profit, competition, boredom, or self-enrichment.

While I imagine few of us consciously or explicitly look at the world this way, we are nevertheless being unconsciously and implicitly trained in greed almost every moment of every day. Like me mindlessly grabbing the Christmas tree Reese's off the shelf, we are daily duped into passive complicity with systems and corporations whose hands are soaked in the proverbial and literal blood of the earth and its resources through their unbridled lust for higher profits and lower costs.

When it comes to the food we eat, industrial food corporations are like Windigo cloning factories, sacrificing sustainability and the humane treatment of land, animals, and workers for increased profits and control of the market share. The means by which industrial food corporations do this would turn even the sturdiest stomachs. This means that for their business model to work, consumers (that's us!) need to remain ignorant, too busy and distracted to look beyond the slick label to learn the true cost of whatever product finds its way to our shopping carts. And business is booming. Norman Wirzba names the uncomfortable truth: "We eat with unprecedented ignorance."[18]

And while I agree with Wirzba, I also think there's more than ignorance at play. Wirzba wrote that statement almost twenty years ago. Since then, we consumers have learned a lot about industrial food processes and factory farms where animals are raised knee-deep in their own excrement without even the space in their cell to turn around.[19] Food documentaries, journalists, climate scientists, ethicists, and human and animal rights activists have exposed some of the most extreme violations of the sanctity of the earth. And yet, very little has changed.

Apathy and Complicity

On that fateful day at the grocery store, I put the Christmas tree Reese's back on the shelf. But a few months later, I didn't. I bought it and ate it. And I've done so many times since. My wife and I do not always purchase organic foods, whether mustard or otherwise. And chicken is a regular part of my diet—both free-range organic and big-box store rotisserie. Why is this? Why do I act in ways that are contrary to my expressed values? Why do I knowingly purchase food that has harmed the earth, animals, or human communities on its way to my mouth?

I think it's partly because I have been trained in greed. Greed isn't just a cannibalistic monster jonesing for its next meal. Greed is also apathy about and complicity with the status quo. It is simply easier, more convenient, and more affordable to buy the factory-farmed rotisserie chicken from Costco than roast one myself that I got from a local farm. And in the moment, my convenience, my budgetary limits, and my schedule are simply more important to me than the well-being of distant fields, animals, or workers whom I will never see or meet.

And this is to say nothing of parents doing their best to survive the incessant demands of life, who simply don't have the energy or wherewithal to spend their few minutes of downtime on any given day strategizing how to source local ingredients or researching the practices of concentrated animal feeding operations (CAFOs) that produce the chicken nuggets that are the only thing their three-year-old will eat. Sometimes surviving our season of life is the best we can hope for. And even if in our current season we take survival for granted, just thinking about the vastness and depravity of the industrial food system gets overwhelming very quickly, which incentivizes our apathy. These are the complexities of contemporary food culture in the industrialized world.

To be alive today is to be complicit in systems of destruction and diminishment. Every choice we make at the grocery store or restaurant impacts how land is used, how animals are treated, and whether someone gets paid a livable wage to get that food to us. It's virtually impossible to avoid complicity in environmental injustice.

And yet there is a way through the complexity that avoids the extremes of perfectionist paralysis, foodie condescension, ascetic isolationism, or the willful ignorance of sticking our heads in the sand. We can walk the Sabbath way. To do so begins by steeping ourselves in greed's antidotes: gratitude, wonder, curiosity, contentment. This helps restore our vision to see the world not merely as raw materials that exist to meet our demand for cheap convenience, but as loving and sacred gifts of the Creator who delights in its existence and laments its exploitation.

If training in greed is about seeing the world through a lens of insatiable consumption, the Sabbath trains us to see the world through a lens of inherent sufficiency. Sabbath trains us to see the world not merely as nature, but as *creation*, the work of the Creator.[20] It teaches us that the way to peace and contentment is not found by taking or consuming everything we can reach, but by appreciating what we have and sharing it freely. However, that message is complicated by another formative value in our culture, deeply enmeshed with greed. Scarcity teaches us there is not enough to go around, so we must take whatever we can get.

Training in Scarcity

In the opening scene of *Kung Fu Panda 3*, Grand Master Oogway's peaceful rest in the spirit realm is interrupted by the flying jade weapon of his old friend turned foe Kai, whom Oogway had banished to the spirit realm five hundred years prior due to his insatiable lust to take what was not his. Kai hasn't changed. He spent all five hundred years mastering how to steal the qi, or vital life source, of every kung fu master, since with enough qi he could return to the material plane to continue his violent conquest. As they fight, Oogway tries to reason with Kai, saying, "When will you realize the more you take, the less you have?"[21]

While on the surface Kai was motivated by a lust for power and conquest, at the root of his centuries-long effort was a profound sense of lack. In life, he had been Robin to Oogway's Batman, always feeling like he was standing just beyond the spotlight. His acute sense of lack propelled him to take more and more, but like the Windigo, he was never satisfied. The more he took, the less he had.

We have been trained to see the world as Kai did. Although we live in a time of immense material abundance, we've been trained to be terrified that there simply isn't enough. When we look at the world through the lens of scarcity, all we see is lack and we become frantic to take more and more to assuage our terror of inevitable insufficiency. Whether we ache for more time or money or security or praise or credit or power or love, nothing will satisfy us because our framing lens is focused on lack. No matter how much we take, it's never enough.

One of my favorite biblical stories explores a theology of *taking* (Hebrew: *laqach*, la-KAHKH). Second Kings 5 tells the story of Naaman, the viceroy of Aram, and Gehazi, the duplicitous apprentice to Elisha. The verb *laqach* appears ten times in the story! After Elisha facilitates the miraculous healing of Naaman, he refuses to *laqach* a gift from Naaman in payment for the healing. In Elisha's mind, grace is free; you cannot *laqach* it. But his apprentice, Gehazi, sees the world differently. For Gehazi, nothing is free, and it isn't fair for Naaman to get away with his healing *and* his gold. So he devises a plan to *laqach* some of Naaman's treasures.

After Gehazi returns with his booty, Elisha perceives what he has done in secret and sits him down for a heart-to-heart. Elisha asks him a version of the question Oogway asked Kai, which echoes through the canyons of time to each of us today: "Is there [ever] a time to *laqach*?" (2 Kings 5:26).[22]

The implied answer to Elisha's question is, "No!" The essence of his message, to Gehazi and to us, is, "In the flock of the Great Shepherd, the sheep lack nothing," and "the Kingdom of God runs on the currency of generosity, so taking is incomprehensible." In other words, *there is never a time to take.*

But to us it is *Elisha's* message that is incomprehensible. We can barely go five minutes without *taking* something or other. Consider our speech habits. The verb "take" is a pervasive part of the American English lexicon: we *take* a walk, *take* a break, *take* a nap, *take* a bus, *take* a drink, *take* a picture, *take* a bite, *take* a vacation, *take* our pills, *take* a class. We tell each other "*Take* care." A leader "*takes* charge." We are so committed to taking that we even take things we *leave*: we *take* a pee and *take* a poo! This linguistic phenomenon helps normalize our other more damaging habits of taking, embedding them in the status quo and blinding us to how often we take what is not ours. It makes me want to pay more attention to my words.

Years ago, I preached a sermon on the Naaman and Gehazi story in which I similarly concluded there is never a time to take. I then proceeded to the Communion table, where I quoted Jesus saying, "*Take*, eat: this is my body, which is broken for you" (1 Corinthians 11:24, KJV, emphasis added).

I'm embarrassed to admit I didn't notice the irony until after the service when a colleague inquired, "You said, 'Don't take,' but then Jesus said, 'Take.' Who should we listen to?" Well, probably Jesus! But perhaps it's a matter of translation. The Greek word for "take" in Jesus' statement is *labete*, which can mean both "take" *and* "receive." In fact, *laqach* can as well. But the English word "take" does *not* also mean "receive." Perhaps we should instead translate Jesus' statement as, "*Receive* and eat. This is my body."

At the same time, not all "taking" is created equal. Perhaps the created world itself can teach us something about tender and generative taking. Maybe we are meant to take in the way a plant takes to soil. A plant "takes root" in a way that nourishes its new home even as it's nourished by it. That nourishment empowers its fruitfulness, which it offers the world without reservation. Poet-gardener Ross Gay reminds us, "When we say a plant takes, we really mean it's going to give."[23] Perhaps Jesus meant for us to do *that* in remembrance of him.

From Taking to Giving

It will not be easy to unlearn our cultural formation in the ways of scarcity and greed. We've been given cultural lenses that make everything appear as commodities. We've been taught to interpret the exploitation of land as an unfortunate but necessary consequence of the modern world. We've been told that there isn't enough, that *we* aren't enough, and that the more we take, the more likely we will be to find happiness.

The Sabbath invites us to see and relate to the world differently, to change our posture from taking to receiving and from taking to giving. The Communion table reminds us that when we do so, we re-member Jesus by stitching back together the fragmented parts of his broken body. The Sabbath and the table both remind us that life is a gift, and the universe is abundant. They remind us that we not only have enough, we *are* enough. To live in light of this requires us to unlearn much of what we have been taught. The Sabbath apprentices us on this lifelong journey.

REFLECTION QUESTIONS

- What variables factored most into the food choices you made for your last two or three meals? For example, cost, convenience, ease of preparation, time, nutrition, availability, emotions, social setting, environmental impact, etc. In what ways are these choices reflective or not reflective of your life values overall?

- The Bible's consistent connection between Sabbath and land use raises some uncomfortable truths. In what ways, if any, do you feel challenged or uncomfortable about what you read? What questions arise as you consider the implications these truths might have for you?

- The Windigo is a children's story intended "to build resistance against the insidious germ of taking too much. . . . [The] monster was created in stories, that we might learn why we should recoil from the greedy part of ourselves."[24] What stories or teaching do you recall from your family history that served the same purpose? In other words, how were you taught to understand the dangers of greed? How effective were those stories or teaching in helping you see through greed's glossy exterior to its vacuous heart?

- To look at the world through a lens of scarcity is to see lack. In what area(s) of life are you most aware of seeing your life through this lens? What are you afraid there won't be enough of for you? For example, money, security, love.

Sabbath Practice: Savoring

This practice invites you to slow down and really pay attention to the food you are eating and the people you may be sharing it with. The ideal meal would be one that includes multiple ingredients in a single bite—a salad, a taco, soup with veggies, a rice or grain bowl—but you could do it with any meal.

- Slowly craft a bite you might consider "perfect."
- Eat the bite slowly. Experience the flavors. Notice the textures.
- Now build a different bite with a different flavor or texture focus.
- Eat your whole meal this way. If you are sharing a meal with others, spend a few minutes eating this way before you start chatting.
- During the meal, name two or three things you are grateful for.
- After the meal, reflect on or discuss the following questions:
  - What was your experience of building bites?
  - What did you notice about your food that you hadn't noticed before?
  - How might you bring this practice to experiences that do not include food at all, such as a walk in the park or working at your desk?

12

DISORIENTING GREED AND SCARCITY

Earth's crammed with heaven,
And every common bush afire with God:
But only he who sees, takes off his shoes,
The rest sit round it, and pluck blackberries.
ELIZABETH BARRETT BROWNING, AURORA LEIGH

Maybe what the word rapture *really means is an attention so ferocious that you see the miracle of the world as the miracle it is.*
BRIAN DOYLE, ONE LONG RIVER OF SONG

In the mid-1800s, as Western society was being transformed by the industrial revolution, Rabbi Samson Raphael Hirsch, founder of what would become Orthodox Judaism, asked a prescient question: "What [is] there to safeguard the world against man?"[1] His answer was the Sabbath. The Sabbath keeps in check the human impulse to transform everything we see into what Hirsch called "an instrument of human service."[2] Simply put, part of the Sabbath's purpose is to mitigate the human temptation to dominate and exploit the world.

One obvious way the Sabbath does this is through the sabbatical year and the Jubilee year, which safeguard human behavior against overrunning creation. But, of course, these practices have been largely ignored or rejected altogether in the centuries since Rabbi Hirsch's poignant question.

There is also a less obvious way in which Sabbath safeguards creation against human overuse. Sabbath resists "thingifying" the world by re-personalizing it. By *re-personalizing*, I do not mean that Sabbath magically turns creation into people! I mean that it restores to creation its inherent uniqueness, beauty, and goodness—its personality—which greed and scarcity strip it of in their pursuit of more, bigger, faster.

Sabbath Resists Thingification

"Thing" is a convenient catchall term that can literally be applied to any*thing*. And every*thing* it refers to is flattened, stripped of its uniqueness and personality. A mountain, a butterfly, a redwood, and a garbage bin can all be referred to with the same generic word. And it's everywhere in English. I've already used "thing" six times in this chapter! Now seven!

When creation is thingified it loses its sacredness. A *thing* is abstract; it can be treated in whatever way will achieve the results we want. When animals become *things*, we no longer must honor their inherent dignity in how we raise and slaughter them. When mountains (and the neighborhoods around them) become *things*, their tops can be blown up and the sediment allowed to leach into surrounding streams and groundwater with the justification that it's the most cost-effective way of extracting coal.[3]

But nothing in creation is a *thing*. In fact, Rabbi Abraham Joshua Heschel argues that there is no equivalent for the word *thing* in biblical Hebrew. The word *davar* is often translated as "thing," but this is a mistranslation, more a consequence of English than a meaning inherent to the Hebrew. *Davar* is the word for "word," but it also means "speech, thought, event, matter, promise," and a couple dozen other related meanings—but never "thing." Heschel asks, "Is this a sign of linguistic poverty, or rather an indication of an unwarped view of the world, of not equating reality . . . with thinghood?"[4]

Heschel's rhetorical question points us once again to the importance of sight. How we *see* the world has a significant impact on how we treat it. The Sabbath teaches us to resist thingifying the world and to see it instead as a manifestation of God's love, abundance, and generosity, utterly unique and worthy of our care and tenderness. As the poet Wendell Berry reminds us,

> *There are no unsacred places;*
> *there are only sacred places*
> *and desecrated places.*[5]

The Bible similarly sees the created world and all its creatures as sacred, infused with God's presence and the object of God's unending delight. In Psalm 104 the psalmist can hardly contain his enthusiasm in naming the manifold ways God cares for, delights in, and exults in creation, from feeding the animals to watering the earth to playing catch with Leviathan to providing darkness as a shelter for animals to hunt. The created world is, for God, an endless source of exceeding joy.

Psalm 104 is a poetic riff on Genesis 1, which connects God's sight to creation's goodness. Seven times God "sees" the goodness of creation. Wendell Berry captured the wonder and mystery of this connection in one of his Sabbath poems, which imagines the

> *Time when the Maker's radiant sight*
> *Made radiant every thing He saw.*[6]

And yet, it is the thingification of creation rather than the sacredness of creation that dominates our view. The combination of greed and scarcity, channeled through our economic structures and reinforced by our language, has distorted our eyesight and justified widespread desecration. Under their influence, when we look at the world, we see infinite potential for both possession and abject lack. When we make decisions from that place, desecration becomes almost inevitable.

The Sabbath offers at least two powerful antidotes to greed and scarcity, which help correct our eyesight, enabling us to look at the world and see God's love and presence pulsing in and through it. The antidote to greed is wonder, and the antidote to scarcity is gratitude.

While gratitude may be a logical antidote to scarcity, wonder may be a less obvious remedy for greed. But bear with me. Wonder looks at the world with playful expectation. It repels reduction, counters commodification, eschews thingification. Wonder knows there is always more than what is visible. Gratitude looks at the world from a place of sufficiency; its contentment enables connection and is contagious. The more it gives, the more it receives. A Sabbath practice that intentionally cultivates wonder and gratitude in a culture dominated by greed and scarcity will bloom into a Sabbath posture of abundance, connection, and joy. The invitation, then, is to embrace these antidotes by training ourselves in wonder and gratitude.

Training in Wonder

In emotion scientist Dacher Keltner's book *Awe*, he explores the potential of awe and wonder to transform our everyday lives. Built on the foundation of research spanning two decades, conducted all over the world, Keltner concluded that (spoiler alert!) experiences of awe and wonder are essential to feelings of happiness and well-being.

Although awe and wonder are difficult to define and inherently evanescent, their beauty and power lie in the fact that they can be found *everywhere*. And finding them, according to Keltner, "doesn't require money or the burning of fossil fuels—or even much time."[7] Keltner's research suggests that even just a few minutes of awe or wonder a day will make a statistically significant difference in our experience of wellness and contentment in life. Cultivating wonder dovetails perfectly with both a Sabbath practice and a Sabbath posture. On the Sabbath day we can experiment with wonder so that our hearts remain more present to it in the fleeting ways we might encounter but overlook it during the week.

But what exactly *is* wonder, and how do we *train* for it in our everyday lives? Isn't wonder something that happens *to* us when we see something immense or beautiful or inspiring? If you're asking these questions, you're not alone. It's important to understand what wonder is, because once we do, we discover that there are indeed ways to practice—to train ourselves—in wonder, some of which may be rather surprising.

Defining Wonder

Awe and wonder are the fruit of particular ways of viewing the world. Keltner defines awe as "the feeling of being in the presence of something vast that transcends your current understanding of the world."[8] It is the psalmist standing before the night sky, exclaiming, "When I consider the heavens . . . what are humans?" (Psalm 8:3-4). It is Job responding to the whirlwind, "I declared what I did not understand, of things beyond me I spoke without knowledge" (Job 42:3). It is Mary at the tomb of Jesus realizing the man to whom she speaks is not the gardener, but the risen Christ (John 20:16). Awe is an embodied experience, manifesting as goose bumps, tears, a lump in the throat, or feeling quiet or small (in a good way).[9]

While *wonder* and *awe* are synonyms, one difference between them is that wonder operates on a smaller scale than awe, and therefore may be more regularly accessible. If awe is being stunned by the vastness and mystery of the cosmos, submitting to a profound mystical experience, or feeling the oneness of thousands of people experiencing something remarkable simultaneously, wonder is being captivated by a child's laugh or astonished by the spring's first butterfly. It is delighting in the familiar-yet-ever-new feeling of holding a loved one's hand, pausing to marvel as a woodpecker hammers a branch or an osprey snags a fish from the lake, or soaking in the bittersweet amazement that your baby who was born just yesterday is now graduating from high school. Wonder is curiosity robed in humility, animated by exuberance, and partnered with delight.

Professor Keltner is right: there are a thousand ways we can experience wonder every day. The trick is that to do so *we have to be paying attention.* If we aren't, these simple, daily opportunities for delight will pass by unnoticed and we will continue to live half-asleep to the miracle of each moment. If you're anything like me, most days you're so caught up just trying to make it to the end of the day—or to the weekend or to your next vacation—that you tell yourself you don't have the internal space or energy to be "trained in wonder." There are too many important things that need doing to waste time on anything unproductive. It's safer and easier to just keep your head down and make it through the day.

But if we pause, take a breath, and really think about it, we know that's not the way we want to live. We know there is more we were born to do than put our heads down and make it through the day. Of course, there are seasons when that's the best we can do. But we must resist normalizing sleepwalking through life, and we must resist it with a holy passion. We were put here to flourish and to fly. The Sabbath is our partner and guide on this journey. It reminds us to prioritize wonder and gives us space *every week* to practice it.

While there are countless ways to practice wonder, two stand out as practical ways we can increase our experience of wonder in life. The first practice may seem counterintuitive, but as we will see, intentionally reflecting on our mortality can infuse our daily living with purpose and joy. Embracing the fact of our death can be a doorway to wonder and delight.

Practice 1: Embrace Death as a Doorway to Wonder and Delight

Almost three decades before her death and twenty years before her first cancer diagnosis, Mary Oliver imagined her death as an exercise in getting clear about how she wanted to live. While the prospect of meditating on our death may feel uncomfortable or like the last thing we want to do, it has a long and storied tradition as a spiritual practice.

The Vietnamese American poet Ocean Vuong regularly practices a Buddhist death meditation. For him, regular reflection on his mortality and the finitude of all life is the key to answering the question, "How do we live a life worthy of our breath?"[10] In the Christian tradition, this instinct is mirrored in the Rule of Saint Benedict, the founding document of the Catholic Order of Saint Benedict, which includes this sentence: "Have death at all times before your eyes."[11]

The inevitability of death is not the antithesis of delight but its doorway. My colleague and friend Todd Billings has discovered this during his journey with terminal cancer: "As strange as it seems, coming to terms with our limits as dying creatures is a life-giving path."[12] The poet Ross Gay perceives in death a paradox of joy: "Joy has everything to do with the fact that we're all going to die."[13] Remembering our mortality, our human limits, cultivates curiosity and humility and facilitates connection, essential ingredients for a life drenched in wonder and delight.

Back to Mary Oliver. In "When Death Comes," she reminds herself of her highest values.

> *When it's over, I want to say: all my life*
> *I was a bride married to amazement.*[14]

In another poem, "Messenger," she describes her life's work as a practice of "learning to be astonished."[15] I think this applies to her work *not* as a poet but as a *human being* living what she memorably called her "one wild and precious life."[16]

Amazement and *astonishment* are compelling synonyms for *wonder* and *awe*. To see the world this way is to see with eyes of abundance, to be ever open to noticing the extraordinary in the ordinary. It is not to see the world through rose-colored glasses or to ignore pain and suffering. Rather, it is to see the world as Elizabeth Barrett Browning did, who famously wrote,

> *Earth's crammed with heaven,*
> *And every common bush afire with God:*
> *But only he who sees, takes off his shoes,*
> *The rest sit round it, and pluck blackberries.*[17]

While many of us likely desire to have God speak to us from a burning bush, as God did to Moses, I suspect most of us are so caught up in our lives and so distracted from what's around us that on the off chance we look at a bush, all we see is the bush—or the blackberries—but we miss the burning presence of God pulsing within it. Most of us live our lives in places where the grandeur of creation, which so readily evokes wonder, is visible only on screen savers and social media feeds, so we need to start small in developing ways to see God's presence in the world around us. One way to do this is to take Jesus literally and just "consider the lilies" (Matthew 6:28). This line from Jesus' Sermon on the Mount is an allusion to a death meditation. Two verses later he reminds his listeners that "the grass of the field . . . is here today and tomorrow is thrown into the fire" (Matthew 6:30, NIV).

Probing deeper into the image, we discover, along with Mary Oliver, that lilies live extravagantly in every moment of their short but illustrious lives. They offer us bold beauty, wild diversity, intoxicating aromas. They offer themselves fully to the world for as long as they have life. We can find in that a model for how to live. And it is no accident that lilies symbolize the Resurrection and fill sanctuaries around the world on Easter Sunday. To ponder a lily is not just to ponder abundant life or the reality of death, it is to ponder the hope of resurrection. To see the world sacramentally is to recognize that every created life contains multitudes; a flower is a portal from death to resurrection. How do we cultivate this kind of sacramental vision in our lives? This is the subject of our second practice.

Practice 2: Cultivate a Sacramental Vision

When I say "sacramental vision," what I'm referring to is the way the Bible envisions God's active and ongoing presence in the world, as well as how it perceives God's presence and character being revealed through the created world—as if the veil separating heaven and earth has frayed and shimmers of heaven are shining through. As a theologian, I call this "sacramental theology." It is the exploration of the manifold ways God reveals Godself to us through the created world, but chiefly through the liturgical actions that infuse ordinary elements—such as bread, wine, and water—with extraordinary meaning to facilitate a sacred encounter between God and God's people.

The rituals of baptism and Communion (or Eucharist) do this to teach us that no parts of our lives are beyond the reach of God's love. These sacred and communal actions ripple out, charging our everyday lives with cosmic echoes through what I call the "spillover effect." Every time we sit to eat a meal and offer our thanks for these gifts of God's bounty, we reenact Communion and are invited to recall the boundlessness of God's love. Every time we shower or swim or drink water, we are invited to remember that, in baptism, God has claimed us as God's own, that we belong to God, and that nothing we could ever do will diminish God's love for us.

I recently had the privilege of talking to my ten-year-old niece Anastasia about her upcoming baptism and what this experience meant to her. As I shared with her this idea of the spillover effect at the center of sacramental theology, I asked her to name some of the ways she daily interacts with water. The first thing she thought of was brushing her teeth. In all my years reflecting on this I had never considered brushing my teeth a sacramental act! As our conversation ended, I asked her what she thought might feel different after her baptism. She thought about it for a second and replied, "I never thought I could have a spiritual experience brushing my teeth, but after my baptism I think I will!" That is as profound a statement on the practical implications of sacramental theology as I've ever heard. I wrote it down and taped it to the mirror above the sink where I brush my teeth every evening and morning!

The Eucharist does for food what baptism does for water. It provides a lens through which to see our food that represents an absolute alternative to the industrial lens of commodification and profit potential. It compels us to see our food as God's love-made-edible, and to see beyond the processed product to imagine the hands and hearts and harvest that produced it and brought it to our table. It invites us to remember that just as Communion celebrates the ultimate sacrifice, every meal we eat involves death and life, sacrifice and sustenance.

Cultivating a sense of wonder in the face of this reality might begin with acknowledging in our table graces the manifold ways God cares for us through creation, beginning with the animals and vegetables that died so we might live. To do this is to honor their lives. It is to refuse to take their sacrifice for granted. While it may seem easy to do this for a cow or a chicken or a pig, it may seem silly to acknowledge the sacrifice a carrot or strawberry made for us to live. But only when we are looking at them through the eyes of the Windigo. When we look at them instead through the sacramental lens of the Sabbath, they become agents actively caring for us our whole lives long—portals connecting us to the heart of God.

To see the world sacramentally is to see that *nothing* is ordinary, that there are, in fact, no *things*. This awareness forms the basis for our love of the world, which in turn informs how we treat it and use it. It also helps us to see the reciprocal character of all God created. We begin to understand that our work is to "care for the creation that cares for us."[18] And when we see our lives in this way we understand, along with Mary Oliver, that our work more or less boils down to "rejoicing, since all the ingredients are here."[19] Ultimately, our work "is gratitude."[20] And this is precisely where wonder, amazement, and astonishment lead us: to gratitude.

Training in Gratitude

Gratitude is an antidote to scarcity, to the sense of insatiable lack that topples us out of the present moment, causing us to fall—or flail—into either the past or the future. As we explored in part 2 on time, the currents of our culture steer our course away from the present moment because the present moment is the *only moment* in which we can experience contentment or be fully alive, which tends to be bad for the economy. We are trained to obsess over the past through guilt, regret, or worry—or to fret about the future through anxiety, fear, or dread. At the root of these feelings is an acute sense of lack. Gratitude grounds us in the present and opens us to acknowledge what is true and real beyond whatever past or future negative experience we've become fixated on. Practices that return us to our bodies—such as breathing, smelling flowers, walking, and dancing—also return us to the present moment, which is the doorway to gratitude.

In her book *Wake Up Grateful,* author Kristi Nelson speaks to how her own relationship with gratitude grew during a season of profound physical disorientation: in the wake of a stage IV cancer diagnosis at age thirty-three. The book's opening line says it all: "Not dying changed everything."[21]

Just as it did for Mary Oliver, confronting her death changed everything about Kristi Nelson's life. Only for her it wasn't just an imaginative exercise. The prospect of death strips away our pretense. It lays bare our inherent vulnerability and exposes our radical dependence. All of this can open us, if we are courageous enough, to live *fully awake* on the wild edges of existence. As Nelson's story shows, gratitude, like joy, is not dependent on circumstance. Even in the valley of the shadow of death, gratitude reminds us that all we need is already here.

Mariah and I have learned the transformative power of gratitude over the course of her decades-long journey with chronic illness. When life has truly felt desperate, when all we could see was lack—lack of health, lack of energy, lack of finances, lack of options, lack of time, lack of community, lack of vitality, lack of hope—a simple practice of naming things we were grateful for broadened our tunnel vision and ground us again in reality: we had everything we needed in that moment.

To say this was not to say life magically became easy, or that we replaced our tunnel vision with blindness to hardship, or even that our disappointment or grief or anger were misplaced or inappropriate. Instead, it helped us remember that those things weren't the whole story. It reminded us that while we didn't always have the power to choose our life situations, we had immense power to choose how to respond to them. It reminded us that pining for a different "now" without these problems, which felt so heavy in the moment, only deepened our misery.

When we spoke aloud names of people we loved or things that had gone well that day, noticed the way the light in the waiting room fell so gently on Mariah's open hands, celebrated that we had a reliable car to carry us to appointments, or remembered that people were praying for us, the load lightened, and we began to see our lives differently. "One of the many gifts of perspective," Nelson reminds us, "is that we can significantly change what we see by changing *how* we see."[22]

When we change what and how we see, we begin to change how we act. Gratitude compels us toward love. For Nelson, "Grateful living is a practice of love in action."[23] Gratitude deepens our capacity to love each other and deepens our convictions about loving the earth. And when our gratitude is refracted through a prism of wonder, we realize it's not just that we love the earth, but the earth loves us as well. And this changes everything. Author and botanist Robin Wall Kimmerer articulates it beautifully: "Knowing that you love the earth changes you, activates you to defend and protect and celebrate. But when you feel that the earth loves you in return, that feeling transforms the relationship from a one-way street into a sacred bond."[24] Restoring the sacred bonds between humans and the rest of creation is central to the vision and purpose of a biblical Sabbath.

A Bond of Mutual Care

Through the intentional cultivation of gratitude and wonder, both on the Sabbath and throughout the week, we strengthen the cords of our sacred bond with all of creation. Moreover, we mitigate the effects of our cultural training in greed and scarcity and reawaken the power of our baptismal identity as the beloved children of God, made to flourish and to fly, creatures of earth who are kin of tree and field, animal and vegetable, gripped by the miracle that is every moment of every day.

I think Rabbi Hirsch was right. Well, half-right, at least. Sabbath does safeguard the world against human abuse. But it also does much more than that. Sabbath partners with us in a bond of mutual care. It models for us what faithful and free living looks like. Its ultimate longing is to connect us to creation, and through it to God, to remind us, week after week, that we are not alone, and that we are loved beyond our comprehension.

REFLECTION QUESTIONS

- Briefly recall your activities and experiences over the last twenty-four hours—morning, afternoon, and evening. In what ways, if any, might you have engaged in thingification—viewing or treating a creature, an aspect of nature, or perhaps even a person as something less than sacred? What would be different—in you or in your behavior—if you had viewed or treated that creature, aspect of nature, or person as wholly sacred instead?

- When have you experienced the kind of awe Dr. Dacher Keltner describes: "the feeling of being in the presence of something vast that transcends your current understanding of the world"? How did the experience impact the way you viewed yourself in relationship to others, to the world, or to God?

- What traditions or rituals does your faith community have around the sacraments of baptism and Communion? What connections might you make between those sacraments and your everyday life? Or in what ways might you embrace sacramental living?

- Briefly identify something you are concerned about from the past or are worried about in the future. With that in mind, name three to five things you are grateful for in this moment. They could be anything, big or small. In what ways, if any, does naming your gratitudes shift your perspective on the concern or worry you identified?

Sabbath Practice: Cultivating a Lens of Gratitude

If how we see the world—and the story we make of what we see—lies at the root of greed and scarcity, then a good first step to begin living beyond these challenges is to change the way we see the world. We do that by enhancing our ability to look at the world in ways that generate feelings of contentment, sufficiency, gratitude, and abundance. To that end, this practice is an invitation to look at the world you inhabit every day with new eyes. It is something the whole family could do every week.

- Go to a place you spend a lot of time. For example, your living room, kitchen, bathroom, closet, garage, car, backyard, a park.

- Slow down and *really look* at what is there—each piece of furniture, utensil, or plant.

- Devote fifteen to thirty seconds to feeling gratitude for each object, noting its benefits and all that it gives you that you typically take for granted. For example, you might thank the lamp for providing light, the rug for warmth and comfort, the spatula for ease of cooking, or the coffee mug for enabling your morning routine. Notice a sense of enough-ness growing in you. Give thanks for that too.

- Recall any stories or memories connected to the objects you consider and give thanks for whatever comes to your mind as you remember.

- Next week, repeat the practice in a different place—or in the same one!

13

REORIENTING: PREREQUISITES FOR A LIFE OF GRATITUDE

*Expressing gratitude . . . is a revolutionary idea.
In a consumer society, contentment is a radical proposition.*

ROBIN WALL KIMMERER, BRAIDING SWEETGRASS

*To wake at dawn with a winged heart
and give thanks for another day of loving.*

KAHLIL GIBRAN, "On Love," THE PROPHET

Our formation *against* grateful living has been sustained and aggressive. The impact of a culture of productivity rooted in scarcity can make genuine gratitude feel not just difficult but irresponsible. The implicit question here is, *How can you be grateful at a time like this?* To which the Sabbath counters, *How can you* not *be grateful at a time like this?* Gratitude, like the Sabbath itself, is radically countercultural. In fact, as author Robin Wall Kimmerer asserts, it's "revolutionary."[1]

Kimmerer is right. Gratitude represents a paradigm shift away from the value system of our culture that promotes a reductive, consumptive, competitive, and acquisitive lifestyle, and toward a slower, fuller, connected, and generous lifestyle celebrated by the Sabbath. This paradigm shift won't happen overnight; it happens over a lifetime of learning and unlearning.

I find the language of learning and unlearning replete with playful possibilities. As a way of drawing this book to its close, I will lay out a "gratitude curriculum" that translates the Sabbath sensibilities explored throughout this book into a curricular format. My hope is that this will be a playful, imaginative exercise that weaves together many of the book's themes into a cohesive whole.

I invite you to enroll in a fictional-yet-earnest sequence of three courses that comprise the backbone of an unconventional "Sabbath Degree in Gratitude" (we'll call it an S.Grat²), offered by the fully accredited Sabbath Institute of Grateful Living (or SIGL, which rhymes with *giggle*). Tuition is free. There is a rolling admissions policy. No application is ever denied. Repeat students are welcome. Classes meet from sundown on Friday through sundown on Saturday, every week, whether the students show up or not.

On the pages that follow, you'll meet your professors, engage primary readings, and be introduced to student learning outcomes for each class. As with any curricular sequence, advanced courses build on the foundation laid in introductory courses. These building blocks are called prerequisites and must be completed before taking the capstone course, A Life of Gratitude.

Opening Convocation: The Grateful Life

Prior to the first Friday evening class, every student, faculty member, and staff member attends a worship service led by the president of SIGL—a fictional psalmist whom I imagine penned Psalm 100, which is the text for the opening convocation to establish gratitude as both the starting point and goal of the entire student experience.

> Make a joyful noise to the LORD, all the earth!
> Worship the LORD with gladness;
>   Enter the LORD's presence with joyful shouts!
> Know that the LORD is God.
>   God made us—we belong to him.
>   We are God's people, the sheep of God's pasture.

REORIENTING: PREREQUISITES FOR A LIFE OF GRATITUDE

> Enter God's gates with thanksgiving—
> God's courts with praise.
> Give thanks to God!
> Bless God's name.
> For the LORD is good,
> God's steadfast love endures forever,
> God's faithfulness is from generation to generation.

To open the sermon, President Psalmist asks, "Have you ever seen something so exquisitely beautiful—or heard something so profound—that it sat you back on your heels and filled you with wonder for the sheer fact of its existence? And did you ever see that sight—or hear the same insight—again later and think, 'Meh. It was better the first time'"?

Sensing the movement of the Spirit, the president continues, "It is almost universal that spectacular things lose their power through *familiarity*. We often speak of being desensitized to violence, but what about being desensitized to beauty and wonder, to the sheer miracle of life itself? Sometimes that familiarity can breed, if not contempt, a kind of irritation—either with the familiar thing, or with the wonder and awe of *others* beholding it for the first time. We might call this irritation by way of familiarity a case of *familirritability*.[3]

"I recall catching myself in a moment of *familirritation* during my *second* visit to the Grand Canyon. Overhearing other visitors' gasps of wide-eyed wonder at its unimaginable immensity, I thought: 'Well, what did you expect? It's called the *Grand Canyon*!'

"I wonder how many of us respond similarly to the metaphors in Psalm 100—entering God's gates with hoots and hollers, being God's beloved sheep. Or how many hearts fail to flutter during the Eucharist when the liturgist utters Jesus' reality-altering line, 'This is my body, broken for you.'

"Let me assure you," the president adds, anticipating the sermon's conclusion, "Psalm 100 is not an expression of tired familiarity with the world. It is the expression of one *captivated* by the world, who is incapable of suppressing their wonder and gratitude, who wants others to wake from their slumber and join the miracle and mystery of life with God."

With this, President Psalmist invites you and every incoming student to submit fully to the Sabbath-shaped gratitude curriculum. "It will be harder than you think," the president cautions. "The kind of intellectual and spiritual formation this curriculum requires are different from the sort you encountered in the competitive environment of the modern educational system. Make no mistake, we will have many moments of fun, and we will laugh much and often. But do not let the presence of play imply ease or mindlessness—or an absence of grief and loss. As theologian Willie Jennings has noted, 'Paying attention requires everything.'[4] Meister Eckhart likewise knew that to live gratefully, 'You may have to leave / more than you ever imagined / behind.'"[5]

"But fear not," the president says with kindness. "You will have many wise guides along the way." Then, glancing out the window, noticing three twinkling stars in the night sky, the president turns to you and all the other students and says, "Time to go outside. Your first class begins now!"

GL101: Introduction to Curiosity and Attentiveness

Outside the chapel, your first professor, poet and essayist Annie Dillard, is waiting to welcome you to the first class of the Grateful Living curriculum: GL101: Introduction to Curiosity and Attentiveness. This course has but one very simple student learning outcome. "As a result of taking this course, students will learn how to see with sacramental vision."

Professor Dillard knows the truth articulated by Rabbi Abraham Joshua Heschel, another faculty member: "Our sight is suffused with knowing, instead of feeling painfully the lack of knowing what we see. *The principle to be kept in mind is to know what we see rather than to see what we know.*"[6] But how do we see beyond our knowing?

In her opening lecture, Professor Dillard addresses this question by telling a delightful story from her childhood, recounted in her book

REORIENTING: PREREQUISITES FOR A LIFE OF GRATITUDE

Pilgrim at Tinker Creek. As a young girl, Dillard would often "hide" pennies in plain sight along the sidewalk or in a crook of a tree, and then draw huge arrows labeled "SURPRISE AHEAD" or "MONEY THIS WAY" to lead passersby right to the penny![7] She became "greatly excited, during all this arrow-drawing, at the thought of the first lucky passer-by" about to receive this "free gift from the universe."[8]

As a child, her pennies were real. As an adult, they become a metaphor. She concludes,

> There are lots of things to see, unwrapped gifts and free surprises. The world is fairly studded and strewn with pennies cast broadside from a generous hand. But—and this is the point—who gets excited by a mere penny? If you follow one arrow, if you crouch motionless on a bank to watch a tremulous ripple thrill on the water and are rewarded by the sight of a muskrat kit paddling from its den, will you count that sight a chip of copper only, and go your rueful way? It is dire poverty indeed when a man is so malnourished and fatigued that he won't stoop to pick up a penny. But if you cultivate a healthy poverty and simplicity, so that finding a penny will literally make your day, then, since the world is in fact planted in pennies, you have with your poverty bought a lifetime of days. It is that simple. What you see is what you get.[9]

Throughout the course, you and your fellow students slowly and gently learn to let go of the impoverished and utilitarian lenses you have developed by osmosis throughout your lives—lenses that suffuse your seeing with ignorance masquerading as knowledge or worse, certainty. You learn to fashion *new* spectacles with which to see the world as it is presented in Scripture—as the marvelous, intricate, mysterious, wonderful, and generous love of God made visible.

The final exam is to recite a poem—of your choosing or one you write yourself—which articulates, with a Sabbath sensibility, a way of seeing the world as redolent with God's presence.

GL301: Training for Wonder

The second course in the sequence, Training for Wonder, is taught posthumously (by some miracle) by the late Rabbi Abraham Joshua Heschel. In Training for Wonder, you and your fellow students sharpen your newly developed "penny vision" by cultivating wonder through a rigorous immersion in the practice of blessing God.

This, too, is a challenging task—former students wistfully recall it as "wonder boot camp." Completing the course requires living with wholehearted attention. Rabbi Heschel sees this course as responding to the undertow of two cultural realities—greed and taking one's life for granted. First, training in wonder is an antidote to the "training in greed" you have received just by being alive. Its legacy is desecrated landscapes, mountains stripped bare and their resources pilfered, mass species extinction, global warming, pollution-related illnesses disproportionately impacting communities of color, and more. But not all is lost. Training in wonder counters training in greed by deepening your love for creation and teaching you to see it as God does.

Second, while you and your fellow students have likely been taught since birth to take your life for granted, Professor Heschel counters, "The surest way to suppress our ability to understand the meaning of God and the importance of worship is *to take things for granted*. Indifference to the sublime wonder of living is the root of sin."[10] In this class, students learn to see the sacred behind the veil of the mundane, whether in a glass of water, a slice of bread, in waking from sleep, even in the act of going to the bathroom!

Professor Heschel teaches that cultivating wonder is a two-way street. You are encouraged to cultivate it, but also be open to how an enchanted world can cultivate wonder in you! The passive reception of wonder is captured in a delightful mistranslation of the tagline for a pair of sunglasses: "Go outside and be wondered!" An error evokes an insight. The wild and woolly world can wonder you back to wholeness, if you let it.

This vision of wonder suggests it is neither a luxury nor an add-on to enrich life. It is the very wellspring of worship. But it is more even than that. Author Valarie Kaur reminds you that "wonder is the wellspring for love."[11]

Throughout the class, Professor Heschel draws on Judaism's ancient legacy of blessing God for all of life's encounters—from the quotidian to the spectacular—as a way of steeping students in the sacramental conviction that all of life is *encounter*. Indeed, the course's primary learning objective is: "As a result of taking this class, students will see all of life as an encounter with the presence, glory, and love of God—in creation, in neighbor, in self."

Judaism's blessing tradition apprentices you in responding to each of life's moments with a blessing. There is a blessing for rising from sleep and another for going to sleep. There is a blessing recited before and another recited after studying Scripture. There's another for seeing a renowned scholar (the professor would expect to hear this mumbled at the beginning of every class), another for bread, for wine, and for water, upon hearing bad news, or for affirming God's sovereignty despite uncertainty. There is even one recited after going to the bathroom. The point is to convey how every moment is *flush* with God's presence.

Professor Heschel's opening lecture includes the following exposition on wonder as the gateway to God's presence.

> Every evening we recite: "He creates light and makes the dark." Twice a day we say: "He is One." What is the meaning of such repetition? A scientific theory, once it is announced and accepted, does not have to be repeated twice a day. The insights of wonder must be constantly kept alive. Since there is a need for daily wonder, there is a need for daily worship. . . .
>
> There is no worship, no music, no love, if we take for granted the blessings or defeats of living. . . . We are trained in maintaining our sense of wonder by uttering a prayer before the enjoyment of food. Each time we are about to drink a glass of water, we remind ourselves of the eternal mystery of creation, "Blessed be Thou . . . by Whose word all things come into being." A trivial act and a reference to the supreme

miracle.... Even on performing a physiological function we say "Blessed be Thou ... who healest all flesh and *doest wonders*."[12]

Students in Training for Wonder also learn to embrace a conviction at the heart of both Judaism's and Christianity's sacramental imagination. Namely, to experience "commonplace deeds as spiritual adventures, to feel the hidden love and wisdom in all things."[13] By leaning into sacramental wonder each Sabbath, students learn to see *every* encounter in life as an encounter with the face of God, whether in their child, their neighbor, a maple tree, or their morning cereal.

The final exam in Training for Wonder includes students reciting an ancient Hebrew blessing called *Shehecheyanu*.[14] It roughly translates to:

Blessed are you, O Lord our God, King of the universe.
You are the one who gives us life.
You are the one who sustains us.
You have caused us to touch this moment in time.

In Jewish tradition, this blessing is spoken at the beginning of holy festivals, but also in response to any moment when one encounters a "first"—such as eating the first fresh strawberry each season or seeing a friend after a long absence. This blessing expresses gratitude for God's sustaining presence from the last time strawberry juice stained your fingers to this time. When this blessing is uttered—whether in a moment of joy or injury, wonder or weeping, suffering or surrender—it acknowledges the active, purposeful, and healing presence of God amid the particularities of human experience.

Wonder is a choice, an expression of agency. It is a muscle developed through training. It is a posture you learn to inhabit on purpose. Genuine wonder leads to action in the world. Wonder is the wellspring of worship, and worship is enacted through love of God and neighbor— and the neighborhood includes the whole created world.

REORIENTING: PREREQUISITES FOR A LIFE OF GRATITUDE

GL601: A Life of Gratitude

In the capstone course, A Life of Gratitude, all the pennies you've gathered become like seeds, flowering in your heart as perpetual wonder and bearing the fruit of grateful living. Rooted in the fertile soil of a curious attentiveness to the world, you and your fellow students are now poised to hear the Spirit of God whispering from every corner of your lives: *There is more to see here than meets the eye. Here is yet another trailhead to spiritual adventure.*

A Life of Gratitude is taught by author Robin Wall Kimmerer. The course's primary textbook is her remarkable book *Braiding Sweetgrass*. In it, she draws on three of her primary identities—poet, botanist, and member of the Citizen Potawatomi Nation—to illuminate, among other things, the revolutionary character of gratitude by attending carefully to the lives of plants through the lens of her indigenous traditions. The course has two interrelated objectives intended to synthesize students' learning and channel it into Sabbath-infused living:

1. Develop a lifelong practice of gratitude.
2. Become indigenous to your place.

Her book chapter "Allegiance to Gratitude" forms the backbone of her approach to the course. In it, she models an action-reflection approach to gratitude, inspired by an ancient address borrowed from the Onondaga Nation (also known as the Iroquois or Haudenosaunee Confederacy). It is a mark of indigenous cultures within the Americas (and beyond) to be "rooted in cultures of gratitude."[15] Nonindigenous people have much to learn from indigenous culture, particularly in this regard.

The address is called "The Words That Come Before All Else," or the "Haudenosaunee (Ho-dee-no-SHO-nee) Thanksgiving Address." This "river of words as old as the people themselves"[16] has been translated into dozens of languages. The Onondaga people see it as part of their legacy and give it freely to the world.[17]

Each Friday, class begins with a collective recitation of the thanksgiving address. This practice steeps the students' Sabbath imaginations in the tea leaves of thanksgiving. The address is composed of many stanzas, each gathering and guiding students' collective gratitude toward a different element of the natural world (such as Mother Earth, Fish, the Four Winds, and my personal favorite, the Grandfather Thunder Beings). It is neither a prayer nor a creed. It is an acknowledgment that no one is truly independent, but all live *in dependence.*

Each stanza concludes with the line "and now our minds are one." How powerful to *begin* "all else" by the repetitive acknowledgment that our minds are "one," united in grateful affirmation of the giftedness of all life on earth. In an era of pernicious polarization, uniting around gratitude is not just revolutionary; it's transformative.

It takes a long time to recite the address: between fifteen and twenty minutes of unhurried thanksgiving! The sheer length of time indicates the truth that *there is so much to be thankful for.* Sabbath rest reminds us that there is always time for gratitude—and that gratitude takes time.

Three other "assignments" reinforce the student learning objectives of developing a lifelong gratitude practice. First, you and your fellow students keep gratitude journals and spend time each day—and extended time on Sabbath—intentionally naming what you're grateful for. Second, after soaking in gratitude through journaling, each student tells someone around them something they're grateful for about that person. Students report this practice being challenging at first, but over time it becomes a cherished habit of meaningful connection that they carry into the rest of their lives. Third, students, faculty, and staff partake of a common meal punctuated by unhurried conversation prompted by the question, "What are you grateful for today?"

One SIGL alum recently wrote Professor Kimmerer to thank her for the transformative experience he had practicing gratitude in her class. In the letter, he included the following *gratiku*—a gratitude haiku—written on a Sabbath morning after his gratitude practice:

Sabbath sun rising
Gratitude's my attitude
So grateful for you.[18]

REORIENTING: PREREQUISITES FOR A LIFE OF GRATITUDE

The second course objective is "become indigenous to your place." The metaphor of indigeneity is both poignant and loaded. Indigenous people, customs, languages, and wisdom were systematically erased from Turtle Island[19] throughout the European-American colonial project and replaced with customs and values informed by a colonial worldview of possession and control. For the vast majority of those living on Turtle Island, therefore, *being* indigenous is not possible. Professor Kimmerer's metaphor, then, is paradoxical and provocative. But ultimately it is hopeful. Students learn they can *become* indigenous by unlearning the colonial heritage they have absorbed, and by satiating their Windigo hungers by feasting on gratitude.

Becoming indigenous to a place is to unlearn the heritage of anxious and greedy taking. It is to root your relationship to the earth in the soil of reciprocity. It is to cultivate contentment as an act of discipleship and to steep yourself in sufficiency. It is to recognize, with author and activist Lynne Twist, that sufficiency has little to do with quantity—how much you *have*. Rather, it is "an experience, a context we generate, a declaration, a knowing that there is enough, and that we are enough."[20]

Becoming indigenous to a place is to fall in love with it, to see yourself as incomplete apart from it, to recognize and name and celebrate all the ways your place cares for you, and then to commit to reciprocating that care in kind. In short, becoming indigenous to a place is to care for the creation that cares for you.

The course includes an array of opportunities for students to translate their deepening love into action through various forms of advocacy that are in line with their passions, interests, and spheres of influence. Whether it's sharing nature photography on Instagram to spread delight and awareness, coordinating a neighborhood block party to build community, writing an op-ed celebrating a local landscape threatened by "development," or organizing a call-in drive to their representative about an upcoming environmental bill, everyone learns there are ways they can make a difference by leveraging their skills and passions.

Rooted in the Sabbath values of delight, gratitude, and joy, this unit does not wallow in despair or guilt, nor foment division or cynicism.

These responses are insufficient to sustain a lifetime of loving the created world in public. *Gratitude* and *joy* are often notably absent from ecclesial and political conversations around climate action and creation care, as the course's teaching assistant, author and activist Kyle Meyaard-Schaap, notes in a lecture titled, "Joy Is the Key Word Missing from the Climate Movement." His lecture concludes with this reminder: "For sustained, long-term action . . . we need more than anger. Every one of us needs a sense of agency. We need a community of belonging. We need hope that our actions can make a difference. We need joy."[21]

To become indigenous is to learn to see beyond the guilt and despair. It is to see, with Professor Kimmerer, that "even a wounded world is feeding us. Even a wounded world holds us, giving us moments of wonder and joy. I choose joy over despair. Not because I have my head in the sand, but because joy is what the earth gives me daily and I must return the gift."[22] It is to follow poet Wendell Berry's counsel,

> *Be joyful*
> *though you have considered all the facts.*[23]

The facts are overwhelming. But Meyaard-Schaap reminds us, "We all need joy. And it's there for the taking."[24]

In lieu of a final exam, successful completion of this course—and approval for graduation—is granted when a student can demonstrate the connection between their Sabbath practice and a deep and abiding love for the created world. Successful students do not appeal to Professor Kimmerer's PhD in botany by reciting the Latin names of plants near campus. Rather, they describe how the world helps them feel *alive*, how it fosters gratitude and awakens their delight. In short, they share how they are *caring for the creation that cares for them.*

Graduation: Nourishing a Life of Gratitude

The S.Grat commencement service at SIGL, led by President Psalmist, takes place during the final Friday evening session of the course.

REORIENTING: PREREQUISITES FOR A LIFE OF GRATITUDE

Students, staff, faculty, family, and friends gather around a vast and august table—in the manner of Hogwarts—set up in the field behind campus. Somehow, it never rains on commencement day. Lit by the soft glow of Christmas tree lights and tiki torches, and laden with delicious food—an intentional mix of local and industrial food, to acknowledge the complexity of modern life and signal that everything we eat can occasion our thanks if we bring our full attention to it—the table is a sight to behold. The table is a place of gathering, of belonging, from which all are nourished, and through which all are ushered into a sacred encounter with the earth, neighbor, and the Spirit, as they feast together on God's love made edible.

The climax of the ceremony is a service of Communion in which the gratitude students have sown and grown throughout their degree is gathered and given to God in heartfelt praise. President Psalmist frames Communion this way: "*Eucharist* is Greek for 'thanksgiving.' As theologian Herbert McCabe reminds us, 'When we make Eucharist we are recognising our food and drink as word from God, as the Word of God incarnate, God's ultimate . . . gift to us, the gift of himself and his own life.'[25] We eat the meal with this in mind, so that it will spill over onto the meal we share afterward, to saturate it with a similarly sacramental significance."

After the meal, once gratitudes have been shared and tassels turned, President Psalmist concludes the ceremony with the following words: "As you have learned throughout your coursework, practicing gratitude is revolutionary—and thus it must endure constant resistance. It cannot be learned overnight. Soon, you will leave the walls and grounds of SIGL and truly commence living a life of gratitude. And you are ready. We are so proud of you.

"As you go, remember that true Sabbath gratitude is not dependent upon circumstance or a Pollyannaish naivete. It is a daring act of defiance in a world addicted to scarcity and consumption. It is an innocence born of experience, a sacramental outlook of wonder that evokes worship. It is choosing joy, despite the facts. It is living *as if* we are indigenous to the place we are in.

"Genuine gratitude, like the Sabbath, is a practice and a posture, a way of viewing the world, rehearsed once a week, that reorients us to live differently in it each day of the week. And, like both the Sabbath and the sacrament, its ultimate end is love. Gratitude fertilized by wonder and joy will reap a harvest of love one's whole life long.

"The novelist Marilynne Robinson was once asked by an interviewer what one single thing would make the world in general a better place. Her response was as profound as it was simple: 'Loving it more.'[26] It is for this calling that you have been prepared. The Sabbath will apprentice you in this work every week. I will sleep well knowing you are in the most capable of hands. My friends, go with God. And be grateful."

REFLECTION QUESTIONS

- When have you experienced *familirritability*? Under what conditions did you experience it? How might you have experienced the moment differently if you had been awake to wonder?

- Briefly recall the events of the last twenty-four hours. What are some "pennies" you overlooked? How might you see them through the eyes of wonder?

- Rabbi Heschel connects the Jewish practice of blessing God with training in wonder. How might this tradition reshape your understanding and practice of prayer? How might you sense God's presence in your life and the world?

- What might it mean for you to practice being "indigenous" to the place you live?

Sabbath Practice: Write a Gratiku

A *gratiku* is a haiku that expresses gratitude, wonder, or delight! Haiku is a simple and ancient form of Japanese poetry consisting of three lines (line one has five syllables, line two has seven syllables, and line three has five syllables). Paying careful attention is a prerequisite to haiku; therefore practicing it is a playful way to grow in that area so central to the Sabbath way.

To write a haiku is to practice paying attention to *one thing*, then to playfully yet earnestly respond to it in brief, concise language. The form forces focus of both attention and words. Haikus traditionally focus on nature. For example, here are two haikus I wrote on different Sabbaths.

Radiant maple
Fading life in shades of red
Glory on the ground

Rush of gratitude
The spring's first heron sighting
Little fish beware!

In your journal or on a 3x5 card, write down a few things that evoke gratitude, delight, or wonder in you. Choose one item to focus on, and become very present to it. Capture some of the words that come to you as you hold that image, and fold them into three lines of five, seven, and five syllables.

This is a great activity to do as a family because anyone old enough to count syllables can do it. Share your haikus at the end and celebrate all the creativity! An alternative is to have everyone choose the same thing to write about and then marvel at how all the haikus are different.

The Sabbath Is Calling

Stand at the crossroads and look,
ask for the ancient paths—
where the good way lies—
and walk in it to find rest for your souls.

JEREMIAH 6:16

We come now to the end of our shared journey along the Sabbath way. But every ending is, ultimately, a beginning; every landing pad a launching pad; and every graduation a commencement. And what commences now is your own Sabbath journey. The invitation is to begin translating what you've read in these pages into living, breathing practices in your complex, messy, and beautiful life. I couldn't be more excited for you! You can do this! It won't be easy, but it will be worth it.

I have sought to show that the Sabbath is an essential practice of Christian discipleship. By essential, I mean that it is central and inherent. It is flour to bread or apples to apple crisp. Instead of being an add-on or a one-off practice to try when you feel like it or have time to spare, Sabbath is a primary organizing framework for life. Which means it is directly related to the fundamental aspects of life in the twenty-first century; it speaks prophetically into the complex dynamics of our economic, political, social, and religious experiences, calling us toward life-affirming ways of embodying love, gratitude, joy, connection, stillness, and grace every day of the week.

To say Sabbath is essential is also to emphasize its value and significance as a gift to be received rather than a commandment to be obeyed. I have sought to inspire you to embrace the Sabbath because an obligatory Sabbath of "thou shalt nots" leaves little room for delight, and a guilt-laden Sabbath of shoulds and oughts erodes the Sabbath of its true power. The Sabbath's true power is to reconnect you with what makes you feel most alive, to amplify your delight, and to help you make room in your life to live it *while it's happening*. Sabbath's power is not the power of coercion or control, but the power of love and joy, which draws you to itself and is a wellspring of life.

Walking the Sabbath way will likely be disruptive to your life. But it'll be the *good* kind of disruptive. Disruptive in the way that grace and love and mercy and forgiveness disrupt patterns of diminishment. That disruption is necessary to empower patterns of vitality. The Sabbath's disruption is transformative; it always leads you toward deeper experiences of life. It will disrupt the way you hide behind your accomplishments in a futile effort to stifle the voices telling you you're nothing apart from what you do and what people think about you. It will disrupt your uneasy acquiescence to the rat race—the busyness, the distraction, the exhaustion—and remind you that a deeper sense of aliveness and joy is not only possible but is your birthright. It will disrupt the shame or discomfort you feel around investing in your own well-being and remind you that you can't fully love and care for others if you don't fully love and care for yourself. It will disrupt the scarcity mindset that drives so much of your life—your relationship with time, finances, work, family, even how you view your identity and what you can contribute to the world—and instead cultivate an abundance mindset rooted in the soil of God's infinite love. It will disrupt your resignation to a time-is-money approach to life, work, and relationships, and reorient you toward life-affirming ways of showing up to your life by prompting you to answer the question, *Is this the path of love?*[27]

The good news is that Sabbath won't leave you in a state of perpetual disruption. Just as a caterpillar must fall apart in a chrysalis before being transformed into a butterfly, or how the Israelites needed the wilderness before they could enter the Promised Land, or how Jesus needed to die before he could be resurrected, the Sabbath will disrupt you to remake you. It will do this by helping you create room in your life for the experiences that make you whole, make your heart sing, and fill you with delight for the sheer miracle of being alive in this blessed and broken and beautiful world.

And all of this will take time. Probably a lot of time. Mariah and I have been practicing Sabbath for nearly twenty years, and we still think of ourselves as being at the beginning of our journey. It has been the most significant, transformative, and delight-full journey I've ever been on. While it has been costly at times and we have had to make hard choices, the Sabbath's guidance toward prioritizing delight, gratitude, connection, justice, and joy has made all the difference.

It's now up to you to walk the Sabbath way by cultivating a Sabbath practice week after week and improving your Sabbath posture each and every day. I have no doubt that if you do this, you will move in the direction of abundance, flourishing, contentment, and connection. You will walk the ancient path on which the prophet Jeremiah promised you would "find rest for your souls" (Jeremiah 6:16).

As you begin to walk this ancient path, remember that the Sabbath is no petty overlord demanding perfection and punishing you for every infraction. It is a wellspring of grace and life and love, bubbling up to overflowing with playfulness and delight. It wants nothing more than for you to live your life to the full. Trust in the goodness of the Sabbath. Fall into its open arms. Experiment. Play. Be creative. Adapt. Try something. Then try something else. Take it seriously, but not too seriously.

A Sabbath practice boils down to this: make room and show up. If you do that week after week there is no telling what may happen, who you'll become, and what delights you'll experience along the Sabbath way.

The Sabbath is calling. And I'm just a few steps ahead of you on the trail. Will you come?

Acknowledgments

I feel an overwhelming sense of gratitude for so many people who helped bring the dream of this book to reality. In the same way that the Sabbath won't survive in isolation, writing a book takes a whole community.

I am so grateful for the community of Western Theological Seminary (WTS) in Holland, Michigan, where the ideas and practices in this book have been nurtured. Many dear colleagues supported me in direct and indirect ways. Carol Bechtel planted the seed that grew into this book when she first suggested I teach a class on Sabbath. Kristen Johnson encouraged me to turn the class into a book and allowed me to teach the class more often than she would have liked to test out material. Thank you! I am grateful to the Board of Trustees for approving my sabbatical request to begin writing this book. Chuck DeGroat and Elizabeth Pennock offered timely and sage advice as I was researching the theme of loneliness in part 3. Tom Boogaart, my beloved mentor and friend, read early chapter drafts and was always willing to talk through my questions when I was stuck. And so many other colleagues asked me how the book was coming, and then listened intently to my long-winded responses. I am grateful.

One of the gifts of teaching the Sabbath class was getting to work with some of the finest teaching assistants ever, whose contributions to the class also improved the book. Linnea Scobey's lecture on Sabbath and time helped me craft chapter 6. Emily Holehan's lecture on Sabbath and dualism influenced my approach to chapters 9 and 10. And Larry Figueroa read early drafts of part 3 on Sabbath and dualism and gave invaluable feedback. Even more than your contributions to the book, I'm grateful for your friendship. And to the dozens of students who took the class, your honest and enthusiastic engagement with the material was a boon to me, and your ongoing efforts to integrate rhythms of rest and delight into your lives are humbling and affirming. And to Lex Cummings, whose class project helped me think more creatively and concretely about the practices at the end of the chapters—thank you!

My spiritual director, Celaine Bouma-Prediger, walked with me through the peaks and valleys of writing this book. Your hours of gentle, compassionate listening to my fears and failings became fuel that fed my resilience and empowered me to persist.

I am indebted to the inimitable Rosemerry Wahtola Trommer, who gave me permission to use two of her poems in the book. You are a beautiful soul who has given so much love and surreptitious kindness to the world. I am grateful to know you. And to Wendell Kimbrough for graciously giving me permission to quote the chorus of "You Belong." Your music and your way of being in the world inspire me.

I am grateful for my mom, Linda Joy, who has been an encourager my whole life. You show love by participating in what matters to the people you love. Thank you for reading and responding to early chapter drafts, and for telling all your friends about what your son is up to. Your support means the world to me.

I am grateful for Robert, Evan, and Annah, the Wednesday morning BEristas at Maggie's *Be* Cafe, where many of the chapters in this book were written. I always looked forward to your enthusiastic greetings and was grateful every time you asked me how the book was going! (Maggie's BE Cafe employs people with varying levels of ability in Hudsonville, Michigan).

To Jan Long Harris and Jillian Schlossberg at Tyndale, thank you for believing in the project, for driving to Holland for a brainstorming session early on that proved instrumental in reorganizing the book, and

ACKNOWLEDGMENTS

for all your support and encouragement along the way. And to my dear colleague Winn Collier, thank you for connecting me with Jan, which made all of this possible, and for your lovely and heartfelt foreword. I am grateful for your friendship, your heart, your humor, and your wisdom. To Danika Kelly and Lisanne Kaufmann, who copyedited the manuscript, I am in awe of—and so grateful for—your attention to detail. I take full responsibility for every error in this manuscript. And to Lindsey Bergsma, who designed such a gorgeous cover that captures the book's invitation to rest, connection, and delight with aplomb. I, too, just want to sit beneath the waving branches and rest awhile in the beauty of the world.

I could not have birthed this book without the firm-but-gentle midwifery of editor extraordinaire, Christine Anderson. You are everything I could have hoped for in an editor: encouraging, intelligent, organized, pastoral, and ruthless in keeping me focused on executing my vision for the book. I hereby name you to the Order of Shiphrah and Puah, the great Hebrew midwives (Exodus 1:15-22), whose tenacity and wisdom enabled the survival and liberation of Israel.

And to my beloved Mariah, your partnership in this Sabbath-shaped life is everything to me. Thank you for being my first and most trusted conversation partner. Thank you for supporting me through the ups and downs of this yearslong process of writing. Thank you for letting me read you paragraphs I loved, and then offering feedback that made them even better. Most of all, thank you for committing your life to walking the Sabbath way with me. I couldn't imagine a more delightful companion.

Notes

FOREWORD
1. Jacques J. Gorlin, "The Unifying Role of Shabbat," *Jerusalem Post*, October 24, 2013, https://www.jpost.com/Opinion/Op-Ed-Contributors/The-unifying-role-of-Shabbat-329686.
2. See Exodus 20:10.
3. Mary Oliver, "Today," *A Thousand Mornings* (New York: Penguin Books, 2012), 23.
4. Eugene Peterson, "The Good-for-Nothing Sabbath," *Christianity Today*, April 4, 1994, https://www.christianitytoday.com/1994/04/good-for-nothing-sabbath/.

AN INVITATION TO REST, CONNECTION, AND DELIGHT
1. Jacques J. Gorlin, "The Unifying Role of Shabbat," *Jerusalem Post*, October 24, 2013, https://www.jpost.com/Opinion/Op-Ed-Contributors/The-unifying-role-of-Shabbat-329686.
2. Abraham Joshua Heschel, *The Sabbath: Its Meaning for Modern Man* (New York: Farrar, Straus and Giroux, 2005), 14.

1. WALKING THE SABBATH WAY
1. Anne Lamott, "Sailing into the Sunset," *Salon*, March 14, 2003, https://www.salon.com/2003/03/14/cruise_3/.
2. Ronald Rolheiser, *The Holy Longing*, quoted by Rich Villodas, "Contemplative Rhythms for an Exhausted Culture" (Osterhaven lecture, Western Theological Seminary, Holland, MI, November 6, 2023).
3. Abraham Joshua Heschel, *The Sabbath: Its Meaning for Modern Man* (New York: Farrar, Straus and Giroux, 2005), 14. The quote is from the song *Lekha Dodi*, "Come, My Beloved."

4. John Calvin frequently used the metaphor of the theater to describe the created world as imbued with God's presence, power, beauty, justice, and glory. See, for example, John Calvin, *Commentary on the Epistle of Paul the Apostle to the Hebrews*, trans. John Owen (Grand Rapids, MI: Baker Books, 1999), 266.
5. See his conversation with Catherine Price on the podcast *How to Feel Alive* (17:24 and 28:55), June 25, 2024, https://catherineprice.substack.com/p/a-delightful-conversation-with-ross.
6. Heschel, *The Sabbath*, 89 (emphasis added).
7. Wendell Berry, "X," *A Timbered Choir: The Sabbath Poems 1979–1997* (Washington DC: Counterpoint, 1998), 18.

2. ORIENTING: WHAT IS WORK?

1. Henri J. M. Nouwen, "Being the Beloved: Henri Nouwen at the Crystal Cathedral," Henri Nouwen Society, YouTube, June 25, 2021, https://www.youtube.com/playlist?list=PLq385qyR7NY6513dy9JAWZ7lvGCVgcQ2f.
2. By "colonize," I mean an external agent that claims a territory for itself, often through force, to extract the resources of the colonized for the colonizer's own enrichment. The three cultural lies retain their power over us by feeding on our life energy and keeping us small and weak.
3. Mary Bell, quoted in Harriet Rubin, "Success and Excess," *Fast Company*, September 30, 1998, https://www.fastcompany.com/35583/success-and-excess.
4. Miroslav Volf, *Work in the Spirit: Toward a Theology of Work* (Eugene, OR: Wipf and Stock, 1991), 35–45.
5. What follows is my own analysis, based on the categories Volf develops in *Work in the Spirit*.
6. Norman Wirzba, *Living the Sabbath: Discovering the Rhythms of Rest and Delight* (Grand Rapids, MI: Brazos Press, 2006), 94.
7. Felicia Wu Song, *Restless Devices: Recovering Personhood, Presence, and Place in the Digital Age* (Downers Grove, IL: IVP Academic, 2021), 153.
8. Song, 153.
9. Jocelyn K. Glei, "Productivity Shame," *Hurry Slowly* podcast, May 14, 2019, 2:09–3:37, https://hurryslowly.co/216-jocelyn-k-glei/.
10. See Brené Brown, *Daring Greatly: How the Courage to Be Vulnerable Transforms the Way We Live, Love, Parent, and Lead* (New York: Avery, 2012).
11. T. S. Eliot, "The Rock," *The Complete Poems and Plays: 1909–1950* (New York: Harcourt Brace, 1930, 1980), 96.
12. Brad Aaron Modlin, *Everyone at This Party Has Two Names* (Cape Girardeau, MO: Southeast Missouri State University Press, 2016), 13.

3. DISORIENTING STRIVING

1. Leonard Cohen, "Anthem," track 5, *The Future*, Columbia Records, 1992, album.

NOTES

2. Brian Andreas, "The Gift of You," StoryPeople.com, Story of the Day, November 22, 2016, Pinterest, https://ru.pinterest.com/pin/191121577917161822/.
3. See Ellen F. Davis, "Slaves or Sabbath-Keepers? A Biblical Perspective on Human Work," *Anglican Theological Review* 83, no. 1 (December 2001), 25.
4. See Shai Held, *The Heart of Torah: Essays on the Weekly Torah Portion: Genesis and Exodus*, vol. 1 (Philadelphia: Jewish Publication Society, 2017), 215.
5. Nahum M. Sarna, *Exodus: The Traditional Hebrew Text with the New JPS Translation*, JPS Torah Commentary (Philadelphia: Jewish Publication Society, 1991), 202.
6. Parker Palmer, *Let Your Life Speak: Listening for the Voice of Vocation* (San Francisco: Jossey-Bass, 2000), 11.
7. *Kung Fu Panda 3*, directed by Jennifer Yuh Nelson and Alessandro Carloni (20th Century Studios, 2016), 11:30, https://www.imdb.com/title/tt2267968/quotes/?ref_=tt_trv_qu.
8. T. S. Eliot, "The Rock," *The Complete Poems and Plays: 1909-1950* (New York: Harcourt Brace, 1930, 1980), 96.
9. Lauren Winner, "All Who Labor," *Sojourners* (September/October 2010), https://sojo.net/magazine/septemberoctober-2010/all-who-labor.
10. See, for example, Ross Gay's *New York Times* bestselling book of essays *The Book of Delights* (Chapel Hill, NC: Algonquin Books, 2019).
11. Ross Gay, *Inciting Joy: Essays* (Chapel Hill, NC: Algonquin Books, 2022), 34.
12. Gay, 34.
13. Gay, 35.

4. REORIENTING: WORK, REST, AND DELIGHT

1. Maya Angelou, *Love's Exquisite Freedom* (New York: Welcome Books, 2011).
2. Ross Gay, *Inciting Joy: Essays* (Chapel Hill, NC: Algonquin Books, 2022), 4.
3. Gay, 4.
4. Rosemerry Wahtola Trommer, "Raking the Leaves with Jack," *Hush* (Beulah, CO: Middle Creek Publishing and Audio, 2020), 48–49.
5. Kahlil Gibran, *The Prophet* (New York: Alfred A. Knopf, 1923), 31–32.
6. Gibran, 33.

5. ORIENTING: WHAT IS TIME?

1. These categories are based on the work of John Swinton, *Becoming Friends of Time: Disability, Timefullness, and Gentle Discipleship* (Waco, TX: Baylor University Press, 2016), 21–22.
2. Brad Aaron Modlin, "Cubism," *Everyone at This Party Has Two Names* (Cape Girardeau, MO: Southeast Missouri State University Press, 2016), 28.
3. Benjamin Whorf, quoted in Swinton, *Becoming Friends of Time*, 23.
4. Swinton, 23.
5. David Steindl-Rast, quoted in Wayne Muller, *Sabbath: Finding Rest, Renewal, and Delight in Our Busy Lives* (New York: Bantam Books, 1999), 3.

6. Jocelyn K. Glei, "Productivity Shame," *Hurry Slowly*, May 14, 2019, https://hurryslowly.co/216-jocelyn-k-glei/.
7. Abraham Joshua Heschel, *The Sabbath: Its Meaning for Modern Man* (New York: Farrar, Straus and Giroux, 1951, 1979), 5.
8. While retirees may not feel the force of this in the same ways they did while they worked, I suspect they still feel the effects of the value system that supports this kind of approach to time, which defines a life's value based on one's capacity to produce and move quickly and efficiently through their days. The shame or discomfort at *not* being busy, and the temptation to anxiously rush and fill one's schedule—to *feel* busy and therefore feel *meaningful*—is a time-is-money struggle many retirees must overcome.
9. Judith Shulevitz, *The Sabbath World: Glimpses of a Different Order of Time* (New York: Random House, 2010), 97.
10. David Whyte, "Vulnerability as a faculty for understanding," *What to Remember When Waking: The Disciplines of an Everyday Life* (Louisville, CO: Sounds True, 2010), audiobook, 1:09-1:50.
11. I first learned of this study from Judith Shulevitz, and her treatment of it was helpful and influential to my treatment here. See Shulevitz, *The Sabbath World*, 24–26.
12. Sixty-three percent of those who had plenty of time stopped to help; 45 percent of those who shouldn't dawdle stopped to help; 10 percent of those who were late stopped to help. John M. Darley and C. Daniel Batson, "'From Jerusalem to Jericho': A Study of Situational and Dispositional Variables in Helping Behavior," *Journal of Personality and Social Psychology* 27, no. 1 (July 1973): 105.
13. Darley and Batson, "From Jerusalem to Jericho," 107.
14. Zygmunt Bauman, quoted in Felicia Wu Song, *Restless Devices: Recovering Personhood, Presence, and Place in the Digital Age* (Downers Grove, IL: IVP Academic, 2021), 81.
15. Song, 6–7.
16. Sean Parker, quoted in Song, *Restless Devices*, 57.
17. Song relates this to the psychological term called a "Skinner Box." She notes that researcher B. F. Skinner "famously demonstrated how a hungry rat could be trained to expect a food pellet when it pressed a lever. The unexpected discovery was in finding that a rat was actually more motivated to press the lever when the pellet was delivered intermittently rather than consistently with each press. . . . What became known as 'the principle of variable rewards' was the key to hooking them. And the eureka-moment lies in realizing that it's exactly the same for us as human beings." Song, *Restless Devices*, 53.
18. Jaron Lanier, interviewed in *The Social Dilemma*, directed by Jeff Orlowski-Yang (Netflix, 2020), 1:34:42, https://www.netflix.com/watch/81254224.
19. Shulevitz, *The Sabbath World*, 19.
20. Mary Oliver, "When I Am among the Trees," *Thirst* (Boston: Beacon Press, 2006), 4.

NOTES

21. Jenny Odell, *How to Do Nothing: Resisting the Attention Economy* (Brooklyn, NY: Melville House, 2019).
22. John O'Donohue, "For One Who Is Exhausted," *To Bless the Space between Us: A Book of Blessings* (New York: Doubleday, 2008), 126.

6. DISORIENTING CLOCK TIME

1. Substantive parts of this chapter (especially the metaphors for time) were developed in conversation with a friend and former student, Linnea Scobey.
2. Simon Carey Holt, "Slow Time in a Fast World: A Spirituality of Rest," *Ministry, Society and Theology* 16, no. 2 (2002): 4.
3. "According to this viewpoint man proceeds through time like a rower who moves into the future backwards: he reaches his goal by taking his bearings from what is visibly in front of him; it is in this revealed history that for him the Lord of the future is attested." Hans Walter Wolff, *Anthropology of the Old Testament* (Mifflintown, PA: Sigler Press, 1996), 88.
4. For example, "He enables me to lie down in green pastures / he guides me beside quiet waters / he restores my soul." (Psalm 23:2-3). I am grateful to Linnea Scobey for this allusion to Psalm 23.
5. Michelle Wiegers, "Slow Down," *The Wonder of Small Things: Poems of Peace and Renewal*, ed. James Crews (North Adams, MA: Storey Publishing, 2023), 66–67.
6. It appears first among the great *mo'adim* ("festivals," plural of *mo'ed*) listed in Leviticus 23.
7. Abraham Joshua Heschel, *The Sabbath: Its Meaning for Modern Man* (New York: Farrar, Straus and Giroux, 2005), 8.
8. Heschel, 6, emphasis added.
9. There is a marvelous three-book series called Every Moment Holy that reinforces this truth with liturgies to mark the sacredness of the ordinary. Written and edited by Douglas Kaine McKelvey and illustrated by Ned Bustard, the series includes vol. 1, *New Liturgies for Daily Life*; vol. 2, *Death, Grief, and Hope*; and vol. 3, *The Work of the People*. Another book in a similar vein is Tish Harrison Warren's *Liturgy of the Ordinary: Sacred Practices in Everyday Life*.

7. REORIENTING: TIME IS LOVE

1. Nikos Kazantzakis, *Zorba the Greek: The Saint's Life of Alexis Zorba,* read by George Guidall (London: Faber and Faber, 1961; Landover, MD: Recorded Books, 1996), 7:38:00.
2. Carl Honoré, *In Praise of Slowness: Challenging the Cult of Speed* (New York: HarperCollins, 2004), 14.
3. Honoré, 14–15.
4. Annie Dillard, *The Writing Life* (New York: Harper Perennial, 1989), 32.
5. Rosemerry Wahtola Trommer, "The Question," *All the Honey* (Reno, NV: Samara Press, 2023), 31.

6. Frank Hernandez, "Patience (Herbert the Snail)," *The Music Machine* (Brentwood, TN: Sparrow Song, 1977).
7. I am grateful to my wife for the line "in trusting we learn to trust," which was the name of a piece of art she painted years ago as a reflection on this theme.
8. For an insightful and playful take on applying the core tenet of improv ("yes, and") to living life fully alive, see Catherine Price, *The Power of Fun: How to Feel Alive Again* (New York: The Dial Press, 2021).

8. ORIENTING: WHAT PREVENTS COMMUNITY?

1. *Lars and the Real Girl*, directed by Craig Gillespie (MGM, 2007), https://www.imdb.com/title/tt0805564/characters/nm0165101?ref_=tt_cl_c_11.
2. I am grateful to my friend Randy Woodley for this evocative and resonant phrase. See Randy S. Woodley, *Shalom and the Community of Creation: An Indigenous Vision* (Grand Rapids, MI: Eerdmans, 2012).
3. Tim Kasser et al., "Some Costs of American Corporate Capitalism: A Psychological Exploration of Value and Goal Conflicts," *Psychological Inquiry* 18, no. 1 (2007): 1–22.
4. Kasser, 3.
5. Kasser, 2.
6. Gabor Maté with Daniel Maté, *The Myth of Normal: Trauma, Illness & Healing in a Toxic Culture* (New York: Avery, 2022), 296.
7. Kasser, "Some Costs of American Corporate Capitalism," 3.
8. Vivek H. Murthy, "Our Epidemic of Loneliness and Isolation," Office of the US Surgeon General, 2023, https://www.hhs.gov/sites/default/files/surgeon-general-social-connection-advisory.pdf.
9. Randy Woodley, "Indigenous Theology as Original Instructions," Stoutemire Lecture in Multicultural Ministry, Western Theological Seminary, Holland, MI, September 24, 2018.
10. Dr. David Stubbs, professor of ethics and theology, Western Theological Seminary, personal communication, March 24, 2023.
11. Vivek H. Murthy, *Together: The Healing Power of Human Connection in a Sometimes Lonely World* (New York: HarperCollins, 2020), 8.
12. Murthy, 10.
13. Maté, *The Myth of Normal*, 286.
14. Maté, 287.
15. Genesis 1:4, 10, 12, 18, 21, 25, 31. The final time, God saw that it was *tov me'od*, "very good!"
16. Quoted in Murthy, *Together*, 10.
17. Quoted in Murthy, 10.
18. Quoted in Maté, *The Myth of Normal*, 295.
19. Quoted in Murthy, *Together*, 13.
20. Quoted in Murthy, 13.
21. Maté, *The Myth of Normal*, 295.

NOTES

22. John Swinton, *Becoming Friends of Time: Disability, Timefullness, and Gentle Discipleship* (Waco, TX: Baylor University Press, 2016). See especially chapter 2, "Time and Progress: Disability and the Wrong Kind of Time," 35–53.
23. Ian Hacking, *The Taming of Chance (Ideas in Context)* (Cambridge: Cambridge University Press, 1990), 162.
24. For more, see W. M. Byrd and L. A. Clayton, "Race, Medicine, and Health Care in the United States: A Historical Survey," *Journal of the National Medical Association* 93, no. 3 supp. (March 2001): 11–34, https://www.ncbi.nlm.nih.gov/pmc/articles/PMC2593958/, and extensive bibliography.
25. Hacking, *The Taming of Chance*, 160.
26. Lisa Wade, "Norms, Normality, and Normativity," *The Society Pages* (blog), September 23, 2016, https://thesocietypages.org/socimages/2016/09/23/norms-normality-and-normativity/.
27. Wade, "Norms, Normality, and Normativity."
28. The biblical story of the judge Ehud (see Judges 3:12-30) is a fascinating cultural and theological meditation on left-handedness in the ancient world.
29. Interestingly, the word *siniestra* in Spanish means both "sinister" and "left hand." Talk about normativity! I am grateful to my friend Emily Holehan for this insight.
30. Judith Shulevitz, "Bring Back the Sabbath," *New York Times Magazine*, March 2, 2003, https://www.nytimes.com/2003/03/02/magazine/bring-back-the-sabbath.html.
31. James C. Wilhoit, "Self-Compassion as a Christian Spiritual Practice," *Journal of Spiritual Formation and Soul Care* 12, no. 1 (December 17, 2018), 71–88, https://doi.org/10.1177/1939790918795628.
32. Kristin Neff, "The Space between Self-Esteem and Self-Compassion," February 6, 2013, TEDx Talks, 19:00, (6:35–6:47), https://www.youtube.com/watch?v=IvtZBUSplr4.
33. Psychologist Kristin Neff provides helpful information about practicing self-compassion on her website, self-compassion.org. The practice here is adapted from various sources, including her website, her TEDx talk, and Kristin Neff, "2 Minute Tips: How to Practice Self Compassion," June 19, 2017, YouTube video, 2:00, https://www.youtube.com/watch?v=8lnU4fZ3eiM.

9. DISORIENTING DUALISM AND DISCONNECTION

1. The historical figure Isaiah lived and prophesied in the period prior to the exile to Babylon. However, scholars have pointed out that the final portion of the book that bears his name (chapters 56–66) clearly speaks to the period after the exiles returned to the land, and so was not written by Isaiah but by a community that preserved his writings and prophetic convictions. For the sake of ease, I refer to the one speaking in the passages as Isaiah, though the historical figure is anonymous and unknown.
2. See Isaiah 56 and 58, along with the discussion of each of these chapters below.

3. Walter Brueggemann, *Sabbath as Resistance: Saying No to the Culture of Now* (Louisville, KY: Westminster John Knox Press, 2014, 2017), 48.
4. There was some diversity in the makeup of these laws, which scholars ascribe to two different traditions that make up the Pentateuch, namely, the Priestly source and the Deuteronomic source. Despite the nuances, both prioritized ritual purity in a dualistic way that resulted in definitive exclusion. See a helpful summary in Brueggemann, *Sabbath as Resistance*, 46–57.
5. I am borrowing the phrase "illicit union" from the NRSVUE. The term's precise meaning is unclear. It could refer to a bastard, the child of an incestuous union or of a prostitute, or even a foreigner. See Jeffrey H. Tigay, *The JPS Torah Commentary: Deuteronomy* (Philadelphia: Jewish Publication Society, 2003), 211.
6. For more on eunuchs in the ancient world, see Megan K. DeFranza, *Sex Difference in Christian Theology: Male, Female, and Intersex in the Image of God* (Grand Rapids, MI: Eerdmans, 2015).
7. For example, in Ezra 9 all "foreigners" are barred from the community, even men who were at the time married to Israelites. An Israelite man's only option for remaining a member of the community was to divorce his foreign wife, thereby exchanging her disenfranchisement for his belonging.
8. Introduction to Ezra, *The New Oxford Annotated Bible*, 3rd ed., ed. Michael D. Coogan (Oxford: Oxford University Press, 2007), 671.
9. Brueggemann, *Sabbath as Resistance*, 54.
10. Wendell Kimbrough, "You Belong," *You Belong*, Integrity Music, 2023. Find this and other songs at www.wendellk.com.
11. Brueggemann, *Sabbath as Resistance*, 55–56.
12. Brueggemann, 56.
13. Desmond M. Tutu, foreword, *Forgiveness and Reconciliation: Religion, Public Policy, and Conflict Transformation*, ed. Raymond G. Helmick and Rodney L. Petersen (Radnor, PA: Templeton Foundation Press, 2001), xiii.

10. REORIENTING: BECOMING THE BELOVED COMMUNITY

1. Cierra Chenier, "Congo Square, New Orleans: The Root of the Culture," *Noir 'N Nola*, June 19, 2018, https://www.noirnnola.com/post/2018/06/18/congo-square-new-orleans-the-root-of-the-culture; Michael T. Pasquier, "Code Noir of Louisiana," *64 Parishes*, January 16, 2024, https://64parishes.org/entry/code-noir-of-louisiana.
2. Chenier, "Congo Square."
3. See Kenneth M. Stampp, *The Peculiar Institution: Slavery in the Ante-bellum South* (New York: Knopf, 1956).
4. Joshua Jelly-Schapiro, "In Congo Square: Colonial New Orleans," *The Nation*, December 10, 2008, https://www.thenation.com/article/archive/congo-square-colonial-new-orleans/.
5. Chenier, "Congo Square."
6. Jelly-Schapiro, "In Congo Square." Emphasis added.

NOTES

7. I am thankful to my dear friend Andrew Mead for pointing me to this profound history after traveling to Congo Square as a member of a Telos Group "ReStory US" pilgrimage. For more information, visit https://www.telosgroup.org/what-we-do/immerse/trips/.
8. A. J. Swoboda, *Subversive Sabbath: The Surprising Power of Rest in a Nonstop World* (Grand Rapids, MI: Brazos Press, 2018), 71.
9. Rich Villodas, "Contemplative Rhythms for an Exhausted Culture," Osterhaven Lecture Series, Western Theological Seminary, Holland, MI, November 6, 2023.
10. Vivek H. Murthy, *Together: The Healing Power of Human Connection in a Sometimes Lonely World* (New York: HarperCollins, 2020), 8.
11. Henri J. M. Nouwen, *The Way of the Heart: Desert Spirituality and Contemporary Ministry* (San Francisco: HarperSanFrancisco, 1981), 25.
12. Ross Gay, *Inciting Joy: Essays* (Chapel Hill, NC: Algonquin Books, 2022), 35. See chapter 3, "Disorienting Striving."
13. Walter Brueggemann, *Peace* (St. Louis, MO: Chalice Press, 2001), 14.
14. *The Hebrew and Aramaic Lexicon of the Old Testament*, s.v. מלש, ed. Ludwig Koehler and Walter Baumgartner (Leiden: Brill, 2000).
15. Martin Luther King Jr.'s quote is "Injustice anywhere is a threat to justice everywhere." For a full reading of the letter, see King to fellow clergymen, April 16, 1963, "Letter from a Birmingham Jail [King, Jr.]," African Studies Center, University of Pennsylvania, https://www.africa.upenn.edu/Articles_Gen/Letter_Birmingham.html.
16. Randy S. Woodley, *Shalom and the Community of Creation: An Indigenous Vision* (Grand Rapids, MI: Eerdmans, 2012), 15.
17. See, for example, Michelle Alexander, *The New Jim Crow: Mass Incarceration in the Age of Colorblindness* (New York: The New Press, 2010), and Bryan Stevenson, *Just Mercy: A Story of Justice and Redemption* (New York: One World, 2014).
18. Walter Brueggemann, *Theology of the Old Testament: Testimony, Dispute, Advocacy* (Minneapolis: Fortress Press, 2005), 189.
19. "*Whether it was 'practiced' or not, however, there the provision sits in the text*, the culminating assertion of the God of Sinai . . . who intends a very different regimen of social wealth and social power" than the one defining the terms of our lives today. Brueggemann, *Theology of the Old Testament*, 190.
20. Jesus quotes most of Isaiah 61:1-2.
21. Ellen Davis, keynote lecture at "The Earth is the Lord's" conference, Western Theological Seminary, Holland, MI, September 23–25, 2010.
22. Cornel West, speech delivered at the Askwith Forum, Harvard Graduate School of Education, October 24, 2017, https://www.facebook.com/HarvardEducation/videos/cornel-west-on-tenderness-in-education/10155292829161387/.
23. bell hooks, *Outlaw Culture: Resisting Representations* (New York: Routledge, 1994), 298.
24. He spoke of it in many places, but here is one example: Martin Luther King Jr., *A Testament of Hope: The Essential Writings and Speeches of Martin Luther*

King, Jr., ed. James Melvin Washington (San Francisco: HarperSanFrancisco, 1986), 8.
25. Sam Cooke, "Wonderful World," Keen Records, released April 14, 1960.
26. In 2024, it was nearly 282 million. "2024 Global Report on Food Crises," Unicef USA, accessed June 11, 2024, https://www.unicefusa.org/media-hub/reports/2024-Global-Report-Food-Crises.
27. Al Zolynas, "Under Ideal Conditions," *Poetry of Presence: An Anthology of Mindfulness Poems*, ed. Phyllis Cole-Dai and Ruby R. Wilson (West Hartford, CT: Grayson Books, 2017), 60.
28. To learn more, visit the "5-for-5 Connection Challenge" website at Office of the Surgeon General, U.S. Department of Health and Human Services, https://www.hhs.gov/surgeongeneral/priorities/connection/challenge/index.html.

11. ORIENTING: WHAT HAS THE LAND TO DO WITH SABBATH?

1. Child Labor and Slavery in the Chocolate Industry," *Food Empowerment Project*, January 2022, https://foodispower.org/human-labor-slavery/slavery-chocolate/.
2. Martha Mendoza, "U.S. Is Sued over Imports of Cocoa Harvested by Child Labor," *Los Angeles Times*, August 15, 2023, https://www.latimes.com/business/story/2023-08-15/cocoa-harvested-by-children-child-labor.
3. Wendell Berry, *What Are People For?* (Berkeley, CA: Counterpoint, 1990, 2010), 145.
4. A. J. Swoboda, *Subversive Sabbath: The Surprising Power of Rest in a Nonstop World* (Grand Rapids, MI: Brazos Press, 2018), 126.
5. For more on the Year of Jubilee, see chapter 10.
6. Second Chronicles is the final book in the Hebrew Bible, which has a slightly different order of books than the Christian Old Testament.
7. For other passages making a similar case, see Leviticus 26 and Ezekiel 20:10-26.
8. Norman Wirzba, *Living the Sabbath: Discovering the Rhythms of Rest and Delight* (Grand Rapids, MI: Brazos Press, 2006), 25.
9. John O'Donohue, *Anam Cara: Spiritual Wisdom from the Celtic World* (London: Bantam Books, 1997), 89.
10. O'Donohue, 89.
11. O'Donohue, 89.
12. Robin Wall Kimmerer, *Braiding Sweetgrass: Indigenous Wisdom, Scientific Knowledge, and the Teachings of Plants* (Minneapolis: Milkweed Editions, 2013), 305.
13. Kimmerer, 307.
14. Kimmerer, 308.
15. Kimmerer, 308.
16. Kimmerer, 308.
17. Calvin's term was, in Latin, *theatrum gloriae*. John Calvin, *Institutes of the Christian Religion*, ed. John T. McNeill, trans. Ford Lewis Battles (Louisville, KY: Westminster John Knox Press, 1960), 1.5.8.

NOTES

18. Wirzba, *Living the Sabbath*, 25.
19. See Berry, *What Are People For?*, 148.
20. See Ellen F. Davis, "Slaves or Sabbath-Keepers? A Biblical Perspective on Human Work," *Anglican Theological Review* 83, no. 1 (December 1, 2001): 25–39.
21. *Kung Fu Panda 3*, directed by Jennifer Yuh Nelson and Alessandro Carloni (20th Century Studios, 2016), 2:45, https://www.imdb.com/title/tt2267968/quotes/?ref_=tt_trv_qu.
22. This is the essential question the narrative explores, though it is often mistranslated.
23. Ross Gay, *Inciting Joy: Essays* (Chapel Hill, NC: Algonquin Books, 2022), 99.
24. Kimmerer, *Braiding Sweetgrass*, 305–306.

12. DISORIENTING GREED AND SCARCITY

1. Rabbi Samson Raphael Hirsch, quoted in Judith Shulevitz, *The Sabbath World: Glimpses of a Different Order of Time* (New York: Random House, 2010), 73.
2. Hirsch, quoted in Shulevitz, *The Sabbath World*, 73.
3. For more on the mountaintop removal processes and the human and environmental impact, see iLoveMountains.org.
4. Abraham Joshua Heschel, *The Sabbath: Its Meaning for Modern Man* (New York: Farrar, Straus and Giroux, 2005), 7.
5. Wendell Berry, "How to Be a Poet (To Remind Myself)," *New Collected Poems* (Berkeley, CA: Counterpoint, 2012), 354.
6. Wendell Berry, "III," *A Timbered Choir: The Sabbath Poems 1979–1997* (Berkeley, CA: Counterpoint, 1998), 8.
7. Dacher Keltner, *Awe: The New Science of Everyday Wonder and How It Can Transform Your Life* (New York: Penguin Press, 2023), xvi.
8. Keltner, 7.
9. Dacher Keltner, "Awe and Wonder with Dacher Keltner," *Action for Happiness*, April 27, 2023, educational video, 5:20 to 5:40, https://www.youtube.com/watch?v=ixWg9Ynq_Ts.
10. Ocean Vuong, "A Life Worthy of Our Breath," interview by Krista Tippett, April 30, 2020, *On Being*, podcast, 49:18, https://onbeing.org/programs/ocean-vuong-a-life-worthy-of-our-breath/.
11. Rule of Saint Benedict, quoted in Kristi Nelson, *Wake Up Grateful: The Transformative Practice of Taking Nothing for Granted* (North Adams, MA: Storey, 2020), 4.
12. J. Todd Billings, *The End of the Christian Life: How Embracing Our Mortality Frees Us to Truly Live* (Grand Rapids, MI: Brazos Press, 2020), 11.
13. Ross Gay, "On the Insistence of Joy," interview by Krista Tippett, July 25, 2019, *On Being*, podcast, 8:40–8:43, https://onbeing.org/programs/ross-gay-tending-joy-and-practicing-delight/.
14. Mary Oliver, "When Death Comes," *New and Selected Poems*, vol. 1 (Boston: Beacon Press, 1992), 10.

15. Oliver, "Messenger," *Thirst* (Boston: Beacon Press, 2006), 1.
16. Oliver, "The Summer Day," *New and Selected Poems*, 94.
17. Elizabeth Barrett Browning, *Aurora Leigh* (Chicago: Academy Chicago Publishers, 1992), 265.
18. I am indebted to Tom Boogaart for this insightful phrase.
19. Oliver, "Messenger," *Thirst*, 1.
20. Oliver, 1.
21. Kristi Nelson, *Wake Up Grateful: The Transformative Practice of Taking Nothing for Granted* (North Adams, MA: Storey Publishing, 2020), 1.
22. Nelson, 48.
23. Nelson, 38.
24. Robin Wall Kimmerer, *Braiding Sweetgrass: Indigenous Wisdom, Scientific Knowledge, and the Teachings of Plants* (Minneapolis: Milkweed Editions, 2013), 124–125.

13. REORIENTING: PREREQUISITES FOR A LIFE OF GRATITUDE

1. Robin Wall Kimmerer, *Braiding Sweetgrass: Indigenous Wisdom, Scientific Knowledge, and the Teachings of Plants* (Minneapolis: Milkweed Editions, 2013), 111.
2. It's *not* a "master's" degree; Sabbath is not about mastery.
3. I hereby coin a portmanteau neologism: *familirritability*, and related terms *familirritation* and *familirritable*.
4. Willie James Jennings, *After Whiteness: An Education in Belonging* (Grand Rapids: Eerdmans, 2020), 59.
5. Meister Eckhart, "Behind You," *Meister Eckhart's Book of the Heart: Meditations for the Restless Soul*, ed. Jon M. Sweeney and Mark S. Burrows (Charlottesville, VA: Hampton Roads, 2017), 69.
6. Abraham Joshua Heschel, *The Prophets* (New York: HarperCollins, 1962), xxiv. Emphasis added.
7. See Annie Dillard, *Pilgrim at Tinker Creek* (New York: HarperCollins, 1974), 16.
8. Dillard, 16.
9. Dillard, 17.
10. Abraham Joshua Heschel, *God in Search of Man: A Philosophy of Judaism* (New York: Farrar, Straus and Giroux, 1955), 43.
11. Valarie Kaur, *See No Stranger: A Memoir and Manifesto of Revolutionary Love* (New York: One World, 2021), 10.
12. Heschel, *God in Search of Man*, 48–49.
13. Heschel, 49.
14. Translation: "You are the one who gives us life."
15. Kimmerer, *Braiding Sweetgrass*, 106.
16. Kimmerer, 107.
17. There is no official "version" of the address, which changes slightly depending

NOTES

on context and speaker. Google "Haudenosaunee Thanksgiving Address" to read the address in full or purchase an illustrated booklet of it.

18. I am the grateful "student." ☺
19. Turtle Island is what many indigenous cultures call North America.
20. Lynne Twist, *The Soul of Money: Transforming Your Relationship with Money and Life* (New York: W. W. Norton, 2017), 74.
21. Kyle Meyaard-Schaap, "The Key Word Missing from the Climate Movement," CNN, April 30, 2021, https://www.cnn.com/2021/04/30/opinions/climate-movement-joy-meyaard-schaap/index.html.
22. Kimmerer, *Braiding Sweetgrass*, 327.
23. Wendell Berry, "Manifesto: The Mad Farmer Liberation Front," *New Collected Poems* (Berkeley, CA: Counterpoint, 2012), 174.
24. Meyaard-Schaap, "The Key Word Missing from the Climate Movement."
25. Herbert McCabe, OP, *God Matters* (New York: Continuum, 1987), 85.
26. The exchange is recorded in Lisa Allardice, "Marilynne Robinson: 'Obama Was Very Gentlemanly . . . I'd Like to Get a Look at Trump,'" *Guardian*, July 6, 2018, https://www.theguardian.com/books/2018/jul/06/marilynne-robinson-interview-barack-obama-donald-trump-writer-theologian.
27. Rosemerry Wahtola Trommer, "The Question," *All the Honey* (Reno, NV: Samara Press, 2023), 31.

About the Author

TRAVIS WEST is professor of Hebrew and Old Testament at Western Theological Seminary in Holland, Michigan. His previous books, *Biblical Hebrew: An Interactive Approach* and *The Art of Biblical Performance*, advocate for incorporating performance, embodiment, and play into the process of learning biblical Hebrew and interpreting biblical stories. When he's away from the classroom and the writing desk, he can be found searching for wonder while walking the fields near his house, going to a farmers market, watching a movie, or hanging out with his wife, who is his most consistent source of delight and amazement.